Handbook of
Personnel Selection
and Performance Evaluation
in Healthcare

Donald N. Lombardi

Handbook of
Personnel Selection
and Performance Evaluation
in Healthcare

Guidelines for Hourly,
Professional, and Managerial
Employees

Jossey-Bass Publishers

San Francisco • London • 1988

HANDBOOK OF PERSONNEL SELECTION AND PERFORMANCE EVALUATION
IN HEALTHCARE
Guidelines for Hourly, Professional, and Managerial Employees
by Donald N. Lombardi

Copyright © 1988 by: Jossey-Bass Inc., Publishers
350 Sansome Street
San Francisco, California 94104
&
Jossey-Bass Limited
28 Banner Street
London EC1Y 8QE

Library of Congress Cataloging-in-Publication Data

Lombardi, Donald N., 1956–
Handbook of personnel selection and performance
evaluation in healthcare.

(A Joint publication in the Jossey-Bass health
series and the Jossey-Bass management series)
Bibliography: p.
Includes index.
1. Medical personnel—Recruiting. 2. Medical
personnel—Rating of. I. Title. II. Series:
Jossey-Bass health series. III. Series: Jossey-Bass
management series.
R690.L65 1988   362.1′068′3   88-42792
ISBN 1-55542-106-7

Manufactured in the United States of America

The paper in this book meets the guidelines for
permanence and durability of the Committee on
Production Guidelines for Book Longevity of the
Council on Library Resources.

JACKET DESIGN BY WILLI BAUM

FIRST EDITION

Code 8826

A joint publication in
The Jossey-Bass Health Series
and
The Jossey-Bass Management Series

Contents

Part Three: Evaluating and Rewarding
Employee Performance

Part Four: Resources for Personnel Selection
and Evaluation

Contents

Preface

Over the past several years, two vital areas of human resources management—employee selection and performance evaluation—have drawn the increasing interest of managers in the healthcare industry as well as consumers of healthcare services. Unlike industries whose products are optional consumable items, the healthcare industry "produces" a complex service: the delivery of skilled care to people who are in need of it. Employees in the healthcare field must possess technical skills and factual knowledge, but they must also be equipped with the "people skills" that will allow them to meet the interpersonal needs of patients. Healthcare organizations are realizing that the human touch is not optional but rather an essential component in the "complete healthcare package."

The reduction of financial reimbursement schemes is one of many economic changes that have encouraged the healthcare customer/patient to use comparison shopping in the selection of a healthcare provider. Often, the difference between an organization that attracts clients and succeeds and one that does not and fails is found in the human resource equation. As a consequence, healthcare organizations need to select and retain employees whose work attitudes, people skills, management ability, and team orientation are strong and positive.

At the same time that the business environment is undergoing changes, the healthcare industry is also finding itself the focus of public interest and industry regulation groups. The legal and equal opportunity practices of healthcare institutions as well as the medical and technical competence of healthcare employees in general are subjects of scrutiny. Industrial watchdog and accreditation groups examine performance assessment and promotion practices of healthcare organizations to determine whether fairness and technical merit are the main review criteria. All these pressures notwithstanding, however, healthcare organizations must maximize their selection and evaluation programs for a universally recognized, time-proven reason: great organizations are built on the employ and retention of great people. An organization may spend countless dollars on the newest equipment and the most modern physical plants, but without stellar performers operating the equipment, staffing the plant, and providing the customer/patient with the human interaction essential to quality healthcare, the organization will never achieve true excellence and optimum profitability.

To assemble a staff that can successfully meet current challenges the healthcare organization must recruit and select employees carefully. Once people are placed in jobs, the manager must implement a good performance evaluation system that will ensure accurate assessment of performance based on valid, factual information. Although this is a complex and demanding task, and although the healthcare field currently employs well in excess of two million people, until now, there has been no text that industry managers, supervisors, and executives could use as a pragmatic guide in hiring and evaluating this immense and unique work force.

This book, built on systems that are currently in use in more than one hundred healthcare organizations, was written to fill this need. It is designed to function as a practical handbook that readers can use to immediately enhance their selection and evaluation efforts. Unlike the generic, philosophy-based overviews that predominate in this field, the *Handbook of Personnel Selection and Performance Evaluation in Healthcare* is designed to serve as a comprehensive, practical guide that healthcare managers can apply in their everyday work lives. It provides the conceptual background, practical systems, and ready-to-use approaches that managers need to immediately enhance their programs for recruiting and hiring new personnel and for evaluating the performance of both newly hired and existing personnel.

Who Should Read This Book?

This handbook is designed, first and foremost, for health-care managers at all levels who regularly make hiring decisions or evaluate employees. Such managers and executives often have the most pressing need for the programs described in this book because their jobs require them not only to apply their specific technical expertise but also to assemble, command, and control a staff. This handbook is designed to provide a comprehensive guide to human resources responsibilities, from recruiting candidates through the management continuum to performance evaluation. It is specific to the healthcare industry and deals pertinently with the current issues and challenges involved in the construction and management of effective work groups in healthcare settings.

The second group for whom this book is intended includes human resources professionals in the healthcare field who have been educated in general terms in selection and performance evaluation but who need a resource that deals practically with the nuances of the healthcare field and with the challenges they face every day in this ever-changing business forum.

Scholars and students in healthcare and business curriculums who desire more detailed information than the typical textbook provides will find this book a valuable training manual. It is my purpose to deliver to these students a practical handbook that will assist in the transition between the educational realm and the world of professional responsibilities.

Finally, this book can be fully used by managers working in industries that support healthcare institutions, such as hospital supply, pharmaceutical manufacturing, and other industry groups that relate to healthcare. Because the book focuses on the traits and business approaches of the healthcare industry, managers in related fields will find valuable insights into employee selection and evaluation, human resources managerial approaches, and the philosophies of both their customers and their competitors.

As stated, the need to accurately recruit and select personnel and to effectively evaluate their performance is one that transcends any specific category of healthcare service. The forces that affect the community hospital are similar to those that affect, on a larger scale, the multifacility hospital chain or nursing home consortium. In this book, I share some of the keys to success that my clients from across the healthcare spectrum have been able to utilize in solidifying their selection and evaluation programs. I have described their use of my formulas and shown how they have combined them with their business acumen and common sense, in order to give the reader a working perspective which is industry-specific but broad in terms of applicability and practical use.

Overview of the Contents

Part One presents methods for designing effective systems for selection and performance evaluation. Chapter One provides an overview of the roles selection and performance evaluation play in the current healthcare arena. In this chapter I discuss the specific economic factors the healthcare industry must pay heed to—notably in the acquisition of human resources—as well as the key factors within the industry that affect human resources management. Chapter Two moves from the *need* for effective selection and performance evaluation systems to *development* of those systems. This chapter addresses the practical analysis of the healthcare organization's business environment, the needs and desires of the healthcare patient/customer, the organizational factors that affect selection and performance evaluation, and ways these factors manifest themselves in the design of selection and evaluation systems. Chapter Three explains how to set standards for selection and performance evaluation systems, particularly how to set standards for attitude, people skills, managerial aptitude, and team orientation, all of which combine to provide the reader with a most useful formula for evaluating applicants' potential and employees' performance.

Part Two examines the recruitment, selection, and hiring processes in detail, including recruitment of applicants from outside the organization as well as candidates who are already employees and who desire a transfer or promotion. This section details recruitment and interviewing methods, evaluation strategies, and more. The Quan-Com Interviewing System, which is currently being used widely throughout the industry, is discussed in detail throughout Part Two.

Chapter Four describes a solid recruitment and selection system and analyzes problems that commonly occur in this area. Chapter Five goes on to detail effective recruitment practices, including ways to use internal systems to identify candidates within the organization. Chapter Six illustrates fully how to conduct an interview and get good results. The guidelines provided in this chapter are specific and readily usable and are tailored particularly for the current healthcare setting. Chapter Seven makes the complex task of evaluating the interview manageable by showing first how to identify the technical capabilities and personality characteristics necessary to a job and then, how to rate a candidate on each item. Chapter Eight presents a case study that depicts the entire recruitment and selection process successfully enacted from beginning to end.

Part Three completely covers the performance evaluation process, from setting performance goals and conducting an appraisal discussion to utilizing an effective performance appraisal form (an example is provided in the book). All of the material will be extremely helpful to today's practitioner, who must deal not only with the interpersonal and business ramifications of the evaluation process but also with the requirements of several legal and accreditation organizations. The book provides all of the guidance necessary to construct an evaluation system that will meet these various demands and provide both the manager and the reviewed employee with a performance evaluation program that will help maximize performance. Chapter Nine discusses the requirements for an effective evaluation system. Specific attention is paid to problems that frequently come up in connection with evaluation. Chapter Ten explains in detail how to set performance standards, including management performance planning, performance categories, project management planning, and common pitfalls in the performance planning process. This chapter provides the reader with practical, easily applicable information and further shows how to link the selection and placement processes with performance evaluation. Chapter Eleven demonstrates how to monitor and measure job performance in healthcare, including how to analyze and evaluate indicators of quantitative performance, qualitative performance, and supervisory performance. Chapter Twelve explains how to conduct the performance review session. Topics include the appraisal discussion, the components of an effective performance appraisal form, potential employee reactions in the review session, and the use of communication diffusers to keep the discussion fruitfully on track. Chapter Thirteen discusses the construction of a training and development plan for the employee, providing insight into the types of training available to healthcare professionals and how the reviewing manager can make the most of these opportunities. Chapter Fourteen discusses rewards for solid performance, exploring the options available to the healthcare manager. Finally, Chapter Fifteen offers a comprehensive case study, presenting an all-inclusive, real-life application of all of the approaches presented in Part Three.

Part Four, "Resources for Personnel Selection and Evaluation," is an extremely valuable collection of forms and data that managers can apply to their individual situations. Resource A shows the results of a healthcare consumer survey conducted by my firm, which elucidates customer/patients' perceptions of the important characteristics of healthcare personnel. Resource B is a glossary of communication terms commonly used in and about the selection and evaluation processes. Resource C is a sample survey readers can use to gauge organizational standards in their organizations. Resource D provides forms that have been proven effective in administering a personnel system; the spectrum they cover starts with job analysis and description and goes through placement and the establishment of job objectives. The Quan-Com Selection System for Hourly Employees is reproduced in Resource E. It provides the reader with questions (cues) to use in the interview and analysis indicators (clues) to help in assessing candidates' responses. Resource F is the Quan-Com Selection System for

Managerial and Professional Personnel. It contains the "right questions and answers" for conducting and interpreting interviews. The performance appraisal form presented in Resource G has been cited as the best of its kind by the American College of Healthcare Executives, the American Association of Homes for the Aging, and other industry expert groups. It is reprinted in its entirety for immediate use by the reader. Resource H is a sample survey that readers can use to determine future training and development needs in their organizations. In the total approach this book takes to personnel selection and evaluation—from concepts to practical applications and finally to proven, ready-to-use systems in healthcare personnel selection and performance evaluation—this is the final step.

Acknowledgments

I would like to thank my friends in the healthcare industry without whose input this book could never have been completed. I am particularly grateful to Paul J. Hensler, FACHE, George H. Stevens of Blue Cross/Blue Shield, and the entire Center for Human Resources/InterVista staff. Thanks, also, to the entire staff at Jossey-Bass for the guidance, support, and scrupulous attention to detail they supplied during the publication process.

Finally, I thank my wife, Deborah Ann, and my entire family, from whom I have learned so much about life and received unbelievable support.

Hackettstown, New Jersey   Donald N. Lombardi
July 1988

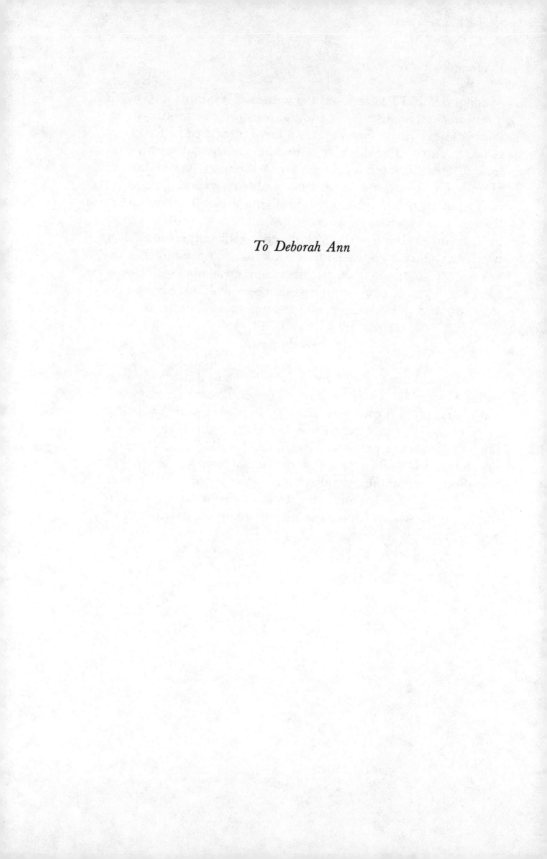

To Deborah Ann

The Author

Donald N. Lombardi is a principal partner of CHR/InterVista, a human resources consulting firm with offices in California, New Jersey, and Oregon. He received his B.A. degree in English (1976) from Florida International University, his M.A. degree in human resources management (1978) from Pepperdine University, and his Ph.D. degree (1983) in industrial psychology from the University of Missouri at Saint Louis.

Lombardi is a regular faculty member of the American College of Healthcare Executives, where his course "Maximizing Managerial Performance" is a regular offering. He is also director of the Management Development Institute at New Jersey's Centenary College and adjunct lecturer at Syracuse University. He has designed and implemented selection and performance evaluation systems for more than fifty healthcare and service organizations and holds more than forty U.S. copyrights on human resources systems. Prior to his consulting work, Lombardi held top personnel positions at American Hospital Supply Corporation and Bristol-Myers Company, where he was instrumental in implementing managerial systems in American, Caribbean, and European operations.

As an officer in the United States Marine Corps, Lombardi instituted numerous educational and personnel management programs, which were lauded by both military and civilian officials. His publications include articles in such diverse periodicals as *Philadelphia Magazine* and *Healthcare Executive*. Clients using his systems span the spectrum from service corporations, such as Jack-in-the-Box and Der Wienerschnitzel, to healthcare organizations, such as the Charlotte-Mecklenburg Hospital Authority and the American Association of Homes for the Aging.

Handbook of
Personnel Selection
and Performance Evaluation
in Healthcare

Chapter 1

Selection
and Performance Appraisal
in Today's Healthcare Arena

By their very nature, employee selection and performance evaluation have always been essential ingredients of a successful healthcare human resources program. Many changes in the industry have increased the importance of these two managerial responsibilities, however. Such factors in the business environment as a decrease in patient benefits, the emergence of several national hospital chains, and shortages of competent healthcare personnel in numerous fields have brought about increased attention to the effectiveness of an organization's selection and evaluation systems. In this chapter, we will discuss some of the specific dynamics currently at work in the healthcare marketplace and explore their impact on the selection and evaluation process.

First, we will take a look at the larger economic factors that have increased the importance of employee selection and performance evaluation in the healthcare industry. We will then look at the industry-specific factors and the changes within the healthcare business forum that have increased the importance of these two processes.

Economic Factors

Several economic factors have contributed to a decline in the amount of basic capital available to most healthcare organizations, requiring today's healthcare managers to pay particular attention to how they are selecting and evaluating their personnel. The first factor is the healthcare industry's shrinking economic base. In the past, the healthcare industry did not have to attack its marketplace aggressively to attract customers—that is, patients—and their dollars. Because of the bountiful employee benefits most patients received from their employers in a given hospital's geographical drawing area, the ability to pay fully for a hospital's services was never a major source of concern. However, with the shrinking of benefits and therefore of the amount of money available for patients to spend, healthcare consumers have become more selective about the kind of services and payment plan they wish to use when medical treatment becomes necessary. Furthermore, whereas in the past a patient would take advantage of benefits to take care of any minor ailment, today's healthcare consumer will seek treatment only for a serious malady.

Another economic factor is the emergence of alternative delivery schemes such as clinics and corporate health maintenance organizations (HMOs), as well as new technology that allows physicians to perform more intricate treatment for patients within the confines of their own offices or clinics. The traditional community hospital has lost important revenues to competitors who ten years ago were nonexistent. The current mania for malpractice suits has also hit the industry hard. Physicians have become reluctant to address certain medical cases aggressively out of fear of litigation, and local hospitals have given up specialty staff and are treading lightly in any medical areas that might invite malpractice litigation. This has had an obvious effect on the patient census at a typical community hospital, since the prospective customer/patient must now look to specialty treatment facilities for services previously provided by the local institution.

With this decline in revenues, it becomes mandatory for the healthcare facility to save the money it has in its coffers and use its operating budget as efficiently as possible. While there are many obvious ways for the administrator or responsible healthcare manager to do this, such as using less expensive equipment, maintaining current facilities rather than developing new ones, and cutting back on other expenditures, the intelligent management of human resources might be the best possible money-saving measure a manager can currently take. The turnover of an employee, for example, who is not able to perform the assigned job competently costs a hospital anywhere from 150 to 285 percent of that employee's yearly salary. This figure is based on placement costs, benefit enrollment, training expenditures, and lost productivity that could have been provided had a competent person been hired. Likewise, an employee not performing up to par who is given an unwarranted favorable assessment costs the hospital in lost productivity. This loss can be compounded in cases where the subsatisfactory employee negatively affects the performance of those he or she works with daily. By bringing down the performance of an entire work group, the employee causes a substantial drain of labor costs and salary expenditures.

Because the money drain created by poor selection and performance assessment is not as readily apparent as other costs, it is often overlooked by management applying traditional cost-saving measures. But by examining the quality of individuals selected and the quality of their subsequent performance, the healthcare manager regulates the expenditure of the human resource budget in a manner that is both judicious and beneficial to the manager's work group and the entire organization.

With this in mind, the healthcare manager must explore the link between selection and performance evaluation. If the manager selects a person who will accept the wage offered for a particular position but in fact may not be able to perform the job expertly, the stage is set for failure. By trying to save some wage expenditures at the outset without ensuring the absolute quality of the employee's ability, the manager is making a critical error that will cost countless dollars in wasted employment costs, through equipment misuse or other types of damage, and possible outplacement and termination costs. Poor selection is a very quick way for a manager to squander budget dollars.

In a similar vein, employees must be assessed and evaluated on the specific job responsibilities for which they were originally selected. For instance, a generic appraisal form that lacks critical scope and fails to require documentation of an employee's performance can easily be used to rate every evaluated employee as satisfactory or better. If a manager uses such a form, an employee whose incompetence costs the institution significant amounts of money may be harbored. By demanding consistent statements of job responsibilities throughout both the selection and assessment phases, the manager can establish a solid system for ensuring that the employee is giving the organization what it needs from the start of the work cycle (selection) to its conclusion (assessment).

Without a comprehensive selection system, people who do not have the necessary talent and abilities often will be hired anyway owing to lack of sufficient interview evaluation. The immediate result is low productivity in their assigned jobs. The long-term effect is a lack of solid performance from those whose jobs are connected to that of the substandard employee, with the overall effect being a crippling of unit performance. Likewise, with a poor performance assessment system these marginal employees often will be allowed to fester within the organization for a significant length of time, costing the institution a great deal in labor costs and lost productivity. This not only drains the capital resources of the organization but has a major effect on the morale and output of previously well-motivated, effective employees. Furthermore, by keeping these employees on the payroll the organization is depriving itself of the opportunity to hire someone more competent and productive.

A solid selection system is a major money-saver in itself. Many healthcare institutions squander large amounts of money by employing placement agencies to identify and select key candidates for many positions. The cost of these services can run anywhere from 20 to 33 percent of the employee's annual salary. This money can be saved if managers learn how to conduct the entire selection process themselves. Such an approach makes sense when one considers that the person who best understands what is needed in a specific position is the manager of that position. The manager, after all, has the insight into what makes a specific person successful in a given position and what kind of personality type is essential for that position as well as within the organization itself. In short, the manager intrinsically knows the type of person needed better than anyone, particularly an outside search/placement consultant. This knowledge, coupled with the proper training and education, allows the institution to save considerable sums in placement fees.

Performance assessment also provides significant opportunities for the individual manager to save money. Poor performance evaluation can cause an organization to needlessly lose capital dollars in two ways: first, the continuance of a salary to a substandard employee, and second, the payment of litigation fees and award judgments to an employee who is improperly and unconstitutionally dismissed. By using a general appraisal form, or worse yet, no formal assessment system at all, the healthcare manager gives the marginal employee the opportunity to stay in the organization and perform marginally. Furthermore, the use of a general or inadequate performance assessment form that is not backed up by documentation leaves the manager and the organization open to litigation of one sort or another from an aggrieved employee. An employee who is dismissed without the required evidence and documentation of poor performance has recourse to an unfair dismissal suit. If the employee belongs to a protected minority, as we will discuss in detail later in this book, the opportunity for recourse is even greater, since countless equal opportunity and antidiscrimination boards will take a case based strictly on lack of documentation. If the organization does not have a solid performance appraisal system in place and working on a daily basis, and the manager is not properly educated in collecting and utilizing performance data effectively, the risk of legal action becomes very high.

The risk of litigation of one sort or another becomes even greater as the industry is singled out more by the media as a target for debate and real controversy over issues such as AIDS treatment and malpractice. As a result of this media interest, the labor boards and Equal Employment Opportunity (EEO) governing powers have redirected their attention to the healthcare business forum. Legislation passed in recent years allows victims of proven discrimination to sue not only the organization responsible for their unfair treatment but also the individual manager. All of these things increase the importance of a healthy selection and performance appraisal system. In order to protect the institution as well as themselves, it is imperative that managers have at their disposal a healthcare-specific selection and performance assessment system that can be readily and justly applied to all employees.

It is important to note that a healthcare institution can easily develop a reputation for discriminatory practices on the basis of the outcome of a single case in which the litigant wins a judgment. Needless to say, if a litigant can prove a case, the floodgates will usually open to several other complainants who want to test the waters while the getting is good. The governing boards in the institution's geographical area will also pay special attention to the offending organization to see if a trend of discrimination exists. It is easy to see how an ill-informed manager who makes a mistake can inadvertently subject an organization to close scrutiny and lawsuits. Despite the manager's good intentions, if the selection and performance assessment system itself is not professionally customized and legally just, the opportunity for negative results is omnipresent.

Because of the economic strife currently suffered by many healthcare institutions, the money available for human resources has predictably shrunk. It is therefore even more important for hospitals to make sure that the money allocated for human capital is in fact invested wisely. It is also essential for organizations to bring in people who are not only competent but also creative and will have ideas for new, revenue-generating services that will attract new patients and customers. With this in mind, it becomes essential from an economic standpoint for the institution to train its managers to select people who will not only maintain a quality status quo but improve on it by adding skills that will provide new, attractive services for the organization's potential clientele. At the same time, the healthcare managers must be able to select people whose creativity does not detract from their ability to function in the organizational hierarchy and meet basic job responsibilities. In order to spend existing dollars wisely, protect the institution from litigation and additional costs, and attract people whose creative abilities will add to revenues, the organization must have a proven, industry-specific selection and performance assessment system.

Industry Factors

Several critical dynamics occurring within the healthcare industry make an effective selection and performance assessment scheme necessary. Perhaps the most obvious factor in healthcare human resources today is the recent change of the average healthcare worker. Today's healthcare worker—in part because of economic factors just discussed—must be a highly dedicated person whose motivation lies primarily in self-satisfaction and the opportunity to do good for others, rather than in money. This is true simply because the pay scales within the healthcare industry are lower than in other industries.

Because of this problem in the American healthcare business sector, there has been an infusion of foreign national workers into virtually every conceivable job position. Notably hailing from the Philippines, Ireland, and other economically depressed and war-stricken countries, these workers are always more willing than their American counterparts to work for the comparatively low wages in American healthcare. For these people, the opportunity to live in the United States and freely pursue personal happiness as well as their career aspirations outweighs the lower wages. These foreign nationals represent a terrific labor pool that is highly motivated, appreciative of opportunity, and unlikely to turn its nose up at wages or working conditions that American workers might find fault with. With the opportunity the institution presents to them comes the beginning of a two-way relationship in which the foreign worker returns loyalty for the initial opportunity to work in the American healthcare society.

The emergence of the foreign worker in the healthcare setting also underscores the need for an effective selection system. Because of the possible language difficulties and cultural differences, it is vitally important to understand completely the range of these workers' experience and how it relates to what

is required in an American setting. They must be able to understand thoroughly the questions asked of them in an interview,
and they must be given the opportunity to represent their
qualifications forthrightly. Potential differences in expertise and
job requirements make a performance evaluation system that
begins on the employee's first day on the job ever more important. It is the responsibility of the healthcare manager to provide clear, complete direction to these eager employees, whose
motivation will be heightened by the fact that the manager is
not only paying attention to them and taking an interest in their
career but providing solid direction on how to attain their work
and career goals.

Throughout the healthcare industry, there is a major
shortage of qualified personnel in certain job categories. This
problem, ever present in the minds of personnel managers and
line managers alike, dominates their thinking when they are
searching for new personnel. Most notable is, of course, the nursing shortage, which has been worsening for the past several years
and has recently become desperate. In 1986, it was established
by the American Medical Association that by 1995 there would
be no less than 25,000 nursing jobs unfilled owing to a lack of
nursing graduates. In essence, things will get even worse before
they get better. Starting salaries for nurses presently range
between $19,000 and $22,000 per annum, with no true opportunity for fast advancement. The nursing profession is often
compared to teaching as a humane profession that is poorly compensated. This creates not only a lack of candidates but a lack
of true job consistency; nurses are apt to leave one institution
for another merely for a 65¢-per-hour raise, or in more extreme
but frequent cases to leave the profession altogether for a more
lucrative field. The first results in a lack of continuity within
an institution's nursing ranks; the second results in a lack of
continuity within the field itself. Widespread apathy exists even
among the entry-level, newly graduated nursing corps. One
nurse recruiter in North Carolina recently told me of a new nursing school graduate coming to an interview dressed in T-shirt
and jeans and interested only in her salary if she was offered
the job. The recruiter explained that the new graduates in her
area are acutely aware of the fact that if they are not offered

an acceptable wage at her institution, they can simply travel to a crosstown institution and, because of the shortage, get the wage and shift hours they desire.

This scenario is repeated from coast to coast, and unfortunately hospitals and other healthcare institutions find themselves hiring these people rather than going understaffed. In order to attract nurses and other personnel where the supply is less than the demand, an organization must have in place a selection system with a recruiting component that can attract qualified, motivated candidates. Furthermore, it must implement a performance appraisal system that provides opportunities for career development and job satisfaction. Without these two components properly in place, the institution reduces the likelihood that it can hire and retain competent workers within the ultracompetitive healthcare labor market.

Another industry factor affecting the selection and performance appraisal systems of healthcare organizations is the "corporatization" of the healthcare field, as evidenced by the emergence of giants such as Hospital Corporation of America, American Medical Inc. (AMI), and other national and regional chains. Many of these corporations have established central control of business policy and human resources management. The problem with these centralized systems is that they may not work effectively in every region. It therefore becomes essential to fine-tune these systems at each significant level. Furthermore, in the corporate scheme there are no guaranteed futures for individuals. A person might be working as an associate administrator in eastern Pennsylvania one year and in the next year be toiling as a department head in a major facility in Tucson. Because of this environment of change, it is essential for the corporation to have one standard selection and performance assessment system, calibrated according to a particular situation or region, so that there is a commonality of candidate qualifications augmented by job-specific data. This practice ensures the credibility and effectiveness of both the internal promotion scheme and the career development programs within these major chains. Without a standardization of selection and performance assessment within these organizations, candidates are liable to be judged and thus rewarded in a biased manner.

A factor that has recently presented itself on the healthcare scene is the scrutiny given performance appraisal systems by the Joint Commission on Hospital Administration. This governing body, which professionally accredits all of the nation's hospitals, has joined with other, similar authorities in placing a premium on performance appraisal. Because of the myriad consulting systems in this area, the healthcare manager must pay special attention to the tenets set forth in Part Three of this book to ensure that his or her system is in accord with the requirements mandated by the Joint Commission as well as the other significant governing groups.

While there are several industry-specific requirements for selection and performance assessment in healthcare, few systems in practice meet these requirements and have been proven on the job. In this book, we will discuss in detail the foremost of these proven systems so that managers will be able to employ them effectively not only to meet the criteria for accreditation but, more important, to select, assess, and retain the people who will do the manager and the organization the most good.

Chapter 2

Developing Effective Selection and Assessment Strategies

In the total scheme of human resource management in healthcare, selection and performance assessment are the two functions that most directly reflect the direction and objectives of the entire organization. The selection process enables the manager to bring in the right people to accomplish the organization's goals. The performance evaluation process ensures that the organization's human resources are meeting these goals with maximum productivity and continuing development. In order to maximize the results of these two essential processes, the healthcare manager must first assess the organization's business environment.

Environmental analysis involves the investigation of the three business environment factors that most affect human resources. The first is the business climate in which the organization currently operates. The second is the customer, or in healthcare the customer/patient, to whom the healthcare organization is providing service. The healthcare manager must understand the organization's customer in order to select the right person to serve that customer and to assess intelligently the employee who provides the service. The third factor is control, the degree to which a healthcare organization can ensure that its employees are eminently aware of the competitive nature of the current healthcare business arena and are therefore intent on giving the hospital high-quality, maximally effective service in return for their compensation.

In this chapter, we will examine each of these environmental factors and specifically explain their relevance to the selection and performance evaluation process. By understanding these factors, healthcare managers will be able to examine their current business environments and adjust their selection and performance assessment efforts accordingly, while at the same time exploring some of the significant phenomena currently affecting healthcare. For example, a recent television commercial shown in the Philadelphia metropolitan area presented a "then and now" scenario inspired by George Orwell's classic, *1984*. In the "then" segment, a Big Brother figure mechanically directed a robotic hospital staff around a crowded emergency room where seemingly grateful patients were treated shabbily. The "now" sequence featured the personal, human touch of the Delaware HMO Group. The commercial is indicative of the changes in the healthcare business arena in the past fifteen years, discussed in the preface and Chapter One. The healthcare manager must now hire and retain employees who realize that an understanding of their business climate, their customer, and the efficient use of their talents and resources is an essential part of healthcare success.

Analyzing the Business Climate

The first environmental analysis category is the overall business climate in which the healthcare organization operates. A fundamental aspect of strategic business analysis and planning, climate analysis is used by marketing and operational experts in anticipating future demands and customer needs. In a similar vein, it is essential for the human resources specialist as well as the line manager who must select and evaluate personnel to understand the business climate and use it as a frame of reference when selecting personnel and setting work goals and objectives. In this section, we explore all of the essential components of the business climate and explain their relevance and use in devising a selection and performance assessment strategy.

Culture. The first characteristic of a particular business climate is the culture—the regional or ethnic background—of the majority of the organization's business community. It is easy to see how a multinational corporation can take into account the differences in language and culture between different countries or regions of the world. Many successful pharmaceutical corporations, such as the Rorer Group, have Taiwanese managers in Taiwan, German managers in West Germany, and so on. A work unit that reflects the culture and regional identification of the local populace engenders a high comfort level between customer and company representative.

This tenet applies to the local hospital as well. By understanding the regional norms and hiring people who either share those norms or fully recognize and respect them, the hospital is telling its customers that their needs will be attended to by "one of their own," someone who understands them and with whom they can feel comfortable. This idea extends to the ethnic composition of a particular business climate. At Holy Cross Hospital in Los Angeles, the telephone caller to the switchboard receives greetings and information in both English and Spanish. This makes both Anglo and Chicano patients feel comfortable with the services of the hospital and reflects the recognition that the local climate is composed equally of two distinct cultures. By hiring people who recognize these cultural needs and who possess skills that can help them meet those needs (such as fluency in both Spanish and English), the line manager is supporting the organization's mission of service to the community.

Figure 1 shows how the healthcare organization operates within the overall climate as a business entity, as well as the vectors of communication that help enhance service and profitability. By selecting employees who have the ability to meet the cultural demands of the organization, and then by assessing their performance in this regard, the healthcare manager is enhancing the quality of service and the credibility of the organization in the local business community.

The cultural factor is related not only to ethnic cultural differences but to regional ones as well. The rural community of northwest New Jersey, for example, is very different from the casino community of Atlantic City, although the two are not far apart geographically. The ailments of the northwest New Jerseyan might be related to a farming accident or perhaps an

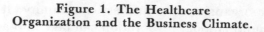

Figure 1. The Healthcare
Organization and the Business Climate.

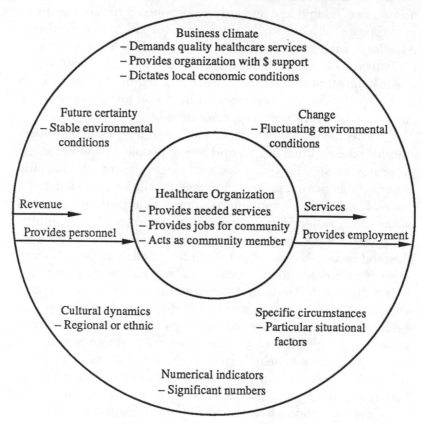

on-the-job injury at one of the local production plants. The Atlantic City healthcare patient might be suffering from alcohol-related injuries, psychological stress (the major malady of casino workers), or perhaps a traffic accident in a city whose road system has not been expanded since the casinos were introduced in the late 1970s. The healthcare manager must hire and effectively direct employees who know the local commerce, their typical customer, and the other factors illustrated in Figure 1.

Change. Change is an everyday reality affecting virtually every aspect of the entire healthcare business. Healthcare is still very much in the midst of widespread change in customer/patient selection and delivery of medical services, the customer/patient's ability to pay for treatment, changes in insurance carrier programs, and the basic apprehensions and expectations of the customer/patient who requires healthcare. The need to keep up with the change in healthcare is evidenced by the plethora of training programs currently available to the healthcare professional in managing change, managing in periods of turbulence and shrinking revenue, and related offerings.

As revenues fluctuate, larger hospital chains become more powerful and prominent, and populations change in size and cultural composition, healthcare managers must be certain that their staffs are able to adapt advantageously to change. The current healthcare business environment is not a good employment opportunity for someone who is rigid and needs a structured, consistently ordered workplace. For example, in 1982 our firm, CHR/InterVista, was engaged by O'Connor Hospital of San Jose, California, to design and implement an employee selection system. In doing our needs analysis, in which we determine the pertinent environmental factors that indicate the profile of the most effective employee, we found that adaptability was the single most needed factor. We came to this conclusion because of the change in O'Connor's business environment, typified by the population explosion attendant on the development of the Silicon Valley computer business center. This change, coupled with the ethnic diversity of the area, the cultural differences between the long-term residents and the newly arrived computer employees, and the basic facility expansion mandated by the increase in population, led to the logical conclusion that O'Connor Hospital had to hire employees who had demonstrated adaptability and flexibility in their approach to their work roles.

Certainty. In every healthcare business scheme there are constant factors that can be built on in formulating business policies in general and selection and assessment schemes in particular. For instance, the hospital business, unlike any other customer-based business, can be sure there will always be an acute need for its services and products; if an organization has provided those goods and services effectively in the past, chances are that customer/patients will use its services again as well as recommend them to friends and neighbors. Likewise, a healthcare organization with a special mission can assess with some degree of certainty the volume of business it can expect and thus anticipate the number and type of employees it needs.

A good example was the opening six years ago of the Estelle Doheny Eye Hospital by the Hospital Corporation of America (HCA), the most progressive research and development entity in the eye care field. The corporation was certain that it would profit by opening a hospital facility that would fully provide progressive care directly to the patient. Upon being selected as the facility's first administrator, Paul J. Hensler engaged our firm to design and implement a selection and performance appraisal system before he hired anyone besides his top reporting staff. He was certain of the prestige the hospital would enjoy, the great need for its services, and his own knowledge of the type of employee needed to serve acute-care patients in a large metropolitan business climate. Using this as a starting point, our staff was able to investigate the other environmental factors quickly and design and install a selection and performance appraisal system. As a result, the institution has become profitable before most new facilities have finished paying their initial debts, and it has a record of low turnover and high employee performance. By intelligently basing his systems on those factors in the business climate of which he was certain, Hensler has created a work organization of unquestionable high quality.

Numerical Indicators. The reliability of climate analysis is rooted in numerical indicators. Numerical indicators of importance to the line manager are patient censuses, shifts in patient populations, and the turnover or termination figures of the staff. For the human resources manager, the significant numerical indicators include the cost per hire, the number of applications submitted, overall organizational turnover, and any demographic figures that give a picture of the available work force and the hospital's chances of attracting, retaining, and developing solid employees. Other important numerical indicators include such aspects of the human resources bottom line as basic expenditures for training and development programs and return on those expenditures in the form of quality training and development and the acquisition of long-term employees.

A structured selection program is usually mandated upon the administration's discovery that the turnover rate of employees has been very high. Because of the high cost of turnover (usually 150–285 percent of an employee's annual salary), the smart organization realizes that quality control must be applied to its selection criteria. Likewise, when all of the performance appraisals in an organization begin to be scored in the "satisfactory" range, employees who perform at an above-average level become frustrated and leave for other employment. Hence, a valid performance appraisal system becomes a necessity for an organization cognizant of the significance of its numerical indicators.

Specific Circumstances. Every healthcare organization has certain conditions in its work environment that can be considered peculiar to its climate. At an American College of Healthcare Executives (ACHE) seminar that I conducted in 1986, fourteen of thirty participants (all administrators or associate administrators) were working in healthcare facilities currently undergoing major construction or physical expansion. Such conditions put additional stress on the healthcare employee, demand extra attention to customer/patients and their visitors, and emphasize the need for employees with a great sense of adaptability and work ethic. Another example might be a healthcare facility that lacks a consistent census. The line manager might have to lay off personnel, or the human resources manager might have to cease hiring altogether. The performance appraisal process at such an institution would have to be particularly effective so that the administration could clearly understand which employees should be retained in a layoff and which ones should be terminated.

A healthcare organization might be operating under the burden of court action, brought about, for example, by a class action discrimination suit. This would require the personnel office to pay special attention to the employment applications and the performance appraisals of members of the offended group. An organization might also have to recognize and react to significant external events, like the influx of a particular ethnic group or other demographic changes in its area. The population base of Northwest Community Hospital in suburban Chicago, for example, which in the sixties had many teenagers, now has few; three area high schools—at one time rated among the highest in the country—have closed in the past eight years. In general, any external environmental factor that may have a significant effect on the business approach of the healthcare institution should be examined by line manager and human resource specialist alike to determine its effect on the selection and assessment functions.

Cyclical activities and seasonal conditions also affect the business environment. For example, the end of the year is the worst time conceivable to recruit personnel because of the preoccupation with year-end business activities and holiday events. On the other hand, February and March are a recruiter's prime time for action, since the holidays are past and people are reexamining their work situations and their desires and professional goals. The early summer is a good time for organizations to conduct performance reviews and appraisals, whereas the late summer is not because typically people take their vacations in between July and early September. The savvy line manager and effective personnel manager take seasonal events into account when planning the timing of certain actions and the employment of selection and performance appraisal strategies.

The healthcare business climate consists of certain cultural dimensions, has change as an ever-present action agent, and demands attention to dynamics that are consistent and can be depended on with a high degree of certainty. Numerical indicators and consideration of specific circumstances are also necessary to the effective healthcare manager's formulation of employee selection and performance appraisal strategies.

Analyzing the Customer/Patient

In order to determine what types of personnel should be hired and developed, a healthcare manager must fully understand the type of customer the institution serves. By understanding that customer/patient, and perhaps more important, the manner in which the organization approaches the customer in gaining and retaining that person's business, the line manager can gain valuable insight into several key dimensions that are helpful in formulating a human resources selection and performance assessment strategy. In this section, we will examine the critical dimensions of customer analysis and show their pragmatic relevance to personnel selection and assessment processes.

Community. The first customer analysis factor is the customer's local community. In a greater sense, the total community itself is the customer, and in establishing a selection and performance assessment strategy the line manager should take this "bigger entity" into consideration. As we discussed in the section on climate issues, the customer community might include a varied ethnic composition or regional distinctions.

   The line manager should also take into account such economic events as layoffs at major local industries that might affect the organization, as well as demographic and social changes that might influence the customer/patient census of the institution. Healthcare would seem to have a unique business advantage in that it is a universally needed service that is always in demand. Indeed, a customer community probably exists for every healthcare institution. However, the institution that always provides a "personal touch" to clients is the one that will consistently enjoy the community's business.

   The marketing survey that our consulting firm, CHR/ InterVista, used for the O'Connor Hospital project (see Resource A) shows the myriad factors healthcare consumers consider when selecting an institution. All of the factors indicate a great need for the successful organization to employ individuals with effective interpersonal skills—or "people skills." The ability to perceive a customer's needs as well as understand his or her cultural expectations is of paramount importance in drawing the customer in and making him or her feel as though the organization really cares about and understands that person. The ability to communicate with each customer/patient—particularly to listen and convey essential information accurately, answer pertinent questions, and in general make the customer feel as comfortable as possible—is inevitably vital to the establishment of solid, long-term customer relations. Additional influential factors include the presence and bearing of individual employees as well as the image the institution conveys to the customer community at large.

By reacting positively to the personal needs of the customer community an institution can establish itself as the "hometown" healthcare organization, even in our present era of alternative delivery services and ultramodern marketing schemes. For example, O'Connor Hospital has maintained a solid relationship with its customer community by selecting and retaining employees who understand its business climate and who also have the people skills needed to make clients feel as though their care and comfort are top priority. A different kind of healthcare organization, the Estelle Doheny Eye Hospital, has been successful by showing its customer community that it has the strength of a major national entity (HCA) behind it and the technology of an internationally renowned research unit to help in its delivery of service to the customer/patient. The Estelle Doheny Eye Hospital, however, also uses a selection and performance assessment system that puts a premium on good people skills and on interpersonal attributes that will help put clients at ease, help them feel that they are being well treated both medically and humanistically.

The healthcare line manager, then, needs to hire people who understand the business climate and also communicate well, are perceptive and sensitive in their judgments, and project a positive image to the organization's customer/patients. Furthermore, by rewarding these attributes through effective performance assessment, the manager can ensure that these vital abilities will be sustained and developed within the organization.

Concept. The concept of a healthcare organization is the publicized image the organization presents to its buying public, the customer community. Concept affects the manner in which the customer community perceives the institution in respect to its overall quality and the premium it places on providing service. With the emergence of new and alternative healthcare delivery systems, particularly with the arrival of HMOs and similar organizations, many healthcare firms of all levels and sizes have taken a serious look at the issue of image making, as well as the stated missions of their organizations. As the example at the opening of this chapter illustrates, many healthcare organizations are actively using the media as an integral part of their effort to aggressively seek out new markets and expand their current customer/patient census.

It is imperative that the line manager regularly examine the concept of the organization in terms of the ongoing performance of current staff as well as future hiring of replacement and additional personnel. By understanding the unique concept the organization presents to its customer community, the line manager can make certain that the staff presentation is congruent with the overall presence of the institution and that employees share a commitment to the organizational concept. By espousing a common understanding of the organization's mission, the line manager can help shape and encourage employee efforts toward the accomplishment of that mission. When an employee is not introduced to the organizational concept at the time of hiring, there can be little identification with or commitment to the institution's goals and concept. In order to select employees with proven organizational loyalty, the line manager must ensure that the employees have a basic understanding of what the organization is all about.

Choice. The most basic tenet of American business is one that has only recently been fully recognized in the healthcare forum— the customer/patient must be able to make an independent choice as to where to receive healthcare services. Until recently, for all practical purposes, the healthcare customer did not have true freedom of choice; the decision as to where these essential services would be obtained was predetermined either by the prescriptions of an employer-provided insurance plan, geographic limitations, or religious affiliation. The emergence of alternative delivery systems, diminishing employee benefits in all industries, and the rising costs of healthcare have all contributed to making today's customer/patient demand a choice of sources for healthcare services.

Nonetheless, it is amazing how many healthcare professionals, especially those who have been in the field for an extended period of time, have failed to face the realities of drastic change and increased competition in their marketplace. No one is immune, and all managers need to take into account that their customer/patients, who have the power to make or break them, now are exercising their options in picking healthcare providers. As the O'Connor customer survey so clearly indicates (Resource A), clients' choices will be largely based on issues involving interpersonal relations with employees. Once again, hiring and accurately assessing employees who can interact sensitively and effectively with the organization's customer/patients is a key factor in engaging the short-term business and long-term loyalty of healthcare consumers.

In some places and under particular circumstances the customer/patient might still have a limited choice of healthcare services. For example, there are still some areas of the United States that are geographically remote and clients there must rely on whatever institution is close enough to provide adequate service. This is also the case in regions of western Canada, notably in the provinces of Alberta and Saskatchewan. In some other cases, insurance carriers for some industrial firms might encourage the customer/patient to patronize one facility as opposed to another, particularly in some of the newer HMO/CHP (community health plan) schemes. Some customer/patients will always feel bound to use the services of their religiously affiliated local institution or the medical center or teaching hospital of their local university or álma mater. In all such institutions, managers will do well to appreciate clients' loyalty and to determine and act on the factors that will help perpetuate this advantage. Here, as in more competitively situated organizations, the line manager needs to take care to hire and progressively direct employees who will amplify the link to the customer/patient through the application of solid people skills.

In all cases, the line manager and human resources specialist should remember that customer/patients will make their choices based on the healthcare institution's ability to understand their needs as people as well as medical patients. In other words, the customer community will respond positively to and support the organization that employs and retains people who demonstrate their understanding of and concern for the community through good communication, perceptiveness, and appreciation of the mutual benefits of a two-way loyalty between the customer/patient and the institution.

Analyzing Organizational Control

In order to complete a comprehensive analysis of environmental factors, the healthcare manager must anatomize the organizational components that affect the providing of services to customer/patients. In understanding components and their interrelationships, the manager can determine the basic business approach and team orientation that current employees and newly hired staff members should take. Figure 2 illustrates the relationship between organizational goals, departmental goals, and individual worker goals. In a successful organization, individual goals should not only *relate* to the departmental goals but should in fact be functional parts that contribute to accomplishing those goals. Likewise, a department's goals and objectives must be established by its manager with the objectives and goals of the total organization in mind. Considering this interrelatedness, the manager's understanding of the organization's mission, credibility, internal chemistry, and competition is essential to his or her development of an effective selection and performance assessment strategy. Resource C contains a survey instrument that the reader can use to determine an organizational profile.

Mission. The mission of a healthcare organization is simply its charter or overall business objective. While most healthcare organizations have as their mission the universal charter of providing competent healthcare to members of their customer community, the widespread change in the healthcare business arena has altered this aspect considerably. For example, the mission of a private hospital is different from that of a community hospital, and both are different from the mission of an HMO or CHP organization, a nursing home, or an acute-care facility.

Figure 2. Relationship of Goals.

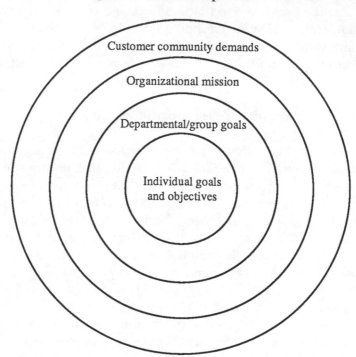

Customer community demands

Organizational mission

Departmental/group goals

Individual goals
and objectives

The mission of O'Connor Hospital in San Jose is to provide a broad range of services to its customer community; the mission of Estelle Doheny Eye Hospital is to provide the best surgical eye care in the world to anyone who needs it.

The mission of the organization must be clearly defined and easily recognized. The line manager and human resources specialist must ensure that new employees understand and respect the organizational mission, and that existing employees maintain their loyalty to the organization and their co-workers in support of that mission. In selecting new employees, the hiring manager might naturally assume that a candidate who has worked at an institution with a similar mission would be more successful in the position than another candidate without such experience. Previous exposure would indeed help in the initial orientation process, but the second candidate might in fact have better long-term potential for the organization. The best approach is for the manager to include the organizational mission among the other environmental considerations, taking candidates' past experience into account but not relying on it as a guarantee of success. This principle will be explained more fully in the chapters on interviewing (Chapters Six and Seven).

Credibility. Credibility is the view, widely held by the customer community, that the healthcare organization represents the best choice for healthcare services. Three factors make up credibility. The first is the "personal touch" discussed earlier in this chapter. Employees with strong interpersonal skills create an internal environment that makes customer/patients feel as comfortable as possible and encourages them, upon their return home, to recommend the facility to friends and neighbors. Since word of mouth is still the most potent form of advertisement, the need to select and retain this type of employee is underscored.

The second component of credibility is the consistency with which the healthcare organization provides reliable, high-quality service. Nothing is more detrimental to the credibility of a healthcare organization than a lapse of consistency, for a consumer will typically focus on poor service and tell others of negative situations.

The final component of credibility is the commitment the institution shows to its customer community in general and to the customer/patient in particular. This is evidenced in the role that the institution plays as a member of the community. For instance, it is hard to think of a successful community hospital that is not a major force in its community's United Way Fund Drive. By promoting community commitment through high-quality business service and community membership and encouraging its employees to support and participate in this effort, the winning healthcare organization builds great credibility with its customer community.

Credibility is hampered by employees who lack true dedication to the cause of helping others, fellow employees as well as customer/patients. The hiring manager must make certain that employees who are hired and retained are dedicated to upholding departmental and organizational standards as well as technically able.

Internal Chemistry and Competition. The chemistry of an organization—the composition of its employees and their ability to work cohesively and effectively as a unit—is the greatest competitive advantage a healthcare organization can have in today's marketplace. The healthcare organization must have a mixture of individuals who are competent in their respective fields and function well together as an integrated team committed to the mission and the success of the entire organization.

Today's healthcare market, with its shrinking revenues and openly competitive nature, demands that an organization provide a team-oriented internal environment that rewards excellence and does not accommodate incompetence or a "me-first" attitude on the part of its employees. This means that the line manager must select people who can work well together and who possess some of the traits of present and past successful employees. By analyzing and understanding the organization's environment fully and using that knowledge to construct a well-tuned, effective selection and performance assessment approach, the healthcare manager is helping to provide the organization with the greatest competitive advantage possible.

Chapter 3

Setting Standards for Selection and Performance Evaluation

The structure, objectives, and personality dynamics of the successful organization today are radically different from those of fifteen years ago. In our present environment of takeovers, daily closings, new ventures, and alternative delivery systems, the healthcare organization must maintain an organizational structure able to provide high-quality service to selective customer/patients, a set of organizational objectives that are aggressive and profit-oriented, and an organizational personality that works successfully with both.

The successful organizational personality comprises four major categories. The first category is the attitude orientation of the organization as a whole and of each employee. The second is people skills, evidenced by the interpersonal strengths of managers and employees. The third is managerial aptitude; each supervisor must be an accomplished leader of personnel and manager of resources, and each employee must be competent in his or her position and progressing toward the next position on the career ladder. The final category is team orientation, necessary to the attainment of the organization's overall mission—to profitably provide healthcare to the customer community.

In this chapter, we will look at the Quantitative Communological Organizational Profile System (Quan-Com System), an organizational analysis formula that over 200 healthcare organizations have used in establishing their selection and per-

27

formance assessment standards. By comprehensively looking at the four organizational personality categories and specifically analyzing their individual components, the reader will be able to use this formula effectively to set employee selection and performance assessment standards for his or her work unit and for the entire organization. By looking at these factors first from an organizational perspective and then at their application to individual situations, the reader will fully understand how to use each of these Quan-Com factors in interviewing and hiring new employees and monitoring the performance of current employees.

The Quan-Com System

The Quan-Com System is based on over fifteen years of research and has been validated both academically (using the Kirkpatrick Formula) and, more important, through practical use by over 200 leading healthcare organizations. It is the recommended system of the American College of Healthcare Executives and has received endorsements from such notable organizations as Harvard University and the American Association of Homes for the Aging. The system is based on research that indicates that each of the four organizational categories—attitude orientation, people skills, managerial aptitude, and team orientation—should be broken down further into four essential components (Lombardi, 1985c). By using a bell curve analysis to determine the relevance of each of these components to a specific job, the healthcare manager can accurately assess the work personality and technical potential of new candidates as well as existing employees in that position.

The Quan-Com System requires that the user first understand the basic bell curve charting of an organizational personality factor. As Figure 3 shows, the bell curve, or "behavioral bridge," is a graphic representation of the fact that too much of a particular trait can be just as detrimental to the work situation as too little. For instance, an extremely energetic candidate for a position might be just as much of a liability in the work situation as one with little energy; such an employee might be hyper-

Figure 3. Bell Curve Plotting of Quan-Com Characteristics.

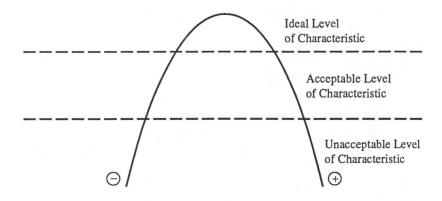

active on the job or a likely candidate for burnout. The line manager must think of job candidates and employees as having behavioral tendencies that carry work liabilities with them. This must replace two misguided philosophies that encourage poor selection and performance assessment.

The first misguided philosophy often held by well-meaning but ineffective managers is that behavior follows a linear scale according to which the perfect candidate is the one who exhibits the most of a particular trait. For example, while aggressiveness is useful in many positions, the most aggressive of a pool of applicants for a particular position might very well be *too* aggressive in his or her business approach. If this tendency manifests itself too often in the work situation, the liability will be that the employee's overaggressive style will alienate others or perhaps offend a customer/patient or visitor.

The second misguided philosophy is that candidates themselves should be asked about their relative strengths and weaknesses. The question "What are your strengths and weaknesses?" is so commonly asked in interviews that it is handled well even by a recent college graduate, who realizes that the weaknesses cited in answering that question should be disguised strengths. Answers such as "I'm a perfectionist, which sometimes causes problems for others" or "I'm a workaholic" in reality indicate strengths. While it is essential to determine the shortcomings of new employees and to ascertain those of existing employees during the performance assessment process, there are more clever ways of doing so, as we will show in the chapters on selection and performance appraisal. What is important to understand in applying the Quan-Com formula is the identification of work personality *tendencies* and the *liabilities* attendant on those tendencies.

Four essential factors must be considered when the Quan-Com organizational analysis formula is applied. The first is the *organization.* The healthcare manager must determine where the organization lies on the bell curve in respect to each of the Quan-Com characteristics. The amount of each characteristic appropriate to each work position is determined with respect to the organization's relative need for the characteristic. For example, while adaptability and flexibility are essential to all organizations in today's healthcare business arena, a newly opened facility might have to be more adaptable than the norm (plotted toward the + side of the bell curve). The manager hiring employees for a new venture would therefore look for people who were more adaptable than average; such employees would be flexible in dealing with the needs of the new venture and synchronized with the organization's philosophy. Someone with a tendency toward inflexibility and a preference for a stable, day-in-day-out work routine would be liable to mesh poorly with the organizational philosophy of adaptability. The survey in Resource C can be used to assess the organization's needs and establish standards.

The second factor is the *position.* The line manager must consider the job description and the basic needs of the work position in calibrating each Quan-Com factor. For example, for the position of internal auditor, the adaptability factor would move to the − side of the bell curve, toward relative rigidity and less adaptability. The positions of new marketing director or training/education specialist, on the other hand, would lie on the + side of the bell curve; an employee with a little more adaptability than the norm would be able to deal effectively with the changing circumstances and the varied personalities one encounters in those two positions.

The third factor is *definition*. Each characteristic is well defined and has been constructed with healthcare line managers and their supervisory needs in mind. Often, one manager's definition of a characteristic differs radically from that of another manager. Therefore, the manager using this system should ensure that all of the people engaged in the selection and performance assessment process—including other managers, personnel recruiters, and the employees themselves—understand each factor's definition and application to each position and to the work group as a whole.

The fourth factor is *situational circumstances*. A healthcare organization may have special conditions that demand consideration in the Quan-Com analysis. These circumstances might affect particular jobs, or the conduct of a job might involve nuances that merit special consideration.

The line manager must remember environmental factors and the aspects of each specific job when calibrating the factors for selection and appraisal. For example, aggressiveness would vary between a nurse working in New York City and another working in tiny Cornwall (population 836), sixty-five miles north of New York on the Hudson River. Aggressiveness would vary further within New York among nurses working in an established facility, one that is still under construction, and one that served many homeless vagrants. In all cases, special circumstances surrounding jobs and significant environmental factors must be recognized and included in the equation.

The four Quan-Com categories—attitude orientation, people skills, managerial aptitude, and team orientation—and the sixteen characteristics they comprise can be outlined as follows:

A. Attitude orientation
   1. Adaptability
   2. Aggressiveness
   3. Perseverance
   4. Work ethic
B. People skills
   1. Communication
   2. Energy level

    3.   Perceptiveness
    4.   Presence or bearing
C. Managerial aptitude
    1.   Creativity
    2.   Delegation
    3.   Independent judgment
    4.   Planning
D. Team orientation
    1.   Cooperation
    2.   Employee relations
    3.   Loyalty
    4.   Technical expertise

With all of this in mind, we will now explore each Quan-Com characteristic by using bell curve analysis, pertinent "real-world" examples, and demonstrated relevance to the selection and assessment process in order to set organizational standards.

Analyzing Attitude Orientation

The first Quan-Com category is the attitude the organization engenders toward establishing and accomplishing its business objectives. At the individual level, it is the attitude that the organization demands from its employees in the pursuit of their work goals. Attitude orientation is usually misunderstood or unintentionally misused, as in the common statement "I don't like that person's attitude." By generalizing this category into one nebulous factor, the offending manager is not fully identifying the characteristic and thus does not have a clear understanding of what it is or how it might affect the business situation.

The four essential components of attitude orientation at the organizational and individual levels are adaptability, aggressiveness, perseverance, and work ethic. The combination of these factors represents the motivation of an employee, the dedication and the mind-set that he or she brings to the job every day. It also represents part of the personality of the organization that the customer public perceives. If the individuals who work for a particular healthcare organization embrace all four of these tenets effectively, the resultant image of the organization in the community will be of an institution that is dedicated to providing quality care to the customer community. In this section, we will look at these four essential ingredients of attitude orientation and demonstrate how to analyze and adjust their application for maximum effectiveness in the selection and performance assessment process.

Adaptability. It is imperative that the successful healthcare organization maintain a high level of organizational flexibility in order to meet the challenges of its changing business environment. By hiring and developing employees with the right degree of adaptability, the organization can ensure that it has the human resources necessary to keep up with the times and meet any new business demands from its customer community. Adaptability is present in organizations and individuals who have a proven ability to perform well under changing business circumstances and to maintain a high standard of work under stress caused by business pressures, such as demands for more services or new programs.

Many healthcare professionals are required to obtain productive work results in situations where declining revenues are the norm. This requires adaptability, as do situations where physical work environments are restrictive or lack equipment or space. Adaptability is also needed by the healthcare worker in order to deal with the plethora of varied personalities that are encountered during the average day, including patients, physicians, and visitors with different backgrounds and agendas. Because the healthcare arena is one in which progress must be made daily in medical services, product development, and technical procedures, the successful healthcare organization must also employ personnel who can absorb and apply new methods and procedures quickly and with excellent results. Adaptability is needed to shift an operating procedure by incorporating new methods that in the long run will benefit everyone involved.

A good example of adaptability in a successful healthcare organization's business strategy and human resources management is the establishment of the first AIDS treatment clinic in the Eastern United States by the Einstein Medical Center, under the direction of Dr. Karen Hein, in 1986. If Einstein Medical Center had not been adaptable enough to create a treatment facility for a little-understood and quickly spreading malady, or if Dr. Hein herself had not been flexible enough to balance her medical and managerial responsibilities, this facility would never have been established successfully.

Figure 4 illustrates the bell curve of adaptability. People who gravitate to the left-hand or − side of the diagram are not flexible at all; their liability is that they will not adapt to the

Figure 4. Adaptability.

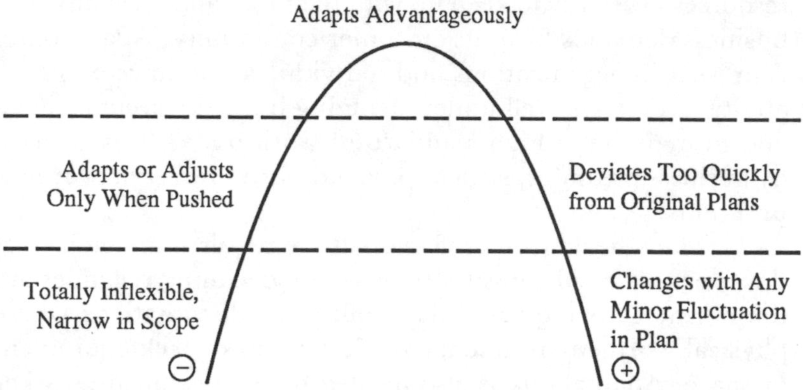

Adapts Advantageously

Adapts or Adjusts
Only When Pushed

Deviates Too Quickly
from Original Plans

Totally Inflexible,
Narrow in Scope

Changes with Any
Minor Fluctuation
in Plan

⊖

⊕

changes in their business environment required by circumstances. On the right-hand or + side of the diagram are found people who tend to change their strategy or approach readily; their liability is that they will forgo a plan that was solid in its first conception. Between these extremes and the top of the graph (which represents the ideal representation of each factor) are varying degrees of representation that can be acceptable in some situations. For example, the point on the − side near the top labeled ''adapts or adjusts only when pushed'' might be an acceptable location for an accounts payable clerk. The healthcare manager should plot the degree of adaptability desired in each position on each of these graphs before selecting a new employee.

The manager should likewise plot existing employees in a similar fashion in order to determine their effectiveness in each category. By determining where the ideal employee in a particular job position fits on each graph, as evidenced by work history and established high level of performance, the manager can also set a standard for each of the positions that report to him in order to select and evaluate employees against a profile of excellence.

Aggressiveness. For an organization to compete with other facilities in proactively attracting customer/patients and to provide customer/patients with the best care possible quickly and effectively, its healthcare managers must select workers with the proper degree of aggressiveness. By hiring and retaining people with positively aggressive tendencies, the healthcare organization will be certain of having employees who are confident in their capability to provide quality service and who will temper their aggressiveness with judgment.

The healthcare professional in a marketing role must be very aggressive in order to attack the marketplace and sell the services of his or her organization. Similarly, a nurse recruiter should be highly aggressive in order to recruit and hire personnel in a field where the demand far outweighs the supply. In a more subtle sense, staff nurses must be aggressive at times in their treatment of patients who are under sedation, for example, or in obtaining the proper records or treatment instructions for those under their care.

In short, successful healthcare workers who are properly aggressive are those who take command when it is appropriate in a business situation—that is, when it will help them provide stellar service to the customer/patient. The work behavior of these people is marked by an ability to be enterprising, to understand what must be accomplished on the job and address that need with positive action. In communicating essential information, they are direct; in collecting information or support needed to get a task accomplished, they are effectively persuasive. People who are insufficiently aggressive usually wind up reacting to situations rather than tackling them proactively. People who are too aggressive, however, often alienate co-workers and even sometimes customer/patients with behavior that is pushy and offensive. Figure 5 illustrates the varying degrees of aggressiveness.

Figure 5. Aggressiveness.

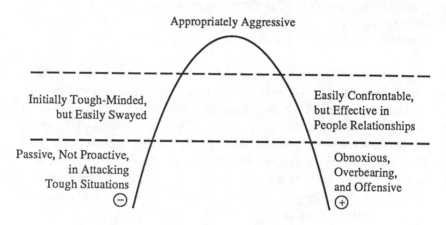

When considering the bell curve graph of aggressiveness and applying it to individual work roles, the healthcare manager should remember that there are some situations that require very aggressive behavior and others in which the worker should be passive. Therefore, the effective manager will look at the entire work role before deciding how aggressiveness fits into it. However, the manager should in no case hire or retain an employee whose natural tendency is to be at either extreme of the bell curve. Such an employee would habitually be either very pushy and obnoxious or very passive and reactive. If this tenet is ignored, the manager will find himself with an employee who tends to either anger or intimidate customer/patients, or one who will not actively seek out opportunities to provide optimum service.

Perseverance. The third component of the Quan-Com category of attitude orientation, perseverance, is the proven ability of a healthcare organization to pursue its desired objectives despite any obstacles. The individual employee shows dedication to the organization by persevering in the accomplishment of a goal. Whatever the fluctuations and difficulties that an organization faces in the daily business arena—an unexpected dip in the patient census, the loss of revenue from a benefactor—the institution must still provide its customer community with high-quality care. Employees must share this dedication to consistency; they must not give up easily or find ready excuses when a set objective is not accomplished.

Several years ago, the administration of Bayshore Community Hospital of central New Jersey instructed us to make sure, while setting the performance appraisal standards, that the management team put a premium on perseverance. The facility is in a growing area of the state, and the increasing census made it natural for the average employee to be sidetracked by a multitude of demands. By incorporating perseverance into its selection and appraisal scheme, the hospital encouraged employees to follow assigned tasks to their conclusion, at the same time intelligently ranking tasks in order of importance and timing requirements. Figure 6 illustrates levels of perseverance in the practical work setting.

Figure 6. Perseverance.

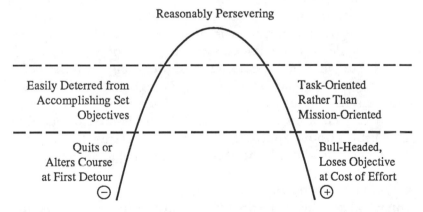

It is important to understand the dynamics of the right-hand or + side of the bell curve, which describes people who are more task-oriented than mission-oriented. Managers should ensure that these employees understand the mission of their work role and how specific tasks will contribute to its accomplishment. They should know what is most important to that mission and persevere in the tasks that are most essential, rather than blindly pursuing a task whose significance has been diminished or removed by changes in the work environment. By understanding what is important and consistently applying their energies and technical talents to the most important tasks, healthcare employees are helping the organization attain a high level of consistent service.

Work Ethic. Genius, said Thomas Edison, is 1 percent inspiration and 99 percent perspiration. This adage expresses well the need for a solid work ethic in the healthcare environment. With nationwide closings of facilities and the current competitive market, today's healthcare worker must join with management in working harder than ever just to survive. Of course, healthcare professionals have historically needed a better work ethic than their peers in other industries. The reasons for this are elementary. Healthcare can often mean life or death; therefore, the stress level in the field is higher than in others. With the exception of physicians, healthcare workers are not compensated as well as most of their counterparts in other fields, and thus they must possess an intrinsic dedication to high-quality service. The dedicated employee with a ''can-do'' approach will give the organization the human resources support it needs for successful existence in today's rapidly changing, almost cutthroat business environment.

A good work ethic is marked by an ability to maintain a realistic, positive approach to all work situations. It is typified by the person who asks himself *how,* rather than *if,* he can accomplish a goal. This person is always ready to perform any tasks that will contribute to the good of the organization. A person who lacks this ''can-do'' philosophy becomes the weak link in the chain of capable and well-motivated human resources. An overabundance of this characteristic, however, can cause suffering from job-related stress and make the employee a candidate for burnout. This is detrimental to the entire work group and perhaps the entire organization, because the behavior of a workaholic is truly oppressive. Obsessive workaholics create job stress for everyone: themselves, their co-workers, their subordinates (in the case of a manager), and in certain instances, the customer/patient. Healthcare managers should examine Figure 7, the bell curve graph of work ethic, and explore its relevance to their selection and performance assessment approach; the organization needs people who possess a well-adjusted work ethic and present neither the liability of performing below an acceptable level nor that of burning out and in the process inhibiting the performance of other workers and colleagues.

Figure 7. Work Ethic.

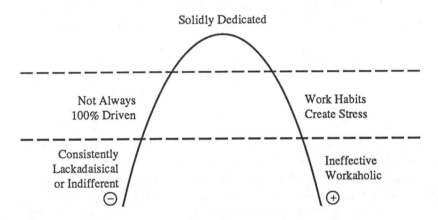

Analyzing People Skills

People skills, the second Quan-Com category, arc the interpersonal dynamics that an organization encourages its employees to apply effectively in the everyday conduct of their work roles. As with attitude orientation, most managers tend to generalize the people skills by assessing a candidate or an existing employee as a "people person" (or "not good with people"). This again neglects the fact that each of the four essential components of people skills is a vital factor in its own way and must be considered individually in order for a selection and performance appraisal strategy to be most effective.

As discussed in the previous chapter and as shown in the customer/patient survey of O'Connor Hospital (Resource A), people skills are elements the customer/patient considers when selecting an institution for healthcare. Because the healthcare business is undeniably a "people business," the personal touch is becoming an increasingly important factor in the customer/patient's choice. People skills are also vital for employees in their interactions on the job, for without the proper amounts of the four people skills—communication, energy, perceptiveness, and presence or bearing—the interaction of the healthcare employee with peers and supervisors will be only minimally effective. In this chapter, we will explore each of the people skills in its entirety and explain its relevance to the selection and performance appraisal scheme of the maximally effective healthcare manager.

Communication. The first component of people skills is communication. This ability is usually rated number one when healthcare managers rank all the Quan-Com factors in order of importance, with the other fifteen alternately being rated close seconds.

In the Quan-Com formula, communication is defined as the ability to express business needs and requirements effectively to all pertinent organizational personnel, including co-workers, superiors, and subordinates, and to customer/patients and visitors. Resource B of this book provides the reader with a complete glossary of over 90 communication dynamics that can be used as a checklist in assessing employees' communication styles on the job and in assessing interview behavior and performance appraisal discussions, as well as any manager-employee discussion. It is easy to understand how communication is essential to the entire spectrum of healthcare management, and the reader is probably personally aware of how good communication can positively, and poor communication negatively, affect a work situation.

Figure 8 illustrates the bell curve application of the communication factor. The healthcare manager should keep in mind that effective listening is an important part of communication, and it is a trait sometimes lacking in employees who think that

Figure 8. Communication.

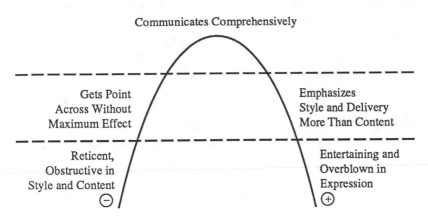

Communicates Comprehensively

| Gets Point Across Without Maximum Effect | Emphasizes Style and Delivery More Than Content |

| Reticent, Obstructive in Style and Content | Entertaining and Overblown in Expression |

they "know it all." The liability of an employee who falls on the left-hand or − side of the bell curve is that he will often make his point in a business conversation in a forgettable manner. On the right-hand or + side of the bell curve, the employee whose communication has "more sizzle than substance" will soon find that none of her communication has the maximum possible effect, as everything is presented in an overblown, overdone fashion. The manager must select and retain employees who communicate effectively and understand the importance of communication in their work roles. The importance of communication, and its prominent role in the selection and performance appraisal process, will be fully explained and underscored throughout this book.

Energy Level. Rabbi David Stern is the administrator of the Beth Israel Home for the Aging in New York City. He is also the star of the large facility's cable television network, hosting its daily talk show and anchoring its news programs. Additionally, he is the organizer of at least half of the resident recreational programs, and during the rest of his time he attends to the basic management of financial, operational, and personnel functions connected with running the facility. Rabbi Stern is the embodiment of a high energy level on the job in healthcare, a most important people skill. Without a suitable degree of energy, a healthcare employee does not work enthusiastically, a problem that is easily discerned by co-workers and customer/patients alike. In order for the healthcare organization to establish and maintain a competitive edge, it must essentially "outhustle" its competition. In order to do this, it must employ human resources who share a notable amount of energy and enthusiasm. The healthcare professional must also possess the vitality and endurance necessary to work more intensely whenever it is demanded by the healthcare organizational environment, where quick, accurate treatment is sometimes the difference between life and death.

Figure 9 shows the continuum of the energy level characteristic, from lackadaisical to hyperactive. It is easy to see how someone on the far right-hand side of the energy level curve would probably be in the same spot on the work ethic curve; such an employee is too energetic and too work-driven and will most likely suffer from job burnout. The healthcare manager must

Figure 9. Energy Level.

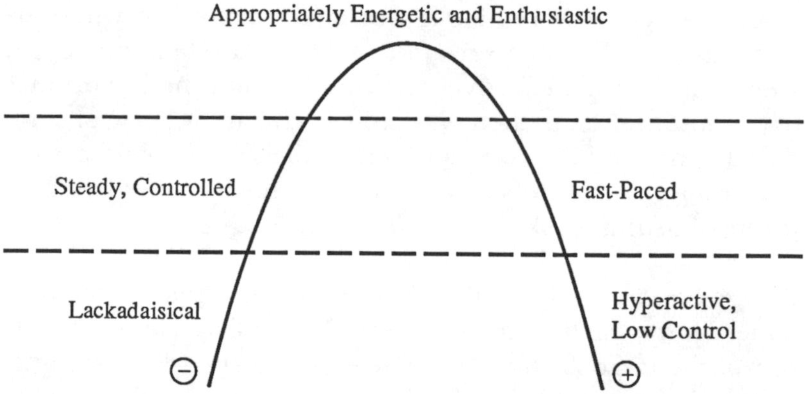

Appropriately Energetic and Enthusiastic

Steady, Controlled

Fast-Paced

Lackadaisical

Hyperactive,
Low Control

$\ominus$

$\oplus$

consider the demands of the position, look at the energy level possessed by the best performer in that particular job, and make the employee selection accordingly. For example, emergency room personnel should have a high energy level to be able to increase the intensity of their work as needed. The ER manager should accordingly hire and retain employees with an energy level that falls just to the right of the center of the graph.

Perceptiveness. The organization must be perceptive enough to know what its customer community wants from it in terms of specific services, how those services should be delivered, and what role in the community the institution should play. Likewise, individual employees must be perceptive in pursuing their work objectives, evidencing comprehensive understanding of the needs of customer/patients as well as fellow workers. Good perceptiveness coupled with good communication skills will yield good results in interpersonal dealings with all members of the health-care organizational community.

Figure 10 illustrates the bell curve of perceptiveness, from insensitivity to interpersonal relations to the state of being too analytical in assessing social dynamics. A good example of the latter is the person who attends a staff meeting and, instead of

Figure 10. Perceptiveness.

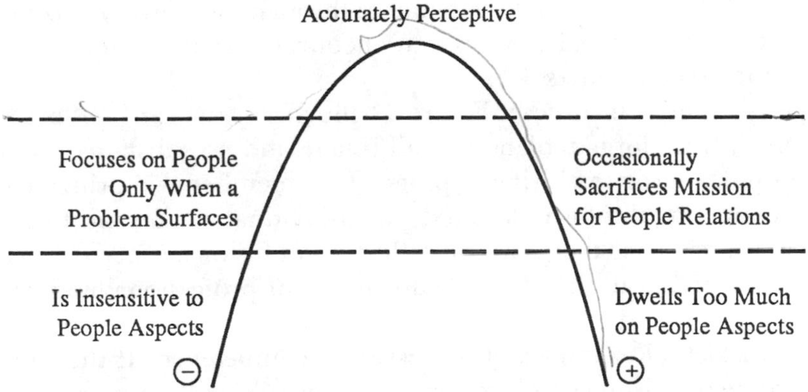

concentrating on *what* was said, spends an inordinate amount of time determining *why* someone said something, or perhaps why someone reacted emotionally to one part of the meeting and not to another. While it is important to understand *why* something was said, this certainly should not be dwelt on to the exclusion of *what* was said and what needs to be done as a result. The liability of an employee who is not perceptive at all is that the critical people issues of a work episode are not addressed adequately; the liability of someone who is overperceptive is that the analysis of the people issues overwhelms the substantive operational and functional aspects of the work situation. In both selection and performance appraisal, the level of perceptiveness must be examined by the hiring or reviewing manager and the potential liabilities fully assessed.

Presence or Bearing. The ability to create a positive impression and make one's presence felt in a business situation is an interpersonal skill needed by the healthcare organization and the individual worker alike. The key in both cases is a presence that projects an aura of competence to the customer community in general and the individual customer/patient. Many healthcare supply companies, such as Johnson & Johnson, American Travenol, and Bristol-Myers, inspire confidence in their customers through their presence or organizational image. Many hospitals, from Valley Livermore on the West Coast to Mt. Sinai on the East Coast, have established images through the delivery of competent professional services that encourage loyalty in their customer communities.

The bell curve in Figure 11 illustrates the range of presence, from forgettableness to all image and no substance. It is important for the hiring manager to remember two principles in applying this formula. First, the individual worker must possess a presence that is a true reflection of his or her personality and conveys to the observer an image of professional competence. Second, the worker must be able to support the image with factual examples of professional competence. If the candidate or existing employee projects more glitter than substance, the manager should apply the tenets of this factor (using the selection systems provided in Resources E and F) and those of communication to determine how valid and "real" the person's presence is. With a phony or "plastic" presence, or without a notable presence at all, it is impossible for the employee to

Figure 11. Presence.

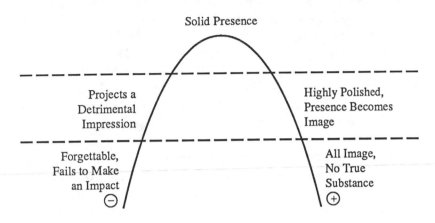

Solid Presence

Projects a
Detrimental
Impression

Highly Polished,
Presence Becomes
Image

Forgettable,
Fails to Make
an Impact
⊖

All Image,
No True
Substance
⊕

make customer/patients feel that they are in capable, caring hands. Even a shy employee can give the customer/patient a sense of security through the professionalism shown in his or her physical appearance and competent work.

Analyzing Managerial Aptitude

The need for solid managerial aptitude—the proven ability to expertly employ all of the physical, financial, and human resources available in the interest of providing quality health-care services—is shared by the organization and the individual healthcare manager. Because of the travails associated with acquiring and retaining good personnel, as well as the difficulty of acquiring and maintaining good physical resources with shrinking revenues, the healthcare organization must manage its total resources more effectively than ever. The individual managers must in turn get the most possible from their available resources. Managers must pay particular attention to the selection and assessment of human resources, as this category is the most qualitative and intangible in nature, and thus the most difficult to manage.

Like the other Quan-Com categories, the four essential factors of managerial aptitude—creativity, delegation, independent judgment, and planning—are usually combined into one general description of a person as a "good (or bad) manager." In this section, we will individually define and fully explain each of the managerial aptitude factors and explore their application to the human resources organizational profile. The reader should consider the relevance of these factors, not only to the hiring and assessment situations he or she encounters with supervisors and employees, but also in respect to his or her own work approach and managerial responsibilities.

Creativity. All healthcare organizations must explore any possibilities for providing new services and thus bringing in additional revenues. Without creativity, there is no organizational growth, and of course without growth, in today's healthcare arena, there will surely be trouble (and perhaps a closing) in the near future. Creativity on the part of the organization is often best inspired by a request for services from the customer community. For example, when the University Hospital of Newark, New Jersey, discovered that its customer community needed more neonatal services, it developed a plan to construct and install a neonatal unit. To finance the unit, the hospital devised a creative scheme of obtaining funds from the state, not from traditional means such as a special legislative bill (which would have taken a considerable amount of time), but from the state lottery system, which at the time was looking for qualified beneficiaries of its fund. Thanks to this financial program, the unit is now in place and serving its customer community competently and profitably.

At the individual level, healthcare managers must use creativity in their management approach in order to consistently provide the best return to the organization on its investment of money, physical resources, and personnel. The manager who uses creativity suitably is one who can innovatively set new plans and business directions that will improve service while using resources more efficiently. This manager is unafraid to take risks on opportunities to improve the status quo and the output of the workplace. Furthermore, this manager also knows how to implement new programs in a way that will realize their maximum benefit quickly and that will also make the powers that be recognize their value. The creative manager not only can see an opportunity and seize it for business gain but can also sell it to the appropriate organizational parties. A good example of the comprehensive use of creativity in the management process appears in the case study in Chapter Fifteen.

Figure 12 shows the range of creativity in a manager's repertoire, from nonexistence to dominating his or her approach without being anchored in reality. The manager who is devoid of creativity is liable to be unable to improve on the status quo and, as a result, to become stagnant and fail to progress and increase profitability. On the other hand, the manager who always gravitates toward the creative angle may spend an inordinate amount of time looking for creative opportunities and lose perspective on what needs to be done from a practical standpoint. The manager who is sufficiently creative and hires and manages employees who can contribute good creative ideas and suggestions on appropriate occasions is the manager who will give the organization an asset that will help maximize the all-important bottom line.

Figure 12. Creativity.

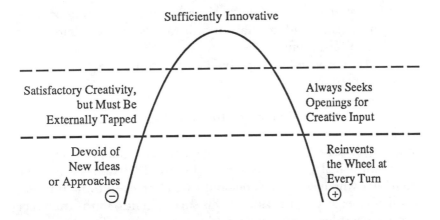

Delegation. A solid healthcare organization is one in which every member is committed to the overall organizational goal of providing high-quality healthcare at all times. In order for each member to contribute the full benefit of his or her expertise and for the managers and directors of the facility to take full advantage of their own technical strengths as well as those of their subordinates, the organization must use a good system of delegation. From the top administrator down to the lowest-ranked supervisor, managers and supervisors must assign work to each employee in an effective manner, freeing themselves to maintain a "big picture" perspective on their jobs without having to supervise their employees from an inappropriately and unproductively close vantage point.

A manager who is a good delegator can assign responsibility and authority to individual employees, utilizing their talents to improve the speed and efficiency of service to the customer/patient. This manager can effectively work through people to accomplish desired ends. The manager who is a solid delegator uses a simple four-part formula to delegate work effectively:

1. Identifying the task to be accomplished and outlining a general plan for its accomplishment
2. Selecting from all of the available human resources the best person to accomplish the task on the basis of technical expertise and past performance
3. Explaining the task fully to the employee, indicating possible approaches and special circumstances that will aid in its accomplishment
4. Arranging a follow-up strategy and timing expectation for completion

The complete formula for setting goals and objectives, and in essence delegating the entire scope of the employee's yearly goals and objectives, is covered comprehensively in Chapter Ten. The delegation bell curve, shown in Figure 13, travels from the manager who never delegates and tries to do everything himself, foolishly neglecting the skills of his subordinates, to the manager who always distributes work and responsibility. The latter person usually does not want to take responsibility for her work group and for anything that might turn out negatively. There

Figure 13. Delegation.

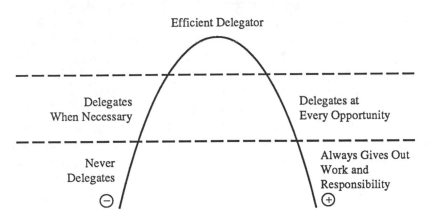

Efficient Delegator

Delegates
When Necessary

Delegates at
Every Opportunity

Never
Delegates

Always Gives Out
Work and
Responsibility

⊖

⊕

is a wider range of efficient delegation than of other managerial traits; for example, a good chief executive officer (CEO) would delegate at every opportunity in order to maintain his all-important "big picture" perspective on his operation. On the other hand, a rookie manager would delegate only when necessary, thus giving herself the maximum opportunity to learn as much as possible about her job and its responsibilities. She could then delegate progressively more work to the subordinates she feels are the most qualified.

In a survey conducted by our firm, CHR/InterVista, in 1985, we discovered that over 70 percent of a nationwide group of 250 managers felt that of the sixteen Quan-Com factors, delegation was the one that needed the most improvement in their own managerial approaches. They tended to delegate infrequently because they wanted to make sure the job was done right, an understandable problem given the high work ethic and commitment to quality that is shared by healthcare managers. However, to maintain consistent quality and instill a broad range of expertise in employees, the manager must be an effective delegator.

Independent Judgment. In order for all members of an organization to contribute their full efforts, it is essential that each employee have a proper amount of independent judgment. This is as true for the administrator—who often must make decisions that will affect the entire organization and its interaction with the customer community—as it is for the housekeeping manager—who must independently schedule and implement a mobilization of employees every day in order to provide the best institutional environment for the customer/patient.

Healthcare managers and supervisors who have solid independent judgment are capable of ascertaining goals and using available human resources to set into motion programs that will achieve those goals. They are self-starting, that is, they do not have to be externally motivated, and they make judgments and decisions and accomplish tasks without undue reliance on others. Without independent judgment in its managers and employees, the healthcare organization moves slowly and stagnantly because it depends on one central source for direction and motivation, usually the top administration, which cannot possibly know all of the operational nuances and opportunities for improvement of each work group. On the other hand, an organization whose managers have too much independent judgment will find every department going in a different direction and no central control or accomplishment of organizational objectives. Therefore, an appropriate balance must be achieved

Figure 14. Independent Judgment.

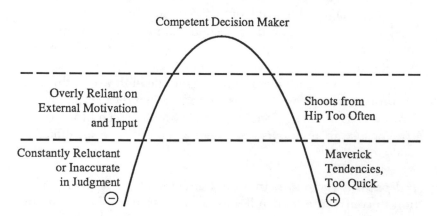

between the two extremes illustrated in Figure 14. It is vital for employees, as well as managers, to possess a proper degree of independent judgment; the employees are the experts in their own work roles and therefore know best how to use their energies effectively. However, too much independent judgment on the part of employees can confront the manager with a work group whose efforts are unproductively scattered and whose members are potentially rebellious.

Healthcare managers should look at the degrees of independent judgment as they appear on the bell curve in Figure 14 and as they are delineated in Resource F. They should determine how well independent judgment has been utilized by their work groups, reporting supervisors, and themselves in the pursuit of maximizing work performance.

Planning. Finally, the healthcare manager with good managerial aptitude is a good planner, able to set goals and design activities to attain them. Like the healthcare organization itself, the manager must strive to foresee events and processes that will have an effect on his or her work group and plan accordingly. With the daily changes in the healthcare environment, it is often difficult to set specific, concrete plans far in advance. It is possible for the effective healthcare manager, however, to set long- and short-range business objectives and a course of action that will achieve those objectives. Furthermore, an able healthcare manager can determine a set of specific job assignments for his employees that will help meet future business demands and actively set targets for work accomplishment and a plan for reaching them. Figure 15 shows the bell curve for the planning factor. The continuum ranges from the scattered, ineffective manager who does not plan well to the overstructured manager who cannot alter a set plan to accommodate changes in business conditions.

The manager who does not plan at all is liable to be unprepared for future business demands and have to react to them ineffectively. Similarly, the manager who stays locked into a plan also is incapable of meeting new business demands that require a different strategy. The manager should plan the performance and direction of each employee and should hire people

Figure 15. Planning.

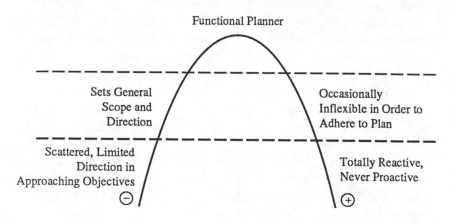

who can plan work activities effectively. Chapter Ten provides specific direction in planning and establishing work performance objectives and activities.

Analyzing Team Orientation

In order for all of the members of a healthcare organization to work together effectively as a unit, they must possess a team orientation. This is the desire to be part of a winning organization and to contribute one's individual expertise in the interest of helping the organization become a high-quality entity. Often described as being "a good team player," team orientation actually consists of four essential ingredients—cooperation, employee relations, loyalty, and technical expertise. This section will explore all four of these factors completely, so that the reader can assess the team orientation he or she needs to inspire in each employee in order to transform them into a maximally effective work group.

Cooperation. All successful business organizations, in healthcare as well as in other industries, have an employee population that realizes that each member is dependent on the others in one way or another for success. This realization generates in turn a spirit of cooperation among all of the organization's members, punctuated by an openness of communication and a commitment to each other and to the common goal of organizational excellence. Without cooperation, organizations can easily become fragmented and divided into groups that do not contribute to the common good. The result of this fragmentation is, of course, a lack of high-quality productivity from the organization as a whole.

The left-hand side of the bell curve graph in Figure 16 locates the uncooperative employee. On the other end of the spectrum is the worker who is cooperative and open with other employees to the extent of undermining his or her own performance. One example is the employee who is cooperative in group activities in order to mask her inability to handle the demands of her own position. Another example is the employee who is so open with other members of his work group that he incorrectly shares information that should have been kept confidential. Truly cooperative employees in a healthcare organization are highly motivated to give selfless service to co-workers, customer/patients, and organizational goals. They put themselves and their own personal wants second; the first priority in their work scheme is a solid commitment to other members of the organization who benefit from their particular talents and abil-

Figure 16. Cooperation.

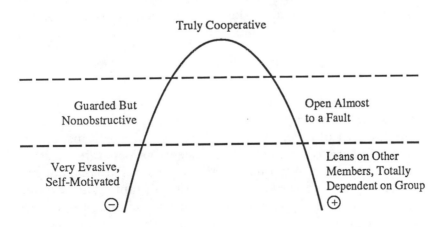

ities and to the prime beneficiary of their work efforts, the customer/patient. In order to build an effective work team, the healthcare manager must hire and retain employees who are truly cooperative.

Employee Relations. Part of the charter of every healthcare manager and supervisor who manages employees daily is the management of employee relations. It is not only essential for the manager to use human resources fully as an integral factor in accomplishing goals; the healthcare manager must also establish a cohesive team spirit for the employees. By creating and maintaining a workplace relationship with subordinates that inspires group participation and team spirit, the manager can generate maximum effectiveness and productivity while enhancing motivation and growth.

Employee relations translate into peer relations when applied to the individual, nonsupervisory employee. A simple question should be asked when considering this factor: Can this employee or job candidate, on the evidence of past work roles and performance, work well with employees who have different personalities but a common objective? If employees cannot get along with peers and other team members, the manager will spend more time resolving interpersonal conflicts than providing meaningful direction for productivity. Figure 17 shows the continuum of employee relations on the bell curve, from the employee or manager who cannot motivate others to the one who is the "company social worker," who spends more time on interpersonal relations than on doing his or her job. Both types of manager or employee are unproductive, since their inability to deal with others in proportion to their responsibilities greatly hinders their output. Healthcare managers should consider their own positions on the bell curve and attempt to maintain an employee relations program that uses human resources as an integral part of accomplishing objectives, not as a disproportionately large consumer of their talents and energies. Hiring people who are professional in their approach and skilled in getting along with co-workers and other significant organizational members makes the task of maintaining solid employee relations much easier.

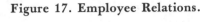

Figure 17. Employee Relations.

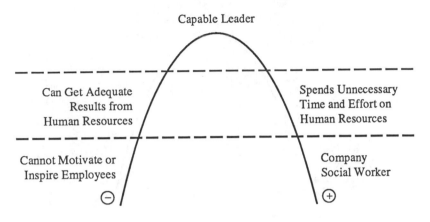

Loyalty. The healthcare organization must demonstrate its loyalty and its moral obligation to its customer community through the provision of stellar healthcare. Likewise, it should have on its personnel rolls people who are loyal to the organization and to that humane objective of giving their fellow human beings needed healthcare service. Loyalty is a major factor in the team orientation of a successful healthcare organization, and it must be shared equally by all members of the organization.

People have many basic loyalties: to their families, their religious beliefs, and their moral convictions. In a secondary sense, they are loyal to their community, their state or region, and perhaps to their bowling team or the San Francisco Giants. Organizational loyalty is the commitment of the healthcare employee to work hard on behalf of the organization, to represent its best interests, giving the needs and demands of the organization and its customer/patients top priority at all times. An employee who is truly loyal to the organization is dedicated to the organization's social cause and business objectives and to those in the organization who share the same commitment to excellent healthcare.

The continuum of loyalty from the radically subversive, self-centered employee to the blindly loyal employee is shown in Figure 18. The liability of the person on the left-hand side of the graph is easy to understand; such a person can cause

Figure 18. Loyalty.

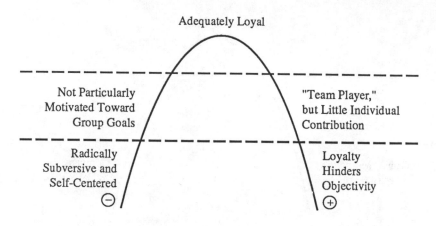

Adequately Loyal

Not Particularly
Motivated Toward
Group Goals

"Team Player,"
but Little Individual
Contribution

Radically
Subversive and
Self-Centered
⊖

Loyalty
Hinders
Objectivity
⊕

trouble, alienate fellow workers, and, if he or she is charismatic enough, motivate others to oppose or subvert authority. The employee on the right-hand side of the graph might be swayed in judgments that have to be objective by loyalty to a favorite supervisor or the old way of doing things. This person, who may mean well, lets misguided or excessive loyalty become a subjective factor in making an important business decision that demands objective, rational thought. In both cases, the employee is a distinct performance liability, and healthcare managers must accurately assess their job candidates and existing employees to ensure that misplaced or misguided loyalty does not hinder performance. Employees with well-placed, adequate loyalty have a primary commitment to giving the organization the best performance possible, without letting secondary, personal loyalties impede their productivity.

Technical Expertise. All healthcare employees, whether managerial or subordinate, must possess a certain degree of technical ability in their fields. In order for the healthcare organization to be successful, it must be composed of competent professionals who possess a superlative amount of accrued and formal knowledge of their trade or technical specialty. Moreover, unless hired for a research position, they should be able to use that technical knowledge pragmatically in order to set business plans and solve work-related problems. Figure 19 shows the bell curve of technical expertise. Without technical expertise, the institution suffers from incompetence, which in turn can destroy the organization's professional reputation. Employees who are pure technicians, however, cannot be useful internal resources for others; under these circumstances, conflict arises easily and the opportunity to create a horizontally integrated, broad-based service organization is lost. The manager should hire and assess employees on the basis of technical contributions, according to their accomplishments in past work roles and their attainment of current, well-measured work goals and objectives.

Figure 19. Technical Expertise.

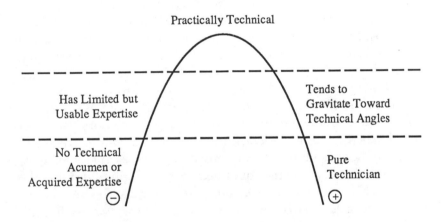

Practically Technical

Has Limited but
Usable Expertise

Tends to
Gravitate Toward
Technical Angles

No Technical
Acumen or
Acquired Expertise

Pure
Technician

Healthcare managers can determine a profile for success in any employee position by considering the entire range of the four Quan-Com categories and the sixteen factors. Then, by applying the tenets of solid selection and performance assessment that are provided in the rest of this book, managers can hire and retain the human resources who can give them and their organizations the best possible performance.

Chapter 4

Requirements for Successful Recruitment and Selection

The primary function of any healthcare organization's human resource program is the effective recruitment and selection of managers and skilled employees. Without a solid recruiting base, the organization has no personnel foundation upon which a successful structure can be built. Although recruiting and selection come to the attention of administration executives and line managers only when an existing position becomes vacant, a truly effective recruiting and selection system is constantly in action from the day the institution opens its doors, using an established system of identifying the critical characteristics of a position, considering the organization's values and objectives, and intelligently selecting qualified people. Figure 20 shows the entire chronology of recruitment, selection, and assessment.

In order to obtain the maximum return on its human resources investment, the organization must make optimum use of its selection and hiring efforts. The cost to the organization when an employee leaves a position before completing one year of employment is extraordinary; the cost when an employee leaves after three years without a skilled replacement can be even greater, when one considers recruiting and placement costs, benefits enrollment, and business opportunities missed because of downtime between the employee's departure and the orientation of a replacement. In another sense, a healthcare organization that does not hire competent employees in the beginning of the work cycle subsequently squanders all of the money spent

**Figure 20. Chronology of
Recruitment, Selection, and Assessment.**

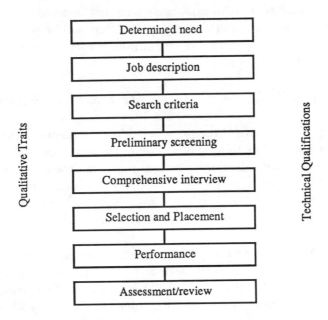

not only on salaries but also on training and development. If human resources do not have the potential to develop further into progressive work positions, such expenditures are wasted. Furthermore, a lack of promotable employees forces the organization to recruit from outside sources, incurring additional recruiting and hiring costs.

The biggest financial risk of not hiring employees who are technically competent and suited to the organization is the inability to provide the customer community with the best possible healthcare service. If customer/patients receive inadequate service, they are likely to take their dollars to a competitor, and the organization not only loses customers but leaves itself open to legal action. The adage that an organization is only as good as its people is particularly true in today's healthcare business environment.

In this chapter, we will explain the essential dynamics of a successful healthcare recruiting and selection system and look at some of the common problems associated with this tremendously important managerial responsibility. We will specifically explore some successful approaches to this process, including a practical, proven interviewing system that will help managers ensure that they are getting the maximum return on their human resources investment.

Common Problems in Healthcare Employee Selection

The dynamics of the present healthcare business environment, among other things, have created several obstacles to the recruitment and selection efforts of most healthcare organizations. In this section we will identify those problems for the reader's recognition and consideration. Subsequent chapters will provide some constructive approaches to these problems.

Lack of Skilled Personnel. A healthcare manager searching for a nurse or for someone competent in medical records finds a dire lack of qualified personnel. This lack of skilled personnel exists at a national level in nursing, medical records, radiology, and several other key technical fields. In fact, managers often find themselves taking the first remotely qualified person they can find, in the hope that the person can perform at an acceptable level in a job that has probably been vacant for an extended period of time.

Additionally, certain areas do not have a sufficiently large pool of available human resources from which to draw less highly skilled workers. For instance, Bayshore Community Hospital on New Jersey's Atlantic shore must compete with all of the resort area's motels and restaurants for housekeeping and cafeteria workers. In communities where the population consists mostly of retired people, like parts of Florida and Arizona, a similar problem exists, as it does in particularly affluent areas, where there are few candidates for hourly work.

Healthcare institutions in this predicament must try alternative ways of recruiting. Some try to draw workers from other communities by making it worth their while to travel some distance (often by public transportation) to the facility for their workday; others utilize intense school recruiting, as discussed in Chapter Five. In all cases, the healthcare manager must examine the basic work force and the number of skilled specialists available in the hiring environment and select an appropriate recruiting strategy.

Poor Job Descriptions. Recruiting managers often have a difficult time deciding which job candidate to select because they do not know practically what they are looking for. The job description might be outdated and thus fail to reflect accurately what the position requires. The job description might be too general to delineate effectively what is needed day by day in the position. On the other hand, the description might be too specific, emphasizing a single responsibility of the job at the expense of a comprehensive overview of what is involved in the position. Without an accurate, current job description, the hiring manager cannot possibly gauge the candidates for the job accurately and intelligently.

The job description should be a timely, clearly stated overview of the critical duties of the position. As the case study in Chapter Fifteen illustrates, it is the starting point for the selection and assessment processes. Without an adequate job description, the manager begins the candidate search at a disadvantage.

No Available Internal Candidates. In a truly effective healthcare organization, the first place the hiring manager should look for a candidate for an open position is within the organization. When people who are working hard and effectively on behalf of an organization discover that a job has been filled—a job that they would have liked to apply for, had they known it was available—the organization might find itself with another job opening, one created by an ignored employee's departure. The healthcare organization should facilitate a good internal candidate system by employing three strategies.

First, it must hire at every level and whenever possible people who are not only competent in the jobs they are hired for but also have the potential to qualify for promotion. In doing so, the organization is establishing a backup system for future growth, which, augmented by a solid training and development program, enables the organization to "grow its own" human resources. This also alleviates the expenses of both the turnover and the replacement of disgruntled employees who were denied promotional opportunities. Only by hiring people with potential, and then nurturing that potential with good training and development strategies and effective performance assessment, can an organization implement this natural system of employee promotion.

Second, the organization must employ a comprehensive bidding system, which is easy to implement and ensures that no employee can claim to have been denied a significant career opportunity. A bidding system consists simply of a set of job descriptions of positions currently vacant, posted on a set of bulletin boards that are easily seen by employees in the course of the workday. The employee fills out a bid request, stating his or her interest in being considered for the position, and the employee's personnel file is reviewed by the manager hiring for the position. An important feature of the bidding system is that the internal candidate receives the same consideration that the external candidate receives. Qualified employees should be interviewed; unqualified employees should be told why they do not meet the requirements of the position and counseled appropriately on how they might develop themselves more fully for future consideration. If the personnel department and its human resources specialists are truly doing their job, they should have an immediate sense of who in the organization might be qualified for a promotion and coordinate the consideration of that internal candidate effectively.

Finally, a good internal candidate system relies on an effective performance assessment system. Since the performance appraisal is the salient part of an existing employee's personnel file, it is important that the appraisal be a valid reflection of that employee's talents and abilities. Without an accurate assessment, coupled with an effective interview, an unqualified employee might be unduly given a chance at a promotion, or a deserving one might miss out on such a chance. By using the performance assessment approach explained fully in Part Three, as well as the interviewing dynamics in Chapters Six and Seven, hiring managers and their counterparts in the successful healthcare organization can develop a valid and credible internal selection system.

Sociological Trends. Several sociological trends of the 1980s must be considered and confronted by the healthcare manager hiring new personnel. The first is the widespread emergence of the dual-career family. The healthcare manager must realize that a candidate who is offered a job will consider, among other things, the effect that taking that job might have on the employment and career of the candidate's significant other. While managers are prohibited by Title VII law from asking specific questions about family situations, most candidates at some time in the selection process will volunteer information about their spouse or partner and perhaps their partner's career. Smart managers should take the opportunity to help the candidate explore opportunities for the candidate's partner in the geographical area and give the candidate and the partner any leads they might have. The manager has to realize that in a dual-career family, if both parties are not reasonably happy, the partner the manager employs will probably not be as effective as possible. By honestly helping both members in the recruiting situation, the manager is both earning the employee's goodwill and helping that employee to be content with his or her decision.

Shifting demographics also have had a drastic effect on the selection process. The rise of the Southwest United States, the depression in oil-dependent Texas and Louisiana, and the development of Silicon Valley and Route 128 outside Boston are just a few of the population dynamics that have effects on customer/patient censuses as well as available work forces. The rise in overall employment in the 1980s has put more people to work and left fewer people likely to accept minimum-wage employment in the housekeeping or food service departments of a healthcare organization.

Another recent development is the rise of major chains such as Hospital Corporation of America (HCA). The dominance of these chains has shrunk the pool of available managerial talent somewhat. This is because these large chains are not only effective in their recruiting efforts but also can provide the sharp, high-potential young manager with all of the opportunities for advancement and geographical change that a nationally based, multifacility conglomerate can offer. There are top-quality regional chains, such as the Charlotte-Mecklenburg Hospital Authority, that on a regional basis offer the young manager the same opportunity. This puts the local community facility, for example, at a distinct disadvantage in managerial recruitment.

With the emergence of these chains comes a "second tier" of executive management that is not present in the local facility's hierarchy. Regional operations directors who monitor the conduct of facilities in a particular geographical area are one example of second-tier managers. Staff positions in marketing, personnel, and finance are also more numerous in the larger chains. Thus, the recruiting manager at a smaller facility must first identify likely management candidates who might be more interested in a local opportunity than in a position with a large chain, and then aggressively recruit and select the best of these candidates.

No Structured Interviewing and Selection System. Many managers suffer from the lack of an effective selection system. Without a good selection system, three major problems arise. First, individual candidates are not assessed completely or accurately; the result can be a bad hire followed by a quick turnover. Second, the manager might unwittingly violate an employment statute or an equal opportunity/Title VII law, leaving the organization open to costly legal action. Third, a manager who does not use a structured interview approach cannot firmly direct or adjust his or her efforts and may therefore conduct the interview incompetently. Line managers, who interview less often than personnel specialists, have an even greater need for a structured approach. The manager who interviews competently not only makes better selections but also conveys, through his behavior, an aura of competence that will help give the candidate the impression that her potential boss is a well-schooled professional. After all, to the candidate, the interviewer *is* the organization; he represents the professionalism and competence of his organization and is the prime factor on which the candidate bases her initial impression.

In the next section, we will discuss the dynamics of an effective recruiting and selection process and introduce and explain to the reader the most effective selection program in the healthcare business arena today.

Dynamics of an Effective Recruiting and Selection Program

There are several dynamics at work in an effective recruiting and selection strategy in a successful healthcare organization. These dynamics are:

1.   Good internal recruiting
2.   Good external recruiting
3.   Structured interviewing system
4.   Proven interview assessment technique
5.   Relevance to job demands
6.   Adherence to all legal standards
7.   Effective follow-up strategies

Good Internal Recruiting. A solid job description system and a well-run bidding system give the healthcare organization a worthwhile internal recruitment system. The effectiveness of this system is enhanced by a talented human resource department that is adept at identifying with the line manager opportunities for developing high-performance employees. By analyzing performance appraisals and other meaningful indicators to identify deserving candidates for development and promotion, the healthcare organization creates an effective backup system and is able to cut external recruitment costs.

Good External Recruiting. Even organizations with successful internal recruiting systems occasionally need to recruit externally. For instance, a stellar employee is an attractive prize to competing institutions, which may lure that employee away with money and other employment incentives. Therefore, the ability to recruit well externally as well as internally is a necessary component of an effective recruitment and selection approach. In the next chapter, we will discuss a full range of proven recruitment strategies for the times when healthcare managers must go outside their organizations for human resources.

Structured Interviewing System. A healthcare organization that uses an interviewing strategy emphasizing good communication dynamics and job-related questions is one that gets the best human resources its recruitment market has to offer. Without such a system, line managers who are not well-versed in interviewing technique may do several things that render their selection efforts meaningless. For example, they might ask a question that requires little more than a yes or no from a candidate and thus provides little insight into the candidate's background and ability. Queries such as ''Do you have experience in a staff nurse function?'' should be replaced with open-ended cues such as ''Tell me about your experiences in a staff nurse function.'' In a similar fashion, a poor interview strategy might contain a plethora of case-study questions, such as ''Suppose that you were the only nurse on duty and such and such happened, what would you do?'' A better approach would be for the interviewer to say, ''Tell me about a tough operational problem you had to solve at your current job.'' This type of open-ended question puts the onus on the candidate of deciding first, what is a ''tough operational problem,'' and second, how to present clearly the problem and the real solution he or she employed. This approach reveals more realistically the candidate's technical expertise, communication ability, and several other of the sixteen Quan-Com characteristics the manager should be assessing. Merely asking the candidate to solve a hypothetical, general problem will do little more than show some general technical competence on the part of the candidate.

Another poor interviewing technique that a structured system avoids is the overuse of easy-to-answer questions that demand little thought on the candidate's part and, as a result, give the interviewer little insight into the candidate's capabilities.

On the other side of the coin, the interviewer might have only two or three general questions ("Tell me all about yourself, starting with high school") that invite the candidate to tell a general life story without revealing the dynamics on which the interviewer can make an accurate assessment. By using the structured selection system described in the following chapters and in Resources E and F, the reader can immediately begin using structured selection in his or her hiring efforts. The system is comprehensive and chock-full of proven questions that are open-ended, rooted in job-related criteria, and provide the interviewer with a broad perspective on the candidate's potential for success.

Proven Interview Assessment Technique. A structured interviewing system requires a proven method of analyzing and assessing interview responses. The interview assessment method must also be commonly used and accepted by everyone using it, so that all parties involved in hiring are using "the same sheet of music." This ensures that in multiple interviews—where the candidate sees several organizational members independently—as well as panel interviews—where several organizational members interview the candidate at the same time—all interviewing managers judge the candidate on the same factors. By using a common set of interview assessment indicators (or, as they are known in our system, "clues"), the management team can make a collective determination on the right candidate for the job.

In the case of a position where hiring is frequent, such as a general service worker, housekeeper, orderly, or hourly cafeteria worker, the manager may select a set of queries (cues) and interview indicators (clues) from Resource E of this book. This set of questions and answers, coupled with a good job description, will give the department manager a consistent, easy reference guide to interviewing and assessing candidates for the position. At the executive level, administrators can keep a similar set of cues and clues in the personnel files of their key reporting systems for easy reference and use as managerial positions become vacant owing to turnover or promotion. The various uses of our selection system will be developed further in the following chapters.

Relevance to Job Demands. Any questioning and assessment procedure should possess four fundamental qualities in order to be meaningful and truly useful. First, the questions asked should elicit specific information about the candidate's range of technical expertise, as well as his or her attitude orientation, people skills, and team orientation. In the case of a supervisory or managerial candidate, the questions should elicit information about managerial approach and ability. In all cases, evidence of the candidate's abilities should be apparent in the examples and explanations the candidate provides in response to these careful questions.

Second, the questions should elicit answers that provide insight into how the candidate will fit into the institution's overall organizational personality. It is critical for healthcare managers to analyze and understand their particular organizational personality and environment so that they have a credible frame of reference in matching candidates to the whole organization as well as specific positions.

Third, the interviewer should have a set of follow-up questions, also known as rejoinders, that will guide the candidate into expanding or clarifying an answer. These rejoinders should be used when the interviewer needs more information to make an assessment on a response to a question, or to ensure that the candidate has provided as much information as possible. This aids the interviewer in discovering everything about the candidate that will help to determine whether that candidate will be the best possible selection for the position.

Finally, the interview should enable the interviewer to determine whether the candidate will become a likely candidate for promotion. In other words, the selection approach, using the right questions and interview assessment techniques, should provide insight about the candidate's potential to meet the demands of progressively more demanding positions. As we have stated, the more that an organization is able to groom its existing human resources for promotion, the more effective it becomes and the more it saves in recruiting and turnover costs.

Adherence to All Legal Standards. It is essential for a healthcare organization's interviewing scheme to conform to all parameters set by local, state, or federal law. One of the biggest potential money drains on any business organization is the settlement of a legal action in which the organization is found to be at fault in the treatment of a job candidate or an existing employee. Because of the plethora of laws governing employment-at-will, fair job dismissal, and other facets of employment, it is imperative for the human resources and healthcare line managers at least to be aware of the basic dimensions of those laws so that they do not place themselves or their organization in jeopardy.

In a well-constructed interviewing program, all set questions and methods of assessing candidate response are formulated with consideration given to all pertinent legal requirements. The most prominent legal requirements affecting employment are the set of antidiscrimination laws prescribed by the federal statutes of Title VII. Failure to comply with these laws, whether intentional or unwitting, can result in a class action lawsuit against the offending manager and, in most cases, against the institution as well. Figure 21 illustrates the range of these laws and the kinds of questions they prohibit and permit. For further reference, the reader should consult the guide prepared by David Twomey of Boston College (Twomey, 1986).

Effective Follow-Up Strategies. Finally, a good interviewing and selection system should have as its final component a follow-up strategy that performs three tasks. First, the follow-up strategy must meet the need to respond to those applicants who have not been selected for a given position. Letters should be sent to these candidates within two weeks after their interviews. The letters should thank them for their time and interest and state that their applications will stay on file in case a suitable opening evolves. Most good personnel departments will keep these applications on hand so that their recruiting specialists can review them before starting an at-large, all-out external recruiting campaign for an open position. By reviewing past candidates along with internal candidates, the institution can save itself money in recruiting and selection costs. A prompt response to rejected candidates is not only a professional courtesy, it is also fundamental to a good public relations policy. By not responding

Figure 21. Equal Opportunity Employment Guidelines.

Topic	Prohibited Questions	Permissible Questions
1. Age	Any that reveals age of candidate	None
2. Race	Any concerning race, color, eye color, etc.	None
3. National origin	Any that reveals ancestry, birthplace, or native language	Only regarding language skills needed for job
4. Sex	Any that indicates candidate's sex	None
5. Marital status	Any forcing disclosure of past or present status	None
6. Family/ child care	Any that reveals the number and ages of children or specific child-care arrangements	Any to determine freedom to travel or work long hours
7. Education	Any regarding the racial or religious affiliation of the school	Any regarding majors, degrees, and so on
8. Arrests and convictions	All concerning arrests, and all non-job-related questions about convictions	Any regarding job-related convictions
9. Handicap	All phrased in a way that discourages open discussion of possible limitations	Only job-related

promptly to these candidates, the organization earns the ill will of a customer community member, whose word-of-mouth assessment of the institution to his friends and peers might not put the organization in a good professional light. Furthermore, the interviewing manager is liable to find herself barraged by phone calls from applicants wishing to know their status in the selection process.

Second, the interviewing manager should follow up quickly with the candidate of her choice and set up a slate of secondary interviews. This slate will include another meeting with the interviewing manager as well as any other significant organizational members who might work closely with the candidate if he is selected. In the secondary interview (in which all members use the same interview tool), the manager can make certain that her first impression of the candidate was a valid one as well as benefit from the input provided by other interviewers. The candidate will also get the feeling that the organization is professional enough to follow up quickly and that the selection decision and his candidacy are important enough to involve several key organizational players.

The third part of a good follow-up strategy is the answering of any questions the candidate has and the handling of any concerns he raises. For example, the interviewer should handle appropriately the candidate's questions about benefits, wages, or perhaps even specific job responsibilities. For her part, the interviewer should establish potential starting dates for the candidate and try to find out how interested he is in accepting an employment offer.

The employment offer is, of course, the ultimate follow-up to the interview. The offer itself should be extended over the phone, followed closely with a written offer consisting of the salary, a benefits brochure or description of the organization's benefit plan, and the proposed starting date. A date by which the candidate should decide on the offer—a deadline for acceptance—should also be included. The letter should close with a statement of the interviewing manager's excitement at the candidate's potential employment and the commitment of her organization and herself to the candidate's future career development.

With a good recruitment and selection strategy, complete with intelligent recruiting and an interviewing strategy structured on the requirements of the job and the work organization, healthcare managers help to ensure that their organization has human resources that will truly provide the maximum return on investment. Resource D contains several administrative forms that managers can use in personnel selection. In the following chapters, we will look in detail at the approaches that will make this a reality. The recruiting, interviewing, and candidate assessment techniques delineated in the next three chapters and the related case study will provide managers with a system that they can use immediately to optimize their employee selection efforts.

Chapter 5

Effective
Recruitment Practices

The first component of a successful healthcare recruiting and hiring system is the identification and attraction of qualified people. All too often, line managers who are not involved with recruiting and hiring on a daily basis find that the most difficult part of the search and interview process is finding suitable candidates. Internal candidates are ignored, poor outside candidates somehow make it into the interview, or confusion exists as to the very nature of the job requirements themselves. In this chapter, we will discuss how to analyze and generate both internal and external sources of candidates, and how best to utilize each source.

Internal Recruitment

People who are already in the employ of the firm and who would grow by promotion or transfer into another position are prime candidates for recruitment. For these employees, many organizations use what is commonly referred to as a bidding system. Many practical-minded managers abhor such a system, feeling the obligation to interview any employee who applies to be a burden and a waste of time. Unfortunately, if internal candidates are not reviewed as thoroughly as external ones, they will have a legitimate grievance against the organization. Inaccurate job descriptions are also responsible for a good deal of the confusion and wasted time that these managers resent.

The responsibility for maintaining a good internal bidding system falls on the shoulders of three organizational parties.

First, the top management or administration has a legal and moral obligation to allow all of its existing employees the opportunity to move up in the organization, provided they are qualified. Second, the human resources department, if it indeed is on the ball, will provide those opportunities in the interests of employee development and saving money on recruiting. Finally, the line manager is responsible for getting the best person for the job; often that person is in the same organization, or even in the same department or section, as the manager. If a workable performance appraisal system is in place and development plans are established, it is easy for all three of these parties to decide whether internal possibilities exist. If not, then a good bidding system that adheres to the tenets of clarity and fairness is necessary.

The fundamentals of an effective bidding system are:

- Posting of all open positions
- Opportunity for qualified employees to bid on positions
- Solid performance evaluation system to assess internal candidates
- Manpower planning system to identify potential candidates
- Screening and interviewing of all internal applicants
- Appropriate response to all internal candidates

In practice, the bidding system should be the same as the external recruiting policy. The job description of an open position is posted, with specific information about the scope of the job, the skills it requires, the pay structure, and the reporting relationships. Interested parties should fill out a form that allows for review of their employee files, augmented with any updates on training or education. Following screening by the personnel office, the line manager should shorten the list of internal candidates to three or fewer who are unquestionably qualified to be interviewed and evaluated. Feedback to both the successful and unsuccessful candidates, with acceptable, believable reasons for the final selection, is critical to this scheme. Lack of feedback can cause friction between employee and organization. For example, one of our clients used a bidding system only for appearances' sake; when the employees discovered how they had been deceived, one of the most demanding labor unions in the country was able to organize them. As one hourly employee put it, if the hospital had not had a bidding system at all, it would have risked less labor trouble than it got with a fraudulent system that insulted the employees' intelligence.

After all of the internal possibilities have been explored, the line manager's next move is to explore outside sources of qualified personnel. The rest of this chapter will examine outside recruitment and how to find the right recruitment strategy.

External Recruitment

The second group of candidates for recruitment are qualified people from outside the organization. With the continuing shortages of nurses and other highly visible professionals, healthcare organizations have become increasingly creative and aggressive in identifying and utilizing new external sources of talent. Their efforts to meet an ever-growing demand for qualified personnel have been augmented by a renewed commitment to traditional recruiting sources. In this section, we examine the ten most viable of these new and rediscovered sources and weigh the advantages and liabilities of each, considering its relevance to an organization's objectives, the regional factors it involves, and its financial implications. These ten sources are:

1. Job fair
2. Media
3. School liaison
4. Government
5. Professional affiliations
6. Walk-in desk
7. Foreign liaison
8. Agencies
9. Competition
10. Employee referral

Job Fair. A traditional method of hospital recruitment that has been adopted by several pharmaceutical and industrial health corporations is the job fair. In its classic form, the job fair is primarily an open house at which the candidates not only can learn about the organization in general, but also can discuss career opportunities in their particular fields with knowledgeable personnel—who, ideally, are also clever recruiters. Normally, the job fair is held in the organization's facility itself, in a large cafeteria or similar space, and is advertised extensively in the local newspapers and occasionally in a trade magazine or similar publication. Large metropolitan hospitals, which usually attract a great many candidates, sometimes hold job fairs at a centrally located hotel or convention center. While this approach does not allow candidates to see the facility firsthand, it gives the organization the opportunity to interview a large number of candidates at a neutral site, as well as allowing it the luxury of subsequently inviting into the facility only those candidates who are most qualified. This approach decreases the occasional petty theft and vandalism that unfortunately happen often at on-site job fairs openly advertised in newspapers.

The organization that advertises an open-house job fair in the community must realize that many candidates who do not have the requisite skills mentioned in the advertisement will attend in the hope that a position commensurate with their skills will be available. Obviously, this can benefit the organization by increasing its candidate bank; unfortunately, it does so at the expense of time that could have been spent interviewing candidates more qualified for the advertised positions. An axiom for organizations advertising job fairs is to be as specific as possible in describing the open positions and their requirements. Some of the institutions we have worked with have stated in their advertisements that only people who met the printed list of requirements would be interviewed, and they have in fact posted personnel at the registration desk who direct qualified applicants to the appropriate interviewing booths and politely ask all others to fill out an application, have a brochure and a refreshment, and "we'll be in touch if anything opens in your field." When these quality control methods are used, the job fair is a useful recruitment tool.

Media. A time-honored but only somewhat effective method of recruiting is the use of regular media coverage, from advertisements of positions to occasional feature stories that may generate the working public's interest in the organization. This approach has given life to a whole new facet of journalism, the "Healthcare Advertising" section, which appears in the Sunday edition of newspapers ranging from the *New York Times* to the *Allentown Daily Express*. Healthcare is the most visible of the service industries that are predicted to dominate the American economy in the twenty-first century; newspaper coverage from every angle will therefore increase, and must be managed effectively by the new wave of hospital public relations specialists working hand in hand with administrations and human resource departments. With increasing visibility, the presentation of job specifications and related information becomes ever more important. The perception of an organization held by potential employees, as well as by potential patients, is almost always based primarily on the media presentation of the organization.

The institution that uses media advertising as a recruitment device must consider several questions. First, is the publication one that potential candidates will see? Second, and just as important, is the publication regarded as a high-quality product? A hospital in a northeastern city that advertised extensively in a local paper was dissatisfied with the quality of the candidates elicited by the ad campaign. After spending a good part of its budget, the hospital discovered that the paper it had selected was considered to be a sensationalistic tabloid and that a disproportionate number of its readers lacked jobs or skills. By moving its advertisements to a more respected paper, the hospital soon drew candidates of the caliber it sought.

Another important consideration is the wording of the advertisement itself. Unclear ads with ambiguous descriptions of qualifications and responsibilities are self-defeating; unfortunately, they are also prominent because of the haste in which so many ads are often written. The advertisements that seem to be most effective are clear and eye-catching and detail the job specifications, salary range, and application requirements (such as résumés, references, and licenses). As always, the key is in planning, where adherence to these guidelines will save both money and time.

School Liaison. Another practice, which seems to be particularly useful in recruiting nurses, is the use of a school liaison. This practice can take several forms. Some of the organization's key personnel may teach continuing education classes at a particular school, an appointed liaison may work hand in hand with the school's placement officers, or the organization may simply make its presence known at strategic functions such as career days. Since schools and colleges have been somewhat sluggish in providing more health-related curricula, aggressive approaches by healthcare institutions are even more important. Some advanced healthcare firms have taken a cue from their industrial counterparts like Dow Chemical and IBM, and now lend or encourage their managerial personnel to fill adjunct teaching positions at targeted schools and colleges. Usually, these organizations have in place a solid tuition assistance program, an important component of this strategy. These organizations demonstrate to the student that education is vitally important in their credo. The combination of a benefit program and the classroom presence of managerial staff is very effective in attracting diligent students and aspiring professionals. Furthermore, the teacher/manager can evaluate applicants firsthand and have infinitely more insight into their character and potential than in the traditional selection situation.

With the other two school liaison strategies, the margin for error is somewhat greater. In dealing with placement personnel, the organization's recruiter is subjected to a great deal of sales pressure. Placement personnel are normally evaluated primarily on the number of graduates they place in jobs directly from school; hence, they attempt to place as many students as possible, the marginal candidates as well as the stellar graduates. Large institutions hiring great numbers of candidates become prime targets of what is becoming known as the "wholesale placement" officer. Likewise, at the occasional career-day functions, the organization's recruiters must be eminently aware of and resistant to overt sales pitches not only from placement personnel but also from students who paid more attention to sessions on "how to impress a recruiter" than they did to their core curriculum classes. A safeguard in all of these approaches, however, is that the reputation of the school is usually a very accurate barometer of the quality of its graduates.

Government. Another type of recruitment is the use of federal, state, and municipal government agencies that might provide worthy candidates. The recruiter must again remember that the placement worker at an agency is being paid to place applicants, the marginal as well as the superior. The federal government sometimes provides accurate statistics on various job categories, which can offer useful information about the availability of workers. Healthcare giants such as Johnson & Johnson and American Hospital Supply have been using this battery of statistics for years in wage analysis and other compensation areas. In other cases, the various government agencies provide hospitals with pools of candidates for unskilled jobs. Several veterans' organizations offer similar services in their members' hometowns. While their quality will vary, the government agency system can always provide candidates in quantity.

Professional Affiliations. Another traditional method of recruiting in healthcare is the use of professional affiliations to get leads on qualified candidates. The healthcare business itself has a plethora of professional organizations across the spectrum of both technical and administrative disciplines. Among the larger professional organizations are state and local nursing associations, support service technical groups (which also monitor accreditation in certain areas), and management groups for administrative and supervisory staff. Affiliations with these groups are usually a source of timely, accurate information on the availability and quality of certain human resources; some groups have actually formalized the process for convenient access to their membership.

Many examples demonstrate how efficient these ties can be for both the individual and the organization. The American College of Healthcare Executives, for example, has a membership of more than 30,000 key healthcare managers and administrators. As a member of their regular faculty, who provide the accredited education activities for membership and full fellowship, I have never conducted a session with the organization where business cards and, in some cases, résumés themselves have not been exchanged. In fact, that organization, as well as several smaller ones of its genre, has established a clearinghouse for members wishing to activate their candidacy or post appropriate open positions. An additional benefit of these contacts is that references and informal input on the quality of both candidate and organization are more readily available. This is even truer for technical societies, where the criteria for excellence are even more concrete and quantitative in nature and thus even more easily made known to all members. An organization that has a manager who is an officer in one of these groups can use the affiliation to even greater advantage. We have a client organization that partly solved its nurse recruiting problem when one of its nursing supervisors became president of the state nursing association. The time that the supervisor spent on association work was offset easily by the visibility and the attendant candidate interest generated by the manager's presidential status.

Walk-In Desk. A recruitment practice that seems to be indigenous to large hospitals, particularly in urban areas, is the use of a walk-in desk, at which anyone who walks into the building can apply for work. A personnel professional is assigned the responsibility of distributing and collecting applications and performing daily on-site screening interviews. Most, if not all, applicants have few or no technical skills and are thus qualified only for the housekeeping and unskilled food service functions. This type of system has several pitfalls. First, the people who would use such an easy-access avenue are usually not highly motivated, and they may merely be making the rounds to demonstrate to a family member or a government representative that they are making an effort to get work. Second, the best possible result of this method is the hiring of unskilled laborers, of whom there is a large supply; the expense of manning this desk is a foolish waste of money unless, for some unique reason, there is an inordinate need for unskilled labor. Finally, the person who makes a solid impression in this preliminary screening phase is likely to make a similar impression at the other stops on the walk-in trail and thus may get a better offer elsewhere. In our firm's work with over fifty healthcare firms in the past ten years, no one on our consulting staff has ever known of a good walk-in system that was both cost-effective and efficient. However, in unusual cases, such as start-up operations or recently de-unionized facilities, the walk-in approach becomes a necessary evil.

Foreign Liaison. Many successful organizations have begun to employ recruitment strategies utilized by leading firms in other businesses. One of these methods is attracting and retaining qualified and highly motivated people from outside the United States. While this can be a very costly proposition, several organizations that we have worked with have tried it, with varying results. For example, one of New York City's major Catholic hospitals is located in an area populated primarily by Irish-Americans and recent emigrants from Ireland. To alleviate the hospital's shortage of nurses, which is exacerbated by the hospital's urban location, the director of operations hired a nurse recruiter familiar with Ireland to set up a recruiting office in that country. The recruiter was to select and hire qualified Irish-national nurses whose credentials would enable them to be licensed in the United States and who were more than willing to leave the chaos, economic depression, and regional strife of their environment for the streets of New York City (which some might see as very similar). The Irish nurses have proven to be well motivated and very loyal, owing to their appreciation at the opportunity to start a new life.

In two other cases, this strategy was not quite as rewarding. A client of ours in the greater Los Angeles area recruited several physicians and nurses from various countries in Asia. While they were as highly motivated as the Irish nurses, they had not consistently mastered the skills expected of U.S.-trained professionals. This case underscores the need to analyze specifically the various skill levels and related requirements for certification. In a third case, a hospital in the southeastern United States recruited nurses from the Canadian provinces of Quebec and Ontario with the lure of the fabulous weather and living conditions of their city. This very attraction became the plan's undoing. When the winter months rolled around, the nurses from Quebec longed for their winter carnivals and other Nordic traditions, while the nurses from Ontario missed not only the province's seasonal changes but also the established cosmopolitan flavor of Toronto. Of fifty nurses, only five remained after a year. Obviously, not only do the foreign professionals' skill levels have to meet American standards, but the American hospital's locale must be a marked improvement on the immigrants' previous environment. The financial liability of these schemes dictates that these factors be well analyzed before an organization commits itself to such a plan.

Personnel Agencies and Search Firms. Two organizations established in other industries, personnel agencies and search firms, have recently directed their efforts toward making an impact in healthcare. Personnel agencies, also called placement firms, work primarily on a contingency basis, whereby they are paid only if the candidate they place with an organization in fact works for the organization for at least three months. On the other hand, search firms often charge half their total fee (normally 1 percent per $1,000 of the position's annual compensation, with a ceiling of 33 percent) at the outset of the search for candidates. This is usually accompanied by a guarantee of services against the collected fee. Placement agencies, as a general rule, fill positions that pay up to $50,000 per year; search firms, on the other hand, generally fill positions that pay more. Both types of firm are regulated by state labor departments.

It has become common for these organizations to create departments that supposedly specialize in healthcare. There are at least as many legitimate claims of expertise as there are false ones, and the principle of caveat emptor should be observed. It is critical to remember that the contingency agencies cannot survive without a certain number of placements per month, and the buyer must be able readily to separate a candidate's true qualifications from slick packaging. There are, however, several high-quality recruiting firms whose main business is healthcare. The organization using a recruitment agency should also remember that the best practice is to establish a steady, long-term relationship with a quality-conscious firm and not to be tempted by other agencies' constant offers of price concessions, package deals, and other gimmicks. The number of marketing ploys used by one of these firms is usually an accurate inverse indicator of its overall performance quality.

Another measurement of the quality of a placement firm is its track record in healthcare and its willingness and ability to provide solid references. A reluctance to do so, or a statement like "that information is confidential," is usually a ploy to cover a lack of references. Yet another way to determine quality is simply to examine the account recruiter who will handle the search. The recruiter's amount of exposure to the field, evidenced by his or her creditable use of key technical phrases, is an indicator, as is dexterity in discussing various healthcare organizations and current trends. Of course, the final test is the quality of the initial candidates presented. A good search firm will only present candidates who are "on the money" from the outset. A marginal firm will often send poor candidates to the initial interviewing sessions so that the top candidate, who will be presented later, will look that much better by comparison. Not only is this an expensive method, it is time-consuming and can have devastating effects because of the liabilities that arise when a position is open too long.

Competing Organizations. With all the change in the healthcare arena recently—hospitals closing at an alarming rate and large conglomerates buying out smaller institutions—another emerging source of candidates is the competition. Simply put, recruiting from the competition involves keeping abreast of any activity that might facilitate a large turnover at a nearby facility. Our studies have led us to conclude that healthcare personnel are among the most loyal employees in American business, owing to the nature of the work and the unvarying need for selfless service. However, when change occurs, employees will often consider moving to a familiar competitor rather than working for an unfamiliar conglomerate or new management at their current workplace. Many savvy managers have scouted their competition and have a network they can utilize to "get the scoop" on potential gains in this area.

This approach has several advantages. With a good network, managers can find out which employees would be outstanding recruits. They can gain insight into what would attract a targeted employee and thus be prepared to offer a desirable location and job range. Finally, this recruiting approach is really an appeal to the person's professional self-esteem. The implied message is, this person is so good that you have sought him out and want to bring him to your organization. While most industries have been doing this since the railroad wars of the 1870s, healthcare has just begun to make use of this effective strategy.

Employee Referral Systems. Yet another relatively new recruitment approach borrowed from other industries is the use of employee referral systems. The organization encourages its employees to refer qualified acquaintances to the firm, with the proviso that if the referred person is hired, the employee receives a monetary bonus. The evident benefit of this type of system is that "like attracts like," and good employees will bring in only people like themselves. The opposite, unfortunately, is equally obvious—that is, if the employee is marginal, the referral will also be a marginal candidate. A drawback to this system is that an employee whose referrals do not work out and who therefore receives no bonuses can become alienated. Furthermore, some employees who are successful in this pursuit dedicate more time to recruiting than to their regular jobs.

Recently, I have seen some very thoughtful applications of employee referral systems by our clients. One approach is to give the employee who provides a good referral time off or additional vacation days instead of money. Usually, stellar employees do not use all of their normal sick days, so no time is lost. Another approach is to pay the bonus money in quarterly increments so the employee is motivated to pace his or her recruitment efforts consistently. In all cases, the programs seem to work if the process is kept as a supplemental activity and not a main event, and if the rewards are given in a timely, judicious manner. This method is very cost-effective, and, aside from the occasional bad feelings when a referral does not work out, it is a strong approach to solid recruitment.

Recruitment is the foundation on which the rest of the hiring and selection process is based. While the healthcare business is somewhat in vogue with the working public, we see evidence daily of the lack of truly stellar performers generally and specifically in critical technical areas. Unless high-quality candidates—not just large quantities of applicants—are attracted and evaluated by the organization's staff, the human resources of the organization will wallow in mediocrity. In today's healthcare arena, that is too dangerous a chance to take.

As the adage goes, ''Many are called but few are chosen.'' It is of paramount importance that healthcare managers extract only the best from the many who want to participate in the dynamic growth of our field. After all, only with high-quality people will that growth continue.

Chapter 6

Conducting
the Interview

The most important element in the selection process in healthcare is the conduct of the interview itself. Even if an organization has the best recruiting system in the world, if the line managers are inept in conducting an interview and eliciting maximum candidate response, the entire effort will be ineffective.

The critical concept in conducting the interview is that of flow, an everyday dynamic that has only recently been quantified by behavioral scientists. Flow refers to the human ability to concentrate fully on a particular task to the exclusion of all secondary tasks or distractions. Professional athletes are the best illustration of this concept, which is colloquially described as being "in a groove" or "on a roll." When Martina Navratilova plays at Wimbledon's center court, wins handily, and then honestly tells the television commentator that she did not hear any of the thousands of spectators, she is describing the experience of working at her craft in a state of flow. We working people may experience this state while working on a project we truly enjoy and feel eminently competent about. The phone might ring, a colleague might make small talk while we are working, but we remain absorbed in accomplishing our objective. It is essential for interviewers to strive to get the candidate comfortable enough to achieve a state of flow that will provide them with a natural, comprehensive look at the candidate's background and potential with the organization.

In this chapter we will discuss how to prepare for the interview, how to conduct the interview, and how to select specific questioning strategies for particular situations. By using the approach explained in this chapter and the established formulas that appear in Resources E and F, the line manager and human resource specialist can give their organization a structured, effective, and equitable mechanism for interviewing personnel for any positions in the organization.

Preparing for the Interview

To get the greatest amount of information from the interview, the interviewing manager should prepare for it comprehensively. Everyone has had the experience of walking into an interview and immediately being asked about something prominent on their résumé, like their current position or alma mater. Not only does this tell the candidate that the interviewer is either stupid, disorganized, or uninterested (or all three!), but it also wastes precious time on conveying information when it should be used to discuss specific issues. By being thoroughly knowledgeable about the candidate's background at the outset, the interviewer can get all critical areas targeted for discussion and thus make optimum use of the interview time. This also shows the candidate that the interviewer was interested enough to take time to learn about the candidate, which will enhance comfort and flow and also indicate to the candidate that both the individual manager and the organization itself truly care about people issues.

Preparation incorporates the processes of reviewing all applications and résumés, targeting several for in-depth interviewing, and analyzing a compendium of key factors in each one, as well as the process of choosing appropriate questions in order to adjust the scope and maximize the productivity of the session. In reviewing the list of candidates, it is essential for the manager to critique the submitted applications and résumés by matching the information provided on each one not only with the job description, but also with the Quan-Com profile discussed in Chapter Three. The interviewing manager should review others who have been in the position before, determining their relative strengths and weaknesses and how they fit on the bell curve. The next step is to look at the quantitative or technical qualifications each person presents on the application. These include education, technical expertise, current position, and how the candidate came to apply for the open position.

Does the candidate have all of the academic education and technical training that is necessary for success in the position? Is the institution where the candidate received this training accredited and considered a good school? The manager should give less weight to the school's overall prestige than to its practical reputation in the given field. Also, did the candidate work while attending school? While this is not a guarantee of work ethic and aggressiveness, it is a safe assumption that a student paying for his or her own education at a reputable college by working nights is well motivated and a hard worker. The interviewer should look past the names and images to discern the quality of the candidate's performance in the context of his or her situation. Important indicators include length of time in school, grade-point average, extracurricular activities, and, naturally, relevant work history.

How much acquired technical expertise does the candidate possess? The manager should ensure that all relevant factors are considered, including any expertise obtained outside the healthcare arena that would have value in the field. For example, few guest relations experts have previously worked in healthcare; their work history usually encompasses work in the resort, restaurant, or hotel/motel fields. However, the skills they need in those fields are not vastly different from what they need in the healthcare arena. Certain firms in these fields, like Holiday Inn and Marriott, are considered in human resource circles to have the best recruiting and training functions in their business. The manager should therefore weigh the quality of the organization in which the candidate currently works or previously worked as well as the quality of the candidate.

What are the scope and responsibilities of the candidate's current job? The manager should evaluate the reporting relationships of the position, its financial responsibilities, the physical and human resources it is concerned with, and the teamwork it involves. The analysis systems discussed in Chapters Two and Three are critical to this evaluation. By using them to analyze the candidate's current position, the manager can get a solid preliminary idea of whether the candidate merits an interview.

How did the candidate come to the application process? Was a placement agency involved? Was the candidate referred by an employee? Did the candidate respond to a newspaper ad? The candidate's method should be evaluated against the record of success and failure that the organization and interviewing manager have had with that source in the past.

After reviewing the applications in this manner, the manager interviewing hourly candidates should use the set hourly-worker screening system provided in Resource E or select one question from each of the four categories used in screening hourly candidates. For management and supervisory interviews, the manager should either use the set management interviewing tool in Resource F or select one question from each of the sixteen characteristics, covering all four of the categories. All of the questions, or cues, in these interviewing systems are open-ended; candidates must use their own examples and illustrations in answering them, thus providing as much insight as possible into their approach to business and their daily responsibilities. By utilizing a roster of these questions, coupled with the follow-up rejoinders that also appear in those Resources, the interviewer will indeed put the burden of dialogue on the candidate. Another advantage of using a set roster of questions for a particular position is that all candidates for that position can be interviewed and evaluated uniformly. Not only does this provide consistency and fairness, it also sets the stage for consistent team interviewing and rotation schemes.

Preparing for the interview effectively not only saves time in the interviewing, selection, and hiring phases, but it also enables optimum productivity from the interviewing session itself. In today's competitive healthcare arena, it is essential for the healthcare manager to make the most of the time spent in the interview. Quality preparation is the key to success.

Interviewing Guidelines

In our consulting work we have found that good line managers rarely interview, for the simple reason that they are able to retain good people and maintain a backup system that allows for internal promotion rather than outside recruitment. Because line managers usually interview candidates infrequently, they are prone to making mistakes that can cause poor candidate response and interrupt or divert the flow of the interview. Therefore, we have identified a compendium of guidelines for the line interviewer that will facilitate good responses and put the responsibility for interview flow where it belongs—on the shoulders of the candidate. These guidelines are:

1. Respect the candidate's feelings and self-esteem.
2. Make the candidate as comfortable as possible.
3. Establish time parameters.
4. Listen accurately, actively, and attentively.
5. Be objective.
6. Avoid excessive encouragement or discouragement.
7. Make consistent eye contact.
8. Take notes unobtrusively.
9. Let the candidate do the talking.
10. Ensure that the candidate answers a question completely before moving on.
11. Control excessive rambling.
12. Give the candidate appropriate opportunity to ask questions.
13. Describe the next steps of the recruitment process.

Respect the Candidate's Feelings and Self-Esteem. It is important to understand that the interview represents a microscopic look at how the candidate conducts not only his work life but, in many cases, his life in general. Therefore, the interviewer should remind herself that every candidate deserves her utmost attention and basic respect for applying to the organization and agreeing to share his life story with the interviewer. The interviewer should always make an overt effort to show that she respects the candidate's feelings, accomplishments, and self-esteem.

The interviewer must keep in mind from the beginning of the interview that to the candidate, the interviewer is the organization. As far as the candidate is concerned, he is interviewing and evaluating the organization as much as the organization is interviewing and evaluating him. Many times in the high-action healthcare field line managers will be running from a work situation right into the interview. It is imperative for the line manager, as much as practically possible, to take about five minutes prior to the interview to review the résumé a final time and get ready to represent the organization to a person who is not only a candidate but also a potential patient, visitor, and member of the community and buying public. While ''professionalism'' has unfortunately become an all-encompassing cliché in our field, the interviewing manager should keep in mind the essence of that word—good bearing, fair but firm direction, and good listening and interactive skills—at all times in the interviewing process.

Make the Candidate as Comfortable as Possible. For the sake of developing flow, the interviewer's respect for the candidate should be supplemented by an effort to make the candidate (and the interviewer) as comfortable as possible. This means sitting in an arrangement that both interviewer and candidate are comfortable with and spending the first two minutes making small talk about the weather, current events, a common bond or shared experience that was mentioned on the candidate's résumé (having attended the same alma mater, for example), or another topic that will help set the stage for the interview itself.

At the outset of the interview, the interviewer should explain to the candidate several important dimensions. First, he should mention the fact that he will be taking notes. Next, he should briefly explain the nature of the job at hand and a little about the organization itself. Finally, he should ask the candidate if he can call her by her first name. Using first names heightens rapport and comfort. In monitoring over 14,000 interviews in the past ten years, we have learned of only one case in which a candidate did not want to be called by his first name. The candidate, who held a Ph.D. in physics, wanted to be called ''Dr. ———,'' not ''Jim.'' The university at which he was interviewing prided itself on being an informal, ''down-home'' school and felt that ''Dr. ———'' was not adaptable enough for its purposes. There are other situations (in the military, for example) in which the first-name approach might not be appropriate.

Establish Time Parameters. A very important component of the interview opening is explaining to the candidate the time parameters of the interview. This can be done with something along the lines of "We'll be spending the next twenty-five minutes discussing your background, and then we'll have about five minutes where we can turn the tables and let me answer some of the questions you might have." Once these parameters have been established, the candidate can pace her presentation effectively and budget her "air time" in the interview expediently.

Establishing a uniform interview time period also prevents candidates from feeling that they were cheated out of a fair opportunity to present themselves. Many managers ask our staff in seminars, "If I have told the candidate the time parameters, and they are obviously a mismatch for the job, can I abbreviate the interview?" While this question touches on legal ground, several right answers can be given here. The safest approach is to let the candidate interview fully in the time slot, as he or she might be suitable for other positions in other areas or at some time in the future. Another approach, which is legally a little riskier, is for the interviewer to ask all of the questions he has prepared and, when the candidate is finished, to ask if there is any other information she feels it is important to provide. Following her answer, the interviewer can politely conclude the interview. In both cases, the candidate is given the opportunity to present fully her skills and qualifications.

An alternative, but dangerous, approach is simply to tell the candidate, "Look, I appreciate your interest but unfortunately you're not qualified at all for this position. Thanks anyway and have a nice life." The major problem with this approach is that it violates the basic premise of equal opportunity. For example, if a member of a minority group is given only ten minutes to interview for a position for which, on paper, they appear to be qualified, and a person who is not a member of a minority group is hired on the basis of a full thirty-minute interview, the organization and the manager will both wind up in court. There are lawyers currently advertising openly in newspapers no less prominent than the *Los Angeles Times* that they will represent people who feel they were treated unfairly in either the application or the interviewing process. A person in the Pittsburgh area recently won a decision when he was able to prove that his interview was only one-quarter as long as the interview of the person who ultimately got the job. Clearly, it is ultimately wiser to use the first two strategies and spend the extra time interviewing in the office instead of in court.

Listening Accurately, Actively, and Attentively. The manager should "listen in technicolor" in order to get as much out of the candidate as possible. By not directing his concentration to the candidate's response, the manager runs the risk of not hearing the information fully and correctly, as well as of conveying the impression to the candidate that he lacks interest in the candidate's responses and is just going through the motions. To listen in technicolor means to absorb *all* of the candidate's flow, both verbal and nonverbal. By asking a battery of open-ended questions such as those provided in Resource F, the interviewer is assured of eliciting solid responses and key indicators (or clues, which we will discuss in the next chapter).

Be Objective. Often, the interviewer finds it difficult to keep a neutral stance toward a candidate. For example, if a position has been open for a long time, the interviewer may quickly become disgusted with a candidate whose qualifications are far off the mark. On the other hand, the interviewer might quickly become enamored of a candidate who in the all-important first five minutes of the interview appears to have superlative talents and personality. The liability that exists here is that most interviewers, particularly operations managers, make a firm determination on a candidate in those first five minutes, and often base that judgment on subjective criteria. It is important to remember that the candidate's presence and ability to communicate are the *only* characteristics that can be accurately gauged in the first five minutes. Furthermore, candidates who have been out of work for an extended period are typically in prime interviewing shape; that is, they have interviewed many times recently and are experts in presenting a terrific initial impression, particularly if they have received formal training in image creation courtesy of a placement firm or outplacement counselor.

Interviewers must avoid falling into the trap of subjectivity by reminding themselves that candidates must be able to sustain a genuine, forthright presentation of their qualifications for the entire interview, whether it is a fifteen-minute interview for an hourly position or a forty-five-minute managerial interview. Even if it is 4:30 on a Friday afternoon and the interviewer is ready to spend a long weekend away from the job—a time when a candidate can be tremendously impressive in the first five minutes—the entire interview must be objectively and critically evaluated in order to establish truly the candidate's potential worth to the organization. If the candidate perceives that the interviewer is buying the initial five minutes, the interview is liable to become purely a sales presentation that may gloss over potential weaknesses and danger areas. By maintaining an objective stance for the duration of the interview, the manager guarantees quality responses and decreases the possibility of quick turnover and additional lost time and productivity.

Avoid Excessive Encouragement or Discouragement. The interviewer's verbal and nonverbal responses can lead the candidate to adjust her answers excessively to the feedback from the interviewer. For example, frequent nods and verbal agreement encourage the candidate to continue the particular line of response that is eliciting the positive action. On the opposite side of the coin, if the interviewer arrives at the interview upset (about a missed deadline by one of his existing employees, for example), his negative attitude can transmit itself into the interview and cause the candidate to abbreviate her responses and to receive an overwhelmingly negative impression of the interviewing manager as well as the organization itself. This is another reason that the interviewer must clear his mind completely before conducting the interview.

Another potential problem along these lines is that the interviewer may react negatively to something in the candidate's response. For example, in a hospital that prided itself on hiring veterans, an acute problem arose whenever one of its ex-military managers interviewed a candidate who discussed disagreement with the armed forces or Vietnam or revealed left-wing political sympathies. A similar situation occurred in an urban hospital whose managers were almost all of one religious persuasion. When a candidate not of this particular persuasion was interviewed, the chances of an unbiased, successful exchange were next to nil. When the administrations of these institutions were made aware of their respective problems, they had our firm help correct them by underscoring the need for objectivity in our seminars. The administrators wisely understood both the business liabilities and the legal ramifications of such behavior, as well as the danger of having a stagnant, excessively homogeneous organization.

Make Consistent Eye Contact. In the early seventies, the dynamics of consistent eye contact became part and parcel of studies of body language. While there is as much psychobabble as substance in many of these studies, the interviewer should adhere to a few of their conclusions about the use of eye contact in making the candidate as comfortable as possible. The best rule is for the interviewer to make eye contact in the manner that is most comfortable for him or her. It is amazing how many managers will read a self-help book on body language and eye contact and then adopt an eye-contact technique along the lines of the one used by the Amazing Kreskin. By steering between hypnotizing the candidate and looking constantly at notes or other things, the interviewer should find a median position that both interviewer and candidate are comfortable with.

Take Notes Unobtrusively. When a candidate sees the interviewer taking many notes, she programs her answers in such a way that the interview becomes tantamount to an oral examination. The interviewer should mention at the beginning of the interview that he will be taking notes. He should take notes in a natural sequence and write only essential information so that he can maintain a fluid exchange between himself and the candidate. If the interviewer has a good memory, note taking should be minimal. When notes are taken, the interviewer should record information in any manner he wishes, using a formal or informal shorthand, symbols, abbreviations, or whatever else will shorten the process. Resource D contains scoresheets used by some of our clients that enable both good note taking and uniform scoring.

Let the Candidate Do the Talking. Simply put, a major flaw of line managers' interviewing style is to talk too much in the interview. Not only does this limit the candidate's opportunity to provide information, it often gives the candidate too much guidance on what the interviewer wants to hear. In some of our most effective clients, like Estelle Doheny Eye Hospital and Charlotte Memorial Hospital, the management team has directed the staff, on our suggestion, to allot 80 percent of the "air time" to the candidate and 20 percent to the interviewer. By imposing that standard, the organization is making certain the candidate will get a full opportunity to speak without being tipped off as to what and how to present. The line managers are also instructed not to finish thoughts for the candidate or aid them in any other way in answering questions. One of the benefits of a structured system is that the roster of questions, coupled with rejoinders, prevents excessive participation on the manager's part.

Ensure That the Candidate Answers a Question Completely Before Moving On. If the candidate is given too much leeway, he will dwell on areas he sees as advantageous and quickly dispose of questions he is not comfortable with. If the candidate is allowed to do this throughout the interview, the overall assessment will probably come out too positive. The interviewer must make certain the candidate answers all questions fully, and requestion the candidate in areas that were handled briefly. If the candidate ducks the second probe as well, the interviewer must conclude that the area in question is a marginal one for that candidate.

Control Excessive Rambling. While it is important for the candidate to take charge of the interview and bear the major responsibility for the information presented, it is equally important for the interviewer to keep the candidate from rambling. In open-ended interview schemes such as our Quan-Com System, the aggressive candidate will often seize the opportunity to oversell himself by dwelling on a description of how terrific he is and what a wonderful asset he would be for the organization. While it is essential to let candidates present themselves in their own fashion, as well as to assess what and how they decide to present about themselves, excessive positive rambling can reduce the interview to a human television commercial. By asking another question or using one of the rejoinders described in Resources E and F, the interviewer can bring the candidate back to the point. Less common is a tendency for the candidate to be excessively negative in describing past situations. While certain dimensions of this behavior portray adherence to interpretive characteristics described in Resources E and F, a negative rambling can be as detrimental as positive rambling to the interviewing process.

While the interviewer must control rambling, the candidate should be interrupted as infrequently as possible in order to maintain maximum flow, and then with the utmost tact and brevity. Interruptions should occur only to clarify information or to reconcile information that seems contradictory. In some instances, however, it might be prudent to use a rejoinder or additional question to deliberately interrupt a candidate who is straying from the point of the original question or who is repeating information unnecessarily. It is essential to refocus the candidate's efforts on objectives the interviewer wants covered so that irrelevant or useless information does not take precedence in the allotted time.

Give the Candidate Appropriate Opportunity to Ask Questions. A good rule of thumb is to allow the candidate about five minutes to ask questions at the end of the initial interview, but not to conduct another interview, this time with the candidate in charge. More time should be allotted in the second round of interviews. The manager should listen actively while the candidate is asking questions, because the types of questions a candidate asks are extremely revealing of his or her attitude orientation. For instance, questions about technical aspects of the job can be representative of the candidate's business acumen, whereas questions that revolve around benefits and holidays may reveal the candidate's work ethic or perhaps desire for family security. The interviewer must not analyze these queries too deeply but should be alert for those that provide further insight into the candidate's quality.

Describe the Next Steps of the Recruitment Process. The interviewer should now tell the candidate that the time allotted for the interview has expired and delineate what comes next. If the candidate wants to ask additional questions (which indicates interest and aggressiveness in varying degrees), she should be told that perhaps an opportunity to discuss things further will present itself in the future. Occasionally, a candidate will want immediate feedback on her performance and potential for selection. The interviewer should counter this aggressive ploy by tactfully explaining to the candidate that while the interview was enjoyable and enlightening, there are other candidates to be interviewed before a final decision is made. Subsequently, the manager should tell the candidate that she will receive notification of her status within two weeks from the organization directly. Failure to do this results in aggressive candidates calling on the phone to get information and potential ill will between the candidate and the organization. As we mentioned above, in healthcare word of mouth is the most powerful advertising force; to misuse the follow-up mechanism for an interview foolishly risks bad publicity. With public relations in mind, the interviewer should in all cases at this point thank the candidate and express appreciation for her time and interest.

Interviewing is a strenuous process physically and mentally, and it requires a dedicated effort each time out in order to maintain the quality of flow, direction, and assessment. John Mylinski, the chief recruiter for the Bennigan's restaurant chain, tells me repeatedly that interviewing a daily slate of six managerial candidates for that organization is more taxing than the mountain climbing he does in his off time to relax. Since organizational control and quality are the responsibility of all healthcare managers, it naturally follows that it is the responsibility of all managers to attack the conduct of the interview with the same top effort they apply to all their other responsibilities. Our opinion, supported by countless healthcare managers, is that interviewing may be the managerial responsibility with the most liability, for even the best-laid plans and ideas are worthless if the human resources are less than the best they can possibly be.

Chapter 7

Evaluating the Interview

It is vitally important that the interviewer accurately evaluate the interview dialogue and fully assess the candidate's assets and liabilities for the organization and the subject position. It is in this dimension that the most potential for error lies. Evaluating an interview is really the process of taking a subjective, planned dialogue controlled by a "selling" candidate and matching it up as objectively as possible to a set of job characteristics. At the same time, all of the factual information presented by the candidate—such as previous employment, schools attended, and training received—is subjectively evaluated by the interviewing manager for its applicability to the open position. Added to this mixture of factors is the subjective bias the interviewer might already possess concerning type of background, healthcare experience range, and a host of other facets. Clearly, there is a wide margin for misinterpretation and misjudgment if the structured interviewing process does not have a strong, proven evaluation scheme.

The interview can be evaluated by aplying the Quan-Com categories used to analyze organizational personality (Chapter Three). By using our model of the sixteen essential Quan-Com characteristics, as well as the list of specific questioning and evaluating techniques in Resources E and F, the interviewing manager can make quantitative decisions in the four major categories of attitude orientation, people skills, managerial aptitude (in the case of a management or supervisory candidate), and team orientation. Although the category of technical expertise is normally subsumed under team orientation, evaluating expertise is such an important part of the interview that it will be discussed separately. In this chapter, we will note some typical

99

problems of interview assessment and discuss the use of the four major categories of interpersonal behavior in a structured evaluation scheme.

Common Dangers in Evaluation

As we have discussed, most line managers in the healthcare business interview candidates infrequently, particularly if they have selected long-term employees successfully and have the latitude to provide existing employees with the growth opportunities that decrease turnover. Therefore, it is easily understood why a line manager will often make a poor judgment on a candidate for reasons that are easily seen from an objective viewpoint. Most problems in the interview evaluation are due to what is termed by some the "halo effect" or excessive candidate likability.

Candidate likability is the ability of a candidate to endear himself to the interviewer immediately and thus to sway the interviewer's judgment in his favor. Candidate likability is usually established by three means, all of which are extremely effective and routinely present in the healthcare forum. In the first type of candidate likability, the candidate couples an engaging personality, identifiable by a strong image or presence and a polite, earnest manner, with requisite knowledge of the subject position and an expressed ability to handle its responsibilities flawlessly. The interviewer in effect becomes sold on the candidate and stops working and assessing after the initial five minutes of the interview. The candidate uses the balance of the interview to validate the impression the manager has formed and reinforce his suitability for the subject position.

The second type of likability is created when the interviewer uncovers a factor or set of factors in the candidate's background that is similar to the interviewing manager's personal history and becomes biased in favor of the candidate immediately. This is commonly referred to as "hiring in the same image," and it is a widespread problem that has inhibited growth at several major organizations both in and out of the healthcare arena. It is often seen when a corporation, for example, has a number of managers who graduated from the same college or university and who also have been particularly successful in the organization. Their alma mater becomes, in essence, a seal of approval and its new graduates receive carte blanche treatment in the organization's recruitment process, often including automatic visits by recruiters to the school for initial interviews and subsequent first-class trips for the candidates to the organizational headquarters for secondary interviews. The obvious fallacy of this approach is that while certain schools may have a curriculum or faculty that makes them a good risk for recruitment, there are absolutely no guarantees that such schools will produce winners. An example of this fallacy is the recently publicized fall and acquisition of American Hospital Supply Corporation. During its heyday in the late 1970s, the firm was run mainly by graduates of the midwestern "Big Ten" universities, notably Northwestern, Ohio State, and Michigan. While all of these schools are certainly fine institutions—Northwestern in particular has a superb school in management—the mechanical manner in which the personnel department recruited their graduates and the hiring managers offered them positions eventually resulted in immense turnover of marginal lower-tier managers and stagnation. Furthermore, our firsthand experience has shown that this homogeneous group of midwestern college graduates was totally incompetent and ineffective in dealing with the more ethnically and regionally diverse areas of the country, another major factor in mass turnover.

A third type of candidate likability exists when the hiring manager in effect believes that the candidate is of the same personality type as the manager and thus arrives at the premature conviction that the candidate is "their type of person." This is a trap often set by skilled placement counselors when working on a position for a client with whom they have some familiarity. The candidate can be instructed (or can quickly determine for herself in the interview) where to appeal to the interviewer on an interpersonal level and how to condition her presentation for maximum effect. Two major liabilities exist here. First, the candidate may be playing a role that, simply put, has little or no relationship to her real personality, thus in essence leading the manager to hire an act, not a person. Second, the manager who hires someone solely on the basis of a similar personality is overlooking the requirements of the job and the fact that the personality needed in the open position may be different from that needed in the hiring manager's position.

In all of these cases it is vital that the manager protect himself by adhering to the principles of sound data collection and evaluation. In our seminar work in the hospital industry, I always ask line managers, "How many of you make your judgment on the candidate after five minutes?" Invariably, about 75 percent of the participants reply in the affirmative. This is easy to understand, for the reasons we have discussed in previous chapters. However, it is imperative that the interviewer postpone making the final determination until after the entire interview is over. Virtually anyone in business is capable of making a good impression within the initial five minutes, and this is also the very period of time in which an interviewer, perhaps a little nervous or preoccupied with other matters, is most susceptible to making a judgmental error. All collected notes and perceptions should be qualitatively consistent from the outset of the interview to its conclusion.

It is also essential for the interviewing manager to be flexible and reactive in the interview so that the onus remains on the candidate for control and direction. The manager should make notes of items that are of primary importance and might be forgotten if not noted promptly; only following the interview should the manager attempt to review and assess the entire collection of data. These data should include notes on the objective information the candidate has provided and, perhaps even more important (since much of the objective information is on the résumé and was evaluated during applicant screening), on all of the subjective impressions the manager received of the candidate's management style, approach to business, and even nonverbal behavior. Without trying to become an amateur psychoanalyst, the manager should logically form an assessment of the candidate's style and presentation and decide how it matches the established requirements of the subject position.

In summary, the manager should apply the same diligent work ethic to the interviewing and evaluation process as he does to his other responsibilities in order to ensure successful assessment and placement.

Assessing Technical Expertise

A primary function of the interview is to gauge how much technical ability the candidate possesses, specifically the amount of accrued and formal knowledge of the particular area of the business. Obviously, this dimension takes on added importance in the healthcare field, where, in numerous disciplines, the certain knowledge or mastery of key procedures can in fact spell the difference between life and death. While the résumé or application invariably indicates essentials in this category, it is the responsibility of the interviewing manager to determine the depth of technical expertise, the breadth of technical knowledge, and, most important, the extent of the candidate's ability to draw from that bank of knowledge and apply it expediently and effectively to the situation at hand. The "behavioral bridge" in Chapter Two shows the spectrum of technical acumen. The skilled interviewer in the healthcare field must ensure that the candidate's ability is commensurate with the position's requirements.

Several factors that can be readily evaluated in the interviewing forum should be discussed and assessed by the interviewer. The open-ended, structured approach this book details enables the interviewer to conduct an interview in which virtually all data are related to the use of technical expertise on the job. Some interviewers make the mistake of providing the candidate with a "what if" or case-study situation. The interview should provide an abbreviated look at what the candidate is like most of the time, and a critical determination should be made about how well the stated approaches and demonstrated behavior fit with the job at hand. By using a case-study or closed-ended informational format, the interviewing manager loses a prime opportunity to truly determine the candidate's attributes and potential with the organization. With an open-ended format, where questions are based on professional approaches and experiences rather than on specific, hypothetical situations, the interviewer can more pragmatically elicit data and make a determination on the candidate's suitability for the subject position.

In addition to the candidate's expertise in a specific field or discipline, most healthcare managers desire to learn how well versed the candidate is in healthcare issues and business dynamics in general. Again, an open-ended format lends itself to the accomplishment of this objective, since questions about the candidate's range of knowledge of the business in general and certain current events in particular can be asked and evaluated. A major complaint of many healthcare executives is that recent college graduates and young managers from other industries, for example, have no idea of the day-to-day nature of the healthcare sector and the inner workings of a healthcare organization. It is therefore of the utmost importance that the manager determine whether the candidate has a realistic understanding of what the day-to-day environment of the healthcare setting is like.

If the candidate in fact does not have any "hard-core" experience in healthcare, the interviewer should determine initially if this type of experience is essential; in some fields, like accounting and personnel, healthcare experience is not of paramount importance. In those cases, the interviewing manager should determine if the candidate has worked successfully in environments similar to that of healthcare, in which high stress is the norm and the quality of customer (or patient) service is of paramount concern. In all cases, the candidate should demonstrate proficiency in his or her specialty through the command of technical terms and creditable explanation and employment of skills. The candidate should display not only depth of knowledge but also breadth, including an understanding of dynamics in closely related fields and of how the candidate's specific discipline fits into the organization's "big picture." Another factor to be considered is the methods the candidate uses to keep abreast of new developments and significant changes in his or her field, such as active participation in professional and technical societies or regular reading of appropriate publications.

Professionals who are truly motivated in their field and strive to make high-quality performance a daily standard are those who can practically apply their technical abilities toward the fulfillment of the overall mission of the organization. This includes the ability to explain succinctly technical processes and programs so a layperson can understand their relevance and importance to the overall mission. I can recall a genius-level pharmaceutical research scientist at Bristol-Myers explaining the dynamics of cancer arrest drugs using a napkin, fork, and spoon at a lunchroom table so that I, a *C* student at best in high school chemistry, could understand the basics of the process and use my understanding in my recruiting processes. This ability to communicate displays not only technical ability and understanding of the overall organizational mission but also the confidence to share technical ability in the interest of organizational achievement and solid team orientation.

The line manager is usually the person most capable of determining technical strengths and weaknesses and deciding whether they will be assets or liabilities on the job. The line manager usually has a technical background akin to the candidate's, and in many cases probably had the same job the candidate is seeking. Therefore, she should utilize her entire frame of reference in order to ascertain comprehensively the quality of the candidate's technical ability, from the screening to the résumé and application to the quality of technical questions asked about the position by the candidate at the conclusion of the interview. Resources E and F contain specific questions (cues) and interpretive strategies (clues) that will help the reader make an accurate determination of the candidate's technical ability. Not only do these selection formulas contain probing strategies particularly calibrated toward technical expertise, but *all* of the questions are constructed in such a manner that the candidate's answers will reveal technical ability throughout the interview. In assessing the candidate's technical ability, along with attitude, people skills, managerial aptitude, and team orientation, the healthcare manager serves as a gatekeeper for the organization who allows only the most qualified and promising candidates into the fold.

Assessing Attitude Orientation

Among the behavioral characteristics that the interviewing manager must compare with job parameters and organizational norms are the four aspects of attitude orientation—adaptability, aggressiveness, perseverance, and work ethic. This section will provide some guidelines for assessing and evaluating these critical dimensions.

Adaptability. The first attitude characteristic is the proven ability to achieve the best possible results under changing circumstances, high stress, and adverse physical conditions. People who are truly adaptable in the healthcare setting have no problems relating effectively to varied personalities and are eminently able to absorb new methods and other changes with excellent practical results. Many healthcare professionals point to adaptability, or flexibility, as one of the major personality prerequisites for any position in healthcare, whether at the managerial or hourly level. As a general guide, we will review how a candidate with suitable adaptability will present his or her case in the interview forum.

Adaptable candidates will usually be more than willing to expand their efforts past the limits of their job description; they inherently understand the need for flexibility in the healthcare workplace and have a desire to learn and grow professionally as much as possible. Their level of work is consistently high, evidenced by two critical indicators: their track record, presented on the résumé or application, and their rendition in the interview of their past achievements and accomplishments. Adverse conditions or situations in which a lot of change occurred are not overly detrimental to the adaptable candidate's performance, and no apprehension exists in the candidate's mind about the wide dimensions or varied tasks associated with a given job. If there is a history of geographical change and relocation in the candidate's background, it is anchored by a progression in positions and career growth and success.

The behavior within the interview itself is an excellent barometer of the candidate's strengths and weaknesses in each of these characteristics. How well the candidate reacts to a change in the interview flow and line of questioning is a good indicator of adaptability. An overt desire for structure and patterned, slow-paced questioning is a firm indicator of a need for concreteness and a hesitancy to read, react, and readjust quickly and effectively. The candidate who responds quickly to change in the interview but determinedly returns to a set pattern of response is again likely to be less adaptable than necessary. As we mentioned in Chapter Three, it is imperative to determine what the organizational standard will be for all of these characteristics, considering the requirements, work situation, growth needs, and daily responsibilities of the subject position.

Aggressiveness. The second attitude orientation factor is the ability to take command appropriately by being enterprising, direct, selectively forceful, and effectively persuasive. In an interview, the leadership roles that the candidate discusses are good indicators, particularly if he obtained the roles by competitive selection. The candidate can also discuss fluidly situations in which push came to shove and tactfully describe how he gained the outcome he desired. In general, when discussing work situations, the successful candidate will reveal the use of a good blend of tact, assertiveness, and persuasiveness in the accomplishment of his goals. The candidate will appear to be unafraid to challenge the norm when it is absolutely necessary to do so to maximize performance, but he will in no case allow his aggressiveness to become obnoxious, offensive, or pretentious.

In the interview itself, a suitably aggressive candidate will establish a strong initial rapport with the interviewer appropriately, professionally, and with optimum impact. He will display creditable aggressiveness by stating his case forcefully but pleasantly, and by staying with his original point when challenged by the interviewing manager. After the interviewer has established the tone and pace of the interview, the aggressive candidate will take over by controlling the pace of the exchange and not waiting to be led through the process. In short, he will make his point in the interview with no evidence of offensive or obnoxious tendencies.

Perseverance. The third attitude orientation factor the interviewing manager must accurately assess is typified by candidates who pursue their work objectives tirelessly and to a successful end despite any situational obstacles. Simply put, these people are always willing to do whatever it takes to get the job done and maintain a steadfast, undeniable approach toward that end. A candidate who is appropriately persevering can provide examples in her work history of working through tough problems by utilizing fully the resources at hand, punctuated by a desire to attack problems directly rather than work around them or avoid them completely. While she might be adaptable or intelligently flexible in altering her plan of attack, she will never compromise her objective. At the same time, an effectively persevering candidate will not become hardheaded at the expense of the organization or job mission, and will not often become a victim of tunnel vision. She will not lose sight of the "big picture" for the sake of a minor task. As with all sixteen of these characteristics, the candidate will be intelligent and experienced enough to realize when and in what quantity to apply perseverance.

Within the interviewing forum itself, the candidate will demonstrate a willingness to answer all questions fully and directly, even if the interviewer asks progressively more intense questions or cues. In discussing past work roles, the candidate will present a pattern of not bending to surrounding negativity in the workplace and a consistent ability to bounce back from adversity. A healthcare worker who is persevering will furthermore demonstrate in the interview an innate ability to maintain this approach to work in an environment that is stressful and action-packed, and whose objectives are more or less in a constant state of fluctuation. In this hyperactive work environment, the successful candidate will doggedly attack all responsibilities with the same tireless vigor coupled with a consistent commitment to quality.

Work Ethic. The final attitude orientation factor is apparent in candidates who maintain a consistently sound "can-do" approach to all work situations, and who manifest an aura of capableness and readiness to perform any and all tasks that will contribute to the good of the organization. The first key indicator of work ethic can be found by analyzing the reason the candidate is seeking employment in the organization. A candidate with good work ethic might be relatively satisfied with his current job, but his desire to grow more and seek more challenge and career growth has motivated him to seek greater responsibility with the interviewer's firm. His work background will invariably be illustrated with examples of going beyond the norm in both quality and quantity of productive output, and he will appear almost intolerant of co-workers and subordinates (and in some cases, even superiors) who do not share his high-caliber commitment to quality. Combining work ethic with a strong practical sense of adaptability and perseverance, the candidate will be always willing to put forth any extra effort that is needed to accomplish a task, and in the process make no compromises on the quality of output.

In the interviewing forum, the candidate will present a consistently solid picture of his background and a work philosophy that puts the needs of the customer/patient and organization before any personal needs and goals. He will clearly demonstrate a creditable pride in his work, his organization, and himself as a solid professional, without working so hard that he becomes a workaholic. The ideal candidate adheres to a realistic, constructive work ethic that is beneficial to all concerned.

Assessing People Skills

The second behavioral category that the interviewing manager must effectively assess is that of people skills, the ability to relate interpersonally with all of the cast of the healthcare setting. Since a high premium is placed in today's healthcare arena on guest relations and optimum human resources management, the need for stellar people skills applies to everyone on the organizational ladder, from housekeeper to CEO. In evaluating the candidate, it is imperative that the interviewing manager carefully examine the candidate's command of the four components—communications, energy level, perceptiveness, and presence—of this most important category. While these skills may be the most readily assessed, they are also, because of their subjective nature, most liable to be linked to subsequent turnover and other hiring and placement problems.

Communication. The first component of people skills is the ability to express business needs and desires effectively to all members of the organization in a professional manner. This encompasses the ability to deal tactfully but advantageously with all related external parties, such as patients, visitors, and primary vendors. There are relatively few ways of assessing this quality by exploring the candidate's background. One way is to determine whether the candidate in the past was required to produce written or oral reports or had any other regular responsibility to provide substantial information. The candidate might also be questioned about her perception of the avenue of communication and communicative systems present in her past or current work roles.

Numerous ways exist, however, of assessing the candidate's communication ability during the course of the interview itself. For example, the interviewer should closely monitor how well the candidate uses her full range of verbal skills. All particulars should be gauged, from sentence construction, grammar, and basic presentation of thoughts to style issues such as brevity, conciseness, and editing of ideas and concepts. The interviewer should compare the candidate's verbal skills to the requirements of the subject position and envision how well the candidate's communicative style might fit with those requirements. The candidate should for the most part be succinct and adroit with sensitive information, displaying good judgment and tact when describing subjective information. The candidate should not show any tendencies to embellish, slant, or alter objective information in any manner that might compromise the essence of the message. A candidate who is an effective communicator will appear comfortable in the interview forum, and will not overstate or dramatize any information provided in the interview. When the candidate is given the opportunity to ask questions about the job or organization, the interviewer should closely analyze the quality of the questions and the questioning process used by the candidate as part of the verbal skills assessment.

The interviewer should look at several equally important factors in the candidate's nonverbal style of communication. The candidate should employ a nonverbal style that seems natural and in harmony with the verbal style; hand and facial gestures should be appropriate to the material being discussed. When the verbal and nonverbal aspects of a candidate's communication style appear out of sync, it is a good assumption that the candidate either has been coached or has prepared herself to make an impression on the interviewer that does not accurately reflect her true style. Another factor that should be assessed is the candidate's listening skills, which are presently a popular topic in training and development circles. The interviewing manager should realize that the ability to listen accurately and actively, as opposed to "just hearing" or politely accommodating the speaker, is of the utmost necessity in the healthcare environment. If the candidate, for example, has a tendency to misunderstand interview questions or asks a question at the end of the interview about something that has already been covered, her listening skills are more than likely at an unatisfactory level. As the field becomes even more competitive, making a patient or visitor feel that an organization's personnel "really listen"— and therefore display real concern in its most basic sense— will be increasingly important for the successful healthcare business.

Energy Level. The second critical factor in the category of people skills is a trait considered to be more inherent than developed in a working professional. Energy level is defined as the ability to execute assignments at a steady, fast pace and to increase activity to the maximum when mandated by business situations. An energetic professional possesses suitable vitality and the endurance required for all work assignments, including promotional opportunities requiring greater stamina and range of action. An interesting relationship exists between energy level and work ethic. A person who has a strong work ethic and commitment to his business role combined with a higher than normal energy level usually straddles the line between a highly productive employee and an obsessive workaholic. On the other end of the spectrum, a person with a low energy level and little stamina and endurance is a likely candidate for quick turnover in the healthcare environment, given its daily demands for sustained hard work. A CEO of a large public California hospital told me once that the key to success in his organization was the same, in his opinion, as for a good basketball team. Both must master finely tuned execution in a fast-paced environment; both must have the "three Es"—emotion, enthusiasm, and energy— to be successful. These three factors should be part and parcel of a healthcare worker's practical work philosophy.

In examining the candidate's background and work record, the interviewing manager should attempt to determine if the candidate applies his energy intelligently, and works "smart," not just hard, minimizing the ever-present risk of burnout. An indicator of this facet is evidence that the candidate always works at least the required number of hours and often will spend more time when the work situation demands it. Energetic people are almost always very positive in discussing past situations, and typically will emphasize the positive in a negative situation. Usually, they also can describe and emphasize a need for a lifestyle of activity away from the job.

During the interview itself, candidates will be consistently animated and respond quickly to probes and cues presented by the interviewer. A reasonable degree of appropriate emotion will be expressed throughout the interview. In short, the enthusiasm will be consistent and appropriate, and there will be little if any "lag time" in the candidate's answers. Again, it is critical for the interviewing manager to be aware not only of deficient energy levels but of excessive or undue applications of energy and enthusiastic response.

Perceptiveness. The third component of people skills is a comprehensive understanding of the human relations in the workplace. A perceptive candidate will demonstrate dexterity in dealing with people both inside and outside the organization and show a fundamental ability to anticipate individual concerns and feelings. While this has always been an essential part of a manager's repertoire of skills, with the increased emphasis on good overall people skills for all levels of employees, it is becoming equally important at the nonexempt level as well. Employees lacking this vital characteristic will be unable to anticipate problems in people-related situations and will mishandle situations in which relating well to others is of the utmost importance.

When discussing past and present situations, the perceptive candidate will provide many examples of dealing with tough people problems successfully while maintaining the best possible interpersonal relations. Additionally, she will sincerely stress the importance of people and their intangible qualities to the work unit's mission. She will demonstrate an ability to relate to other personalities and opposing viewpoints, and she will often emphasize the need to examine the worth of all viewpoints and opinions. Balancing this openness is the ability to prevent subjective perceptions from interfering with the objective facts of a situation. Furthermore, while weighing other viewpoints and ideas, the candidate will not quickly abandon her own ideas and opinions, especially if she has a well-developed sense of what is most effective in a given situation.

In assessing the interview dialogue itself, the interviewing manager should first determine how perceptive the candidate is about her own impact in the workplace, taking into account how the candidate presents herself and how aware she seems to be of the effect on others of her managerial style. The interviewing manager should then evaluate how effectively and sincerely the candidate stresses the contributions of others to the accomplishment of professional goals. Genuine warmth in discussing other players and a personable style in general are viable indicators of the candidate's perceptiveness on the job.

Presence and Bearing. The final factor in the people skills category is defined as the ability to create a positive impression and make one's impact felt in any situation with the most favorable results possible. Many organizations frequently refer to this aspect as the person's or organization's image, a term that connotes a practiced impression or a deliberate scheme to create a certain impression. This quality must be examined for two critical components—first, the candidate's true presence and its effect on others, and second, whether the presence will be sustained over the long term.

Virtually all of the indicators in this particular category must be drawn directly from the candidate's behavior and approach in the interview, rather than from examples or situations that the candidate describes in the dialogue. The first question the interviewing manager should ask himself is, "What would my immediate reaction be to this person in our business setting?" It is imperative for the interviewer to match this initial impression with the specific requirements of the subject position, taking into account the people contact the position entails and the reactions the candidate's presence might engender. A telltale sign of the person's presence is how comfortable she seems in the interview and particularly how consistently her presence is in force when the candidate is speaking. The degree of synchronization between the facts the candidate is describing and the emotion she is expressing is another critical indicator of how real the candidate's presence truly is in an everyday business setting.

Many candidates—particularly those who have worked in a highly image-conscious organization like IBM, American Travenol, or Squibb—are shining examples of the corporate image and philosophy of which they are a product. In our work in the fast-food restaurant business, for example, we find that virtually none of the smaller, regional chains like Der Wienerschnitzel or Jack-in-the-Box will hire McDonald's store managers for their organizations. Their reasoning, which I wholeheartedly concur with, is that those managers have been overconditioned not only in the practical methods of the McDonald's organization, but also in a certain presence, which is not in tune with that of the smaller organizations. Likewise, numerous healthcare organizations indoctrinate their personnel with a certain image that in many cases is considered in the industry to be aloof and somewhat condescending. On the positive side, Johnson & Johnson sales reps are often lauded for their down-home, person-to-person approach.

The interviewing manager should ensure that the impression the candidate presents has been tempered with genuineness and expresses the candidate's true personality. The interviewer should seek those candidates who combine an appropriate degree of warmth with a commitment to dependable professionalism that will put the customer's needs and wants at the top of the list of priorities. In summary, the interviewing manager should look for a person with actual impact, not a person whose presence is contrived.

Assessing Managerial Aptitude

The third behavioral category the healthcare manager should evaluate is relevant primarily for supervisory and managerial candidates, although it has some application to hourly and nonexempt applicants. This is the category of managerial aptitude, which encompasses the essential elements of creativity, delegation, independent judgment, and planning. This category is a particularly difficult one to assess, since candidates are usually schooled in management theory and can often deftly weave clichés and jargon into an appearance of supervisory knowledge and competence. The critical interviewing manager must discern both how real the candidate's managerial philosophy is and, more important, how practical and effective it is, as evidenced by past work experience and by successes detailed by the candidate. The sum of these judgments should be compared with what the optimum performance of the job will require.

Creativity. The first component of managerial aptitude is the ability to innovatively employ both quantitative and qualitative strengths to set policy, construct plans, and provide results-oriented direction. Candidates who are effectively creative are unafraid to take risks on new programs that can provide improved benefits, faster service, or better products. The interviewing manager should take into account any examples the candidate presents that indicate a habit of seeking out and utilizing new methods of conducting business that are practically beneficial for both the customer and the organization. Such examples will also display the candidate's technical expertise; the greater a person's technical expertise, the more opportunities he will discover and capitalize on to increase the efficiency of his part of the business. There are many clues in a person's background to the range of his creativity, from academic background to the willingness to take calculated risks in the business setting, even if the approaches used are considered unorthodox or unpopular. Additionally, the candidate must appear to be self-motivated and not to need a great deal of encouragement, guidance, or reinforcement in his efforts to improve the norm through creativity. An overt need for this type of external counseling indicates not only a lack of creativity but, as we will soon discuss, a marked lack of confidence and independent judgment.

In the interview forum, a creative candidate will be able to describe readily any working process, whether technical or general, step by step to a productive end. He will quickly take control of the range of thought and presentation of ideas, rather than having to be led by the interviewer. In displaying analytical thinking, a good candidate will be able to detail processes and procedures clearly and comprehensively; in displaying conceptual thinking, the candidate will express original ideas, opinions, and well-developed perceptions. These creative approaches, however, will always be anchored in a commitment to bottom-line necessities and a realistic desire to get the job done as well as possible. Finally, the candidate will show breadth of thought augmented with a depth of knowledge in any particularly needed area.

Delegation. The second dimension of managerial aptitude is demonstrated ability to assign work, responsibility, and authority in the interest of efficiency and expediency. The candidate who delegates well works through people effectively to accomplish any desired ends. In reviewing the candidate's work history, the interviewing manager should take note of any evidence that the candidate was able to maintain a set procedure for work measurement and task assignment and for ensuring timely completion of assigned responsibilities; the work history should also show an ability to stay cognizant of all of these critical dimensions throughout the performance of a task.

Many candidates with a high work ethic have great difficulty in assigning work to others, particularly in healthcare, where the need for exact, flawless work is ever present in all operational disciplines. A good delegator is perceptive enough to realize the various strengths and weaknesses of his assigned subordinates and support workers and can take advantage of them by delegating effectively. His work history should be replete with examples of working through people effectively and of maintaining ownership of all work assigned to his section by delegating operational responsibility, not final responsibility—in short, by delegating, not shuffling. The interviewer should seek out a pattern of regularly obtaining maximum performance from assigned human resources in all past work roles.

Within the interview itself, the candidate who cites the ability to get tasks accomplished through delegation must be probed further to ascertain how he delegates assignments. The interviewing manager has to remember that most, if not all, managerial candidates will make an effort to portray a certain managerial philosophy and approach. The interviewing manager must ensure that the candidate's responses have depth and are supported by practical examples that demonstrate competence conclusively (inasmuch as that is possible in an interview) in this area. As we discussed in Chapter Three, delegation is considered by many successful healthcare managers to be the most difficult of these dimensions to master.

Independent Judgment. The third facet of managerial aptitude is also considered to be valuable but rare in healthcare managerial candidates. Independent judgment is a candidate's capacity to ascertain direction and to set goals utilizing his own talent and ability. Independent judgment is typified by a person who is self-starting and who makes timely decisions and executes assignments without undue reliance on other parties. Usually, a candidate with strong independent judgment regularly uses an effective mechanism to ensure that desired results are being achieved; in doing so, the candidate consistently achieves goals ahead of target dates. This type of candidate also will have a history of getting involved with tough situations; that is, the candidate is unafraid to be aggressive and creative in particularly challenging situations. This should be tempered with a record of applying these characteristics successfully and appropriately; a candidate branded a "hot dog," "glory boy," or "golden girl" by subordinates or peers can have obvious negative results on both the morale and the performance of the work organization. If the candidate perceives a situation that calls for unique, quick action, he will not hesitate to give it his best shot immediately, without waiting for a second opinion or encouragement from others.

In the interview, the manager should assess the candidate's ability to describe the resolution of a work problem requiring an active response that was both quick and accurate. The successful candidate will respond to these probes and cues directly and without undue hesitation, a solid indicator of an independent approach to both communication and work-related thought. Additionally, candidates with independent judgment often take pride in and readily cite the short turnaround time of their projects. They can reflect on their accomplishments and delineate what they learned from their experiences. Their personalities are marked by consistent ability to explain adroitly the rationale behind their decision making without any hesitancy, ambivalence, or retraction. In short, they quickly make the best decision possible and live with the consequences, negative or positive, without regret or excessive second-guessing. They have developed a true confidence in their decision-making abilities that will give the hiring organization a solid manager.

Planning. The final component of managerial aptitude is the ability to establish both short- and long-term goals for both the individual and the work unit. The sound candidate in this regard can take the initiative in setting a course of action and outline the specific tasks that will achieve set goals. The most telling factor in this category lies in the type and quality of the candidate's career planning, evidenced by the career moves described in the application or résumé. Like independent judgment, this characteristic is applicable to certain hourly or nonexempt employees as well as supervisory ones. The interviewing manager should critically evaluate in both cases the amount and type of movement the candidate has experienced and its overall effect on the candidate's professional progress.

Following this assessment, the interviewer should weigh how well the candidate analyzes objectives and sets a daily or weekly plan for reaching those objectives. An accomplished planner can usually set a good initial plan of attack, perhaps with a secondary or fallback approach in case circumstances make the first plan infeasible. Both on the application and throughout the interview, the successful candidate will be able to explain a solid practice of weighing the targets, setting a course of action, and attaining the goals, whether they are career objectives or on-the-job accomplishments.

The interviewing manager should consider several factors within the interview itself that will help give an indication of the candidate's planning ability. Foremost is the candidate's preparation for the interview itself. For example, the candidate should have researched the organization as fully as possible and have a basic grasp of the firm's mission and operation. The candidate should also have a fair idea of what he or she wants to present as salient requirements for the subject position, again taking into account the need to be adaptable and responsive when the interviewer moves the dialogue in a new direction. The successful candidate will aptly convey his or her goals for the subject position, demonstrating basic knowledge of what is needed. Clearly, a candidate's ability to do this will vary relative to what information is available as well as how clear-cut and realistic the candidate's aspirations and potential are for the job and for a career with your organization. The ability to go past the general concept of planning and into the specifics of planning mechanisms and approaches is important to all of these factors.

In summary, the ideal managerial candidate is able to blend creative thought, delegation, independent judgment, and planning skills into a management philosophy and practice that has been tested and honed by experience, not concocted from business administration textbooks. This combination of talents, along with the others we have discussed, will give the organization managers who will get the maximum long-term return on the resources they are provided with for the benefit of the health-care organization.

Assessing Team Orientation

The ability of all departments and units to work cohesively and synergistically is integral to the mission of any healthcare organization. In order to attain this group motivation and execution, the interviewing manager must seek and hire only candidates who are team-oriented as well as individually qualified technically and qualitatively. The skills of team orientation—cooperation, employee relations, and loyalty—apply to all levels of management and hourly personnel and across the board of technical areas and business disciplines.

Cooperation. The first dimension of team orientation is a high motivation toward selfless service to co-workers, customers, and organizational goals. Cooperation is also evidenced by the individual's perception that the performance of his or her job is part of a service commitment to others; cooperative people are totally committed to doing whatever is necessary to provide high-quality care to the organization's customers. They consistently put group priorities ahead of individual ones. They freely share essential information with those who need it to perform their own jobs, and in no cases do they play political games with important information or, on the other hand, compromise a co-worker or someone else in the organization by discussing confidential issues. Cooperative people also are routinely willing and able to act as a resource to anyone who needs their general or technical expertise in making a valiant work effort. They are not "blamers," never pointing unduly to other people or to circumstances in times of failure. They are accountable for their actions and do not fear retribution, since their actions are rooted in their commitment to the organization.

In the interview itself, a cooperative candidate will convey a perception of himself as a competent part of a whole entity, not as a superstar, by stressing "we" in a given situation rather than "I." He will demonstrate cooperative behavior in the interview, appearing to be at ease and making every effort to answer the interviewer's questions directly, honestly, and completely. This will be particularly evident when the interviewer asks point-blank questions that are open-ended and require a good deal of internalization and thought. Throughout the interview, the manager should get the feeling that the candidate is a straightforward, selfless person who puts the best interests of the organization and those important to its mission at the top of his list of priorities.

Employee Relations. The second factor in team orientation is the ability to create and maintain a workplace relationship with assigned subordinates and co-workers that helps generate maximum effectiveness and productivity. The supervisory candidate who is proficient in this regard is one who can combine human resources productivity with employee growth and development and who utilizes human resources as an integral factor in accomplishing work goals. As we mentioned in Chapter Three, this is a particularly tricky commodity, with potential for misuse; there are tendencies even on the part of talented managers either to minimize employee relations to the point of alienating workers or to concentrate on the personal aspect so intently as to create favoritism or other problems.

As in the case of managerial aptitude, the interviewing manager should try to obtain a sense of the candidate's overall management philosophy and approach and compare it to that which is encouraged and successful in the organization. Specific attention should be paid to the candidate's regard for and utilization of human resources, beginning with a description of what the candidate looks for in current and prospective employees. For example, the interviewer can ask the candidate to describe the best employee she has working for her (or, in the case of an hourly candidate, the best employee she works with) and match the traits she cites with the employee traits the hiring organization encourages. The interviewing manager should key into certain tough employee situations the candidate has had to handle in the past, such as presenting new operational methods, personnel cutbacks, or any other drastic changes to employees. The interviewing manager should try to determine if the candidate has used progressive human resource management methods to her organization's benefit, such as participative management, flextime scheduling, cross-training, or any other creative method that would inspire increased productivity and dedication from subordinates. The manager who is talented in employee relations can present a record of high productivity, accomplishment of definite goals, and low employee turnover.

Within the interview itself, the candidate with sound employee relations will be genuinely enthusiastic when discussing personnel from current and past jobs and will demonstrate pride and satisfaction in being an integral part of their success. The candidate will also express a sense of comfort and confidence in detailing how she established a fair but firm working relationship with subordinates or co-workers from which everyone benefited. The candidate may emphasize clear and concise delivery of direction to subordinates or co-workers.

Loyalty. Many volumes have been written in the management sciences field about this factor, which has engendered as many definitions and philosophies as virtually any management topic. Loyalty, as we define it, is present in a person who is firmly committed to working hard for the organization at all times, representing always its best interests, and giving its needs and overall performance top priority. In short, this person is dedicated to organization and mission.

Many personnel recruiters cite the length of time spent in each job or organization as a primary indicator of loyalty, but in today's hyperactive work environment it is our belief that this indicator is not as accurate as it might once have been. Few if any indicators of loyalty will be found in the candidate's background or résumé; the majority of indicators exist within the interview dialogue itself.

The first consideration for the interviewing manager is where the candidate's deepest loyalty lies. People who seem intent on speaking negatively and bad-mouthing former employees are likely to be self-centered and loyal to the organization only when it is advantageous to their own position. This is also true of candidates who are disproportionately interested in money, social status, work titles, personal recognition, and other rewards, and who rarely cite other people or the organization in the course of the interview. Additionally, a strong loyalty to a religious or political cause or another off-work activity may hinder work performance. The person who displays a basic sense of loyalty in the interview, is honest in discussion, and is not so loyal to another organization or cause that his energies are divided is the desirable candidate.

In summation, the interviewing manager should remember that evaluating the interview is as strenuous as preparing and conducting it, and has as many possibilities for error. By acquiring a good feel for the evaluation criteria discussed in this chapter and delineated in Resources E and F, the interviewing manager can greatly improve assessment of candidates, which in turn will greatly facilitate better hiring and lower turnover.

Chapter 8

Comprehensive Case Study of Recruitment and Selection

In order to give the reader as much insight as possible into the practical application of the recruiting and selection strategy presented in this book, the following case study is provided. The case is based on an actual hiring process executed by a client organization in which a critical human resource need was successfully addressed. Some of the particular dynamics of the case have been altered in order to provide a full picture of the practical use of all the selection criteria presented in Part Two.

The reader should first look at the case as a whole in order to see how all the factors work in concert. The reader can then focus on each phase of the process in order to understand how each segment of the recruiting and selection process works toward the overall result of accurate, effective selection and placement.

Situation

Nick Wright is the regional manager for the West Tennessee Hospital Corporation (WTHC), a chain of seven community hospitals in the Memphis metropolitan area and its suburbs. Nick has worked in the healthcare field for over fifteen years since his graduation from Memphis State University, and for the last five years he has worked for WTHC. He started his career at Presley Memorial, one of the hospitals that is now part of WTHC, and worked there for nine years, receiving regular promotions. After he was named administrator of the facility, the boom in the healthcare industry began and Nick's institution began to suffer from the changes in reimbursement schemes and other revenue losses. Nick enlisted the support of the board of directors for the plan to merge Presley Memorial with the West Tennessee conglomerate. After a three-year tenure as the staff operations director, he entered his current position.

As regional manager, Nick is responsible for the general management of four of the organization's suburban community hospitals. Each of the hospital administrators reports to him, as does a staff of five professionals who provide consulting and technical direction to their counterparts at each of the institutions. On the whole, Nick has a solid staff of people who enjoy their jobs, see their career goals and desires being met, and consider the greater Memphis area a good place to live. Many of the professionals on the headquarters staff and in the facilities themselves worked at one of the seven member hospitals prior to the formation of the conglomerate seven years ago. All see the value of the greater organization, and there are few problems with resentment or the old loyalties that are common in some merger situations.

As the organizational chart in Figure 22 shows, the position of human resources director for the southern region—Nick's area of responsibility—is open. The current human resources director, Tad Wallingford, is about to leave WTHC for a large nursing home conglomerate based in his hometown, New Orleans. This position is critically important to the organization; not only is it responsible for the personnel of four of the organization's facilities, but the person who fills it will be the likely replacement for the corporate vice president of human resources. The current corporate vice president, Red West, will retire in two years. The human resources director for the northern region, Wilma Jenkins, is a well-placed, long-term manager who has stated her desire to stay in her position until her early retirement in four years. Therefore, Ray Keller, the president and chief executive officer (CEO) of WTHC, has instructed Nick to fill the post of human resources director with a person who can be groomed to take the vice president's position in two years and then to hire and select a staff that will provide outstanding personnel services to the employee population of the entire West Tennessee organization. Upon receiving two weeks' notice of Wallingford's

Figure 22. Organizational Chart of the Southern Region, West Tennessee Hospital Corporation.

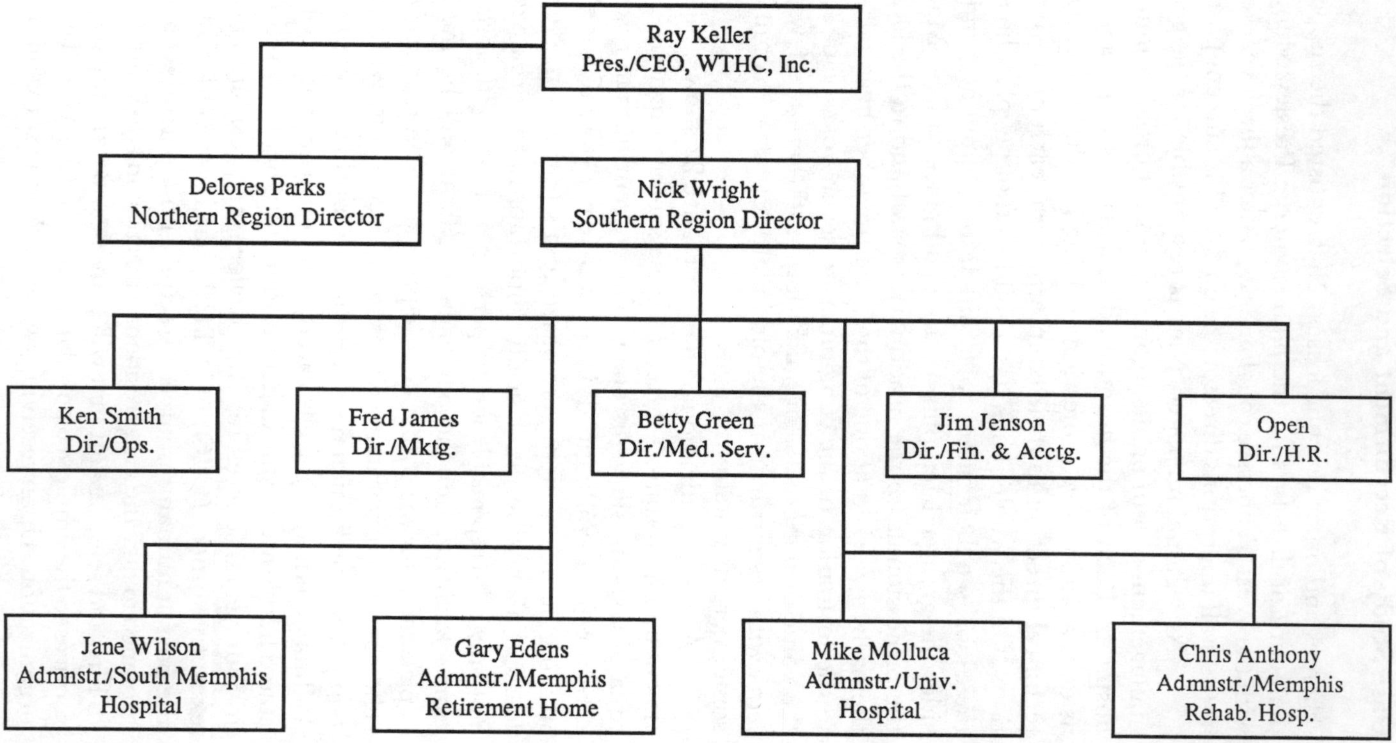

Ray Keller
Pres./CEO, WTHC, Inc.

Delores Parks
Northern Region Director

Nick Wright
Southern Region Director

Ken Smith
Dir./Ops.

Fred James
Dir./Mktg.

Betty Green
Dir./Med. Serv.

Jim Jenson
Dir./Fin. & Acctg.

Open
Dir./H.R.

Jane Wilson
Admnstr./South Memphis Hospital

Gary Edens
Admnstr./Memphis Retirement Home

Mike Molluca
Admnstr./Univ. Hospital

Chris Anthony
Admnstr./Memphis Rehab. Hosp.

departure, Nick takes his cue from his boss and uses his knowledge of healthcare human resources to begin the process of recruiting and selecting a new director of human resources.

Recruitment Strategy

Nick's first step is to analyze the human resources director's position and determine its specific duties and technical requirements. He first reviews the job description on file with the personnel office, as well as the performance appraisal he completed for Wallingford; after reviewing the job description completely, he judges it to be an accurate representation of the position. The human resources director in the southern region has an informal reporting relationship to the corporate vice president of human resources and reports directly to Nick, the regional director. The personnel managers at each of the four regional facilities report to the human resources director in a similar professional capacity. Reporting to the position directly are three manager-level employees and two hourly-level clerical employees. The major reporting relationships are shown in Figure 23.

The major task of the regional director of human resources is to direct the personnel policies and procedures of the four facilities and to provide support and internal consulting services to the facilities' personnel managers as required. The regional human resources director also acts as technical consultant on personnel matters to Nick, the members of Nick's regional headquarters staff, and, in critical situations, the administrators of the four facilities.

The demands of the job description and the previous goals and objectives of the position require the person who fills it to have a command of the five basic skills in healthcare human resources. First, the person must be able to recruit effectively for key positions and to oversee the recruiting and selection practices at all the region's facilities. Second, the person must be able to manage the compensation program effectively to ensure that the wages and benefits programs of the entire region and its member facilities are fair and justly administered. Third, the person must have proven competence at the basics of personnel

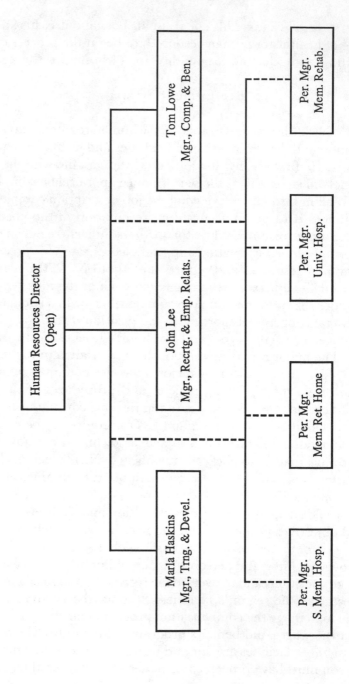

Figure 23. Southern Regional Human Resources Director's Organization.

administration, including the administration of job description and bidding systems.

Nick and the organization think Wallingford was particularly effective at the first three components of the new job; the new director will have only to maintain the status quo and make improvements as needed. In the job's other two duties, training and development and employee relations, Nick feels that Wallingford was of only average effectiveness and sees a distinct need for improvement. In the area of training and development, Nick would like to hire someone who is particularly creative and will generate his or her own needs-specific programs, rather than rely on off-the-shelf, packaged programs, which are not suited to the needs of WTHC. In the area of employee relations, Nick needs someone who can set into motion solid, proactive employee relations strategies, such as quality circle programs and employee suggestion systems. These would be a welcomed (and needed) change from the reactive, anti-union labor relations programs that Wallingford advocated and implemented. Because all the facilities have been de-unionized and the employees are not likely to form another union, a heavy anti-union orientation in employee relations is no longer necessary.

Finally, Nick looks at all of his organizational standards and the environment in which the organization is currently operating. The greater Memphis area has been enjoying a population boom, thanks to the growth of local companies such as Federal Express and the recent relocation of several Fortune 500 companies' headquarters. Nick recognizes the need for a personnel director who has excellent people skills, can adapt to a growing community, and is aggressive enough to implement needed programs in this time of change. The director should also be able to manage a work group effectively and contribute to the regional management team. Taking the job description, his analysis of the sixteen Quan-Com characteristics, and his own knowledge of what is needed in the position, Nick begins his recruitment of a new regional director of human resources.

Nick's first move is to look for candidates within the West Tennessee organization. Only five people in the organization are qualified according to their jobs' and the open job's definitions; therefore, he need not post the job on the organization's formal bidding system. For a position wider in scope, there might be a plethora of suitable candidates not well known to management; in such a case, Nick might use the bidding system. As it stands, he reviews the five candidates who might be suitable for the position.

Three of the candidates report directly to the position, as Figure 23 shows. Marla Haskins, the training and development manager, had been in her job less than a year and has not yet been appraised formally. Because of Wallingford's penchant for off-the-shelf programs, Haskins has been acting as little more than a stand-up trainer for general, fairly ineffective programs. The compensation manager, Tom Lowe, is an effective compensation specialist but has little general experience. John Lee, the recruiting and employee relations manager, is very talented but also very young, only two years out of graduate school. He might be a good backup, however, for the new director, and Nick notes this in his manager's notebook.

The remaining two internal candidates are personnel managers at two facilities in the West Tennessee organization. Bill Holdane is the personnel manager at Bookman Hospital in the northern region, and was brought to Nick's attention by his counterpart, the northern regional director. Jenna Rush is the personnel manager at the University Hospital in Nick's own region. Nick conducts a screening interview with each candidate. After the sessions, he feels both lack the depth of experience needed in the job. He is pleased, however, because the meetings confirmed that both Rush, whom he knew, and Holdane, whom he had never met, are talented people and likely candidates for promotion. He notes them as potential backups and future members of his staff, and sends them memos thanking them for their time and interest. As an additional measure, he telephones all five candidates, expresses his appreciation for their efforts and his faith in them, and appropriately and tactfully explains his reasons for looking outside the organization for a person with more professional experience.

Having exhausted his internal candidate possibilities but gained some insight in the process, Nick now looks to external sources for the new human resources director. Of the sources listed in Chapter Five, neither the job fair, the walk-in desk, nor school liaison is an option, since he needs someone with considerable professional experience. Government agencies are out, since this is a professional, nonhourly position, and there is no need to recruit from a foreign source, since the United States is not short of human resource professionals (although some maintain it is short of *competent* human resources people!).

Nick is left with the choice of a newspaper advertisement, a search firm, employee referrals, or professional affiliations and contacts to generate a list of candidates. Because this position's salary is in the range of $50,000 per year, a high-quality search firm could cost Nick over $16,000. The employee referral option is a long shot, and because of the critical need for a candidate and the sensitive nature of the job, he does not feel comfortable using this avenue. Nick's previous positions were in administration and marketing, and his professional leads in human resources are therefore limited. The competition in his area is not large enough to have an employee skilled in multifacility organizations. Nick considers his two best options to be a search firm and media advertising. Because he would like to screen all the applicants himself, rather than leave them in the hands of an external recruiter, Nick chooses to advertise in a suitable national publication.

With the help of the WTHC public relations specialist, Nick places the following advertisement in *Healthcare America,* a nationally read professional periodical:

Regional Human Resources Director

A major multifacility hospital corporation seeks a regional human resources director. This person will be comprehensively responsible for the administration and management of the human resources function of a four-hospital organizational unit consisting of over 800 employees and supervisors. The successful candidate will have at least seven years of progressive human resources man-

agement experience, and will possess a graduate
degree in human resources management or a closely
related field. Personnel generalist experience in a
healthcare setting is required, preferably in a multifacility organization.

The salary range for this position is $45,000
to $50,000, depending on experience, with excellent
benefits and appropriate relocation costs. Please
apply by sending résumés to:
Box HR/Reg
West Tennessee Hospital Corporation, Inc.
1956 Elvis Presley Blvd.
Memphis, Tennessee 65910

The advertisement, which describes the organization, the position, the compensation, and instructions for applying, generates
over seventy responses. Nick selects five candidates whose education, technical experience, and current jobs meet the requirements of the position for comprehensive interviewing in Memphis by himself and key members of the staff. By running the
ad, Nick has saved his organization about $10,000 (although
reviewing résumés and contacting the five finalists has cost him
the better part of two days); furthermore, he has recruited five
stellar candidates worthy of consideration for the position.

Conducting and Evaluating the Interview

In interviewing the five candidates for the position of
regional human resources director, Nick employed the help of
two headquarters staff executives. Each of the three interviewed
the finalists with the same structured selection approach (Resource F), asking two questions from each major category—
attitude orientation, people skills, managerial aptitude, and team
orientation—and an additional question about each of the particularly needed factors of creativity, technical expertise, and
adaptability. Nick and his peers decided that the best candidate
for the position was Cecilia Jackson, a human resources generalist currently employed at the University of Louisiana's Medical
Center. This medical center is a large facility consisting of three

distinct organizational divisions. Ms. Jackson progressed from manager of training and development to personnel director of the entire 550-person organization. She has held this position for nearly two years.

To show the rationale behind her selection, as well as to illustrate practically the approaches to conducting and evaluating the interview described in Chapters Six and Seven, an abbreviated version of Cecilia Jackson's final interview with Ray Keller, the president of WTHC, is presented on the following pages. Commentary on the essential components of an effective selection interview is presented along with the dialogue.

Keller: Ms. Jackson, I'm Ray Keller, the president of WTHC. Welcome to Memphis once again. I know you visited on your last trip with Nick and two other members of our staff, and I appreciate your time and effort in coming up once again. Today we'll spend about forty-five minutes together, with about an additional ten minutes following our interview for you to ask me any questions you might have about the organization or the position of regional human resources director. I'll take some notes, if you don't mind, and also, would you mind if I call you Cecilia?

Jackson: Not at all, Mr. Keller—if I can call you Ray. (Laughs)

Keller: (Laughs) Certainly, please do. I've read your résumé, Cecilia, and talked to all of the folks you've met here; we're all impressed.

Jackson: Well, thank you. I've been impressed by what I've seen here and what I've learned about the challenge of the position we're discussing.

Keller: Well, good, let's get started then. I wonder if you could begin by giving me a quick overview of your current position, and why you're interested in our position of regional director of human resources.

Keller has opened the interview well, fully explaining the time parameters and agenda for the interview. He has also put Jackson at ease by explaining that he will take notes and establishing the use of first names. By opening with a relatively easy question about Jackson's current role and interest in the subject position, he is setting up a framework and reference point for the rest of the interview. Following this opening, the candidate is ready to present some information comfortably, and Keller can start using his list of questions (Resource F).

Jackson: Well, as you know, I am the director of human resources for the Medical Center of the University of Louisiana, where I've worked for a total of eight years, since I finished graduate school at Tulane University. I was a staff trainer for two years, the training and development manager for four years, and have been the human resources director for the past two years.

In my current job I supervise a training manager, a compensation specialist, and a recruiter, all of whom I've hired in the past two years. You see, Ray, the administration unfortunately terminated my predecessor in the director's position, and as a result two of his staff people decided to leave as well. Furthermore, the third person on the staff, the recruiter, soon left to start a family. So as soon as I took over the position, I had to get right to work.

Keller: It sounds like it was a challenging situation.

Jackson has already shown her loyalty to her current organization through the words and phrases she uses to describe tactfully what was a classic housecleaning situation. Her adaptability is also evident in this answer. By using a rejoinder at this point, along with good eye contact and unobtrusive note taking, Keller will learn more about Jackson's aggressiveness, work ethic, and general managerial aptitude before he needs to ask another question.

Jackson: It was indeed challenging, a baptism under fire in a sense. However, the fact that I was able to hire a good staff quickly—all three people I hired have succeeded to date in their positions—gave me the confidence that I could handle the job. Getting all of the new staff people oriented in their new positions meant a lot of overtime, but in the long run it was worth it, as I had the advantage of having people *I* had selected in key positions, and thus felt as though the total responsibility for the human resources function was truly mine.

So far, we have been able to effect some good results in our two years on the job. Turnover has been reduced by 23 percent, mainly because of more effective recruiting and more structured interviewing. Our wages and benefits programs have stayed just a necessary step ahead of our competition, and this has helped both the turnover situation and the overall morale of the employees. Also, we have promoted extensively from within, which further decreases turnover and related expenses. Our training and development programs have helped with internal promotions, since I feel we have people better prepared to take over key positions. All in all, I feel the program is well in place and will continue to produce good results.

Because the program is in such good shape, almost running itself, so to speak, your advertisement caught my eye. I feel ready for a new challenge that would stretch my abilities further while allowing me to contribute to a bigger, but still high-quality, organization. While I'm basically content at my present job, in a couple of months that contentment, without new challenges, might become boredom.

Jackson's answer stresses accomplishment without egotism, showing a good team orientation in stressing "we" as much as "I." She succinctly describes not only what was accomplished but the rationale behind her achievements, demonstrating both technical expertise and good managerial aptitude. Her work ethic, perseverance, employee relations, and independent judgment are all evident in the hiring and subsequent orientation of her staff and in her willingness to accept the responsibility for her department. Her reasons for pursuing the new job and her well-thought-out career plan show a work ethic that demands more challenge, as well as the ability to plan.

Keller: Well, I believe we have a challenging situation here for the right person. Cecilia, can you tell me about one of the programs you instituted at your current job, explaining it from design to reality?

Keller's rejoinder is neutral but acknowledges the reason Jackson is interested in the position, thus conveying to her that he is actively listening. Nick Wright has pointed to creativity as a key criterion for success in this position; the answer to Keller's question, or cue (taken from the creativity strategy in Resource F), will show just how creative Ms. Jackson is in her work approach.

Jackson: Yes, I will, but I must start with the need for the project and then tell you about the design and implementation. As I mentioned, we had something of a turnover problem at the medical center when I assumed my current responsibilities. After looking at the problem for some time, I realized that not only were the selection criteria inaccurate in most cases, but internal candidates were not being considered first. My plan of action was to decide how to address this problem, and then to implement a program that would encourage the medical center's managers to evaluate internal candidates before initiating external searches.

My approach to this situation involved the installation of two programs. First, I was able to get the administration's support for asking all the managers to complete semiannual manpower development reports, which were graphic indicators of each employee's performance, potential, and promotability. These reports were not very cumbersome, since all they required was information that was apparent on the performance appraisal forms and some thought from the manager on the employee's future career paths, based on those appraisals.

Keller: Was there much resistance from the line managers?

Jackson: Initially, there was some griping, but once the line managers had realized that the program was fairly easy, and once a couple of them had seen that they could save a lot of recruiting time and money by using the reports, the resistance was minimal. In fact, we found that the few managers who continued to complain were behind schedule in completing required performance appraisal forms, so in a way the program identified some additional personnel administration problems we had to address.

After using the manpower development reports steadily for about a year or so, we moved into the second phase of our attack on the turnover problem, which was to use the manpower development reports as blueprints for training and development activities. On each manpower report, the line managers were asked to suggest any training or development activities that they thought might be helpful in enhancing each employee's promotability. This information, combined with the ideas that our training specialist came up with after reviewing the reports, gave us the direction we needed to give the individual employees needs-specific, effective training. The program apparently was well conceived, since last year we had nineteen internal promotions, compared to only three the year before. Furthermore, our outside searches decreased from twenty-two to seven. Another indicator that we are moving in the right direction is the fact that we are conducting more internal training than ever before, and in fact have started a supervisory basic skills course to help address the future need for supervisors at the medical center.

Keller: A supervisory skills program? Tell me more about that.

Jackson's answer is comprehensive and shows not only creativity but also technical expertise and managerial aptitude, in the form of her independent judgment and the thoughtful use of her training manager. Her confidence and perseverance are shown by her pursuit of the internal system despite initial resistance; in fact, she takes the initial negativity and turns it into an advantage by using the complaints of some managers to examine their incompetence in assessing employee performance.

For his part, Keller is maintaining a good interview flow by using opportune rejoinders. He is bringing up a critical area, namely, Jackson's ability to implement some needs-specific training, particularly in the supervisor preparation area. As we have stated, Nick Wright determined from his environmental analysis that the Memphis area, the corporation's customer community, is growing. Therefore, more employees will be needed, as well as capable supervisors who have worked for WTHC and know the organization. The previous approach, buying off-the-shelf, generic training programs, has proven to be ineffective.

By using this rejoinder to elicit more information from Jackson, and by carefully gauging her response, Keller can learn if her talents represent a needed improvement in this area.

Jackson: Yes, of course. Because of my previous experience as the training specialist at the medical center, I realized that all three business units had a critical need for accomplished supervisors in all departments. In fact, the shortage was so bad that when a supervisor left the organization to work somewhere else, the solution sometimes used was simply to combine two departments into one, so that a new supervisor would not have to be hired from outside. I tried to discuss this problem with the human resources director at the time, but for whatever reason he did not share my perception of the problem as a major one, and thus declined to really support the implementation of a supervisory skills training and development program.

Anyway, when I assumed the duties of human resources director, I decided to enlist the necessary support of the administration and install a supervisory skills program. First, I asked my training specialist to look at the notes I had made on the topic and to start researching approaches that might work. He studied programs at other hospitals and healthcare facilities like ours, and he even looked at some of the successful supervisory skills courses promoted by professional educational organizations, as well as those courses that were well attended at local community colleges. Another consideration was determining what kind of training our employees might respond to. For example, it was unrealistic to expect them to attend a full-time, five-day-long program, which would take them away from their duties in a decidedly understaffed organization for a full work week.

After taking two weeks or so to devise a basic plan, my training specialist came up with a series of eight "minicourses." Each minicourse would have twelve participants, would be about three hours long, and would involve the use of video case-study and practical application exercises. All the materials from each minicourse would be part of a large, overstuffed notebook, which, at the conclusion of the last course, would be a complete supervisor's guide for the participant's use on the job. I felt that the content of the courses, as well as the basic design of the minicourses, was a good start. My first move, however, was to link the minicourses together by presenting them as numbered modules. This would allow a regular offering of the entire sequence, and if participants absolutely had to miss a module they could make it up in the next training sequence. Also, I decided that the maximum number of participants in each session would be six rather than twelve, to make sure that they would get the most from each three-hour session.

The next step was to present the program in such a way that managers would not see it as a threat to productivity and participants would see it, simply put, as something special. I felt these two parameters had to be in place, particularly in the initial offering of the program, when our credibility would be established and the program itself would either take off or crash.

To accomplish these two ends, I introduced the programs in an unusual time slot: every Tuesday and Thursday from 11 A.M. to 2 P.M. in the cafeteria conference room. In the first place, this capitalized on the midday period, when the participants would be most alert and ready for a break from their normal workday routine. In the second place, their managers and supervisors would not mind that time slot as much as, for instance, 8 to 11 A.M., when the workday starts, or 2 to 5 P.M., when things are hectically wrapping up on the day shift. The time slot also accommodated workers on the 8 P.M. to 4 A.M. shift, since they could sleep for at least six hours before the program and then have some time afterward before coming back to work. As a "perk," an appealing buffet lunch was served at each session, and we timed the sessions so that lunch was served at the same time that a video was shown, so that people could watch a tape and eat without worrying about actively participating in a discussion. An additional point was that eight sessions, one of each module, could be presented in a single month, representing a potential of seventy-two participants a year.

Fortunately, both the administration and line management were enthusiastic about the program, to the point, in fact, where existing supervisors enrolled in the program out of their own interest. This was especially true after the first three sessions, when interest seemed to snowball. And since the medical center consists of so many diverse work groups, we found that everyone, including our staff, learned a great deal about each other's work roles. This, as you know, helps everyone to understand better how all the jobs and departments fit into the big picture.

At this point, a total of eighty-four people have attended thirteen months of the sessions. We have even received an invitation from Loyola University in New Orleans to present a graduate seminar to M.B.A. students on how we set up the program, so that they can see a "real-world" application of training and development. And as the program has progressed, we have used the participant evaluation forms constantly to fine-tune the content and presentation used in the sessions each month.

Cecilia Jackson's response is a solid indicator of her technical expertise in personnel training and development. Furthermore, it is a great indicator of several of the Quan-Com characteristics. The entire approach to the establishment of the supervisory skills program shows a good range of managerial and professional creativity, as well as strong ability to delegate, evidenced by the use of her training specialist. She aggressively addressed the need for the program, despite the reluctance of her previous boss, whom she once again discusses tactfully, reaffirming her organizational loyalty. Her perseverance is indicated not only by the persistence she showed in establishing the program, but also by the continued monitoring of participant response in the interest of improving the program's content. Her team orientation— notably her cooperation and employee relations—is evident in the manner in which she considered and addressed the time slot of the program and the provision of lunch. In scheduling the program in the middle of the day (as well as toward the middle of the week), she ensured good attendance and provided convenient access to the program for all interested parties, including the existing supervisors whom she had not counted on but who were surely major factors in the program's success. Finally, by providing lunch for the participants, Cecilia used her allotted budget more wisely than a human resources person who bought packaged programs, which cost more and have little specific relevance to these employees' career paths and professional aspirations.

At this point, Keller has received some credible evidence about many of the sixteen Quan-Com factors, notably adaptability and creativity, which are obviously everyday dynamics of Ms. Jackson's work personality. Her ability in training and development has also been eminently proven. Two Quan-Com factors that are not in evidence in the content of Ms. Jackson's responses to specific cues are presence and communication. However, by observing Cecilia Jackson's professional manner and matching it to the indicators of presence (Resource F), Ray Keller can assess her correctly as outstanding in this regard. The organization, presentational style, and conciseness of Ms. Jackson's responses to the questions reflect great communication ability.

Because most of Cecilia's answers have dealt with training and development and employee relations—the two human resources skills that are most needed in this position—Ray can make the assessment that Cecilia Jackson is certainly able in these areas. However, a question is present in Ray's mind about Cecilia's qualifications in the other three basic functions of human resources. To answer that question, he will use the first cue listed in the technical expertise section of the formula appearing in Resource F.

Keller: Cecilia, I've learned a lot about your experiences in training and development and the positive effects they seem to have on employee relations at your current organization. Could you take it one step further and explain your range of experience in the areas of recruiting, compensation, and personnel administration?

Jackson: Surely, and I'll start with my compensation experience, because frankly there isn't much to tell. Except for helping to coordinate wage surveys in my initial employment at the medical center, I had very little experience in wages and compensation administration until I became the human resources director. At that time, I received a practical course in compensation; since I needed to hire a new compensation specialist, I wanted to learn as much as possible about the function. I attended a seminar conducted by Centenary College of Louisiana and read two books on the subject. Furthermore, I called a colleague at another institution who has had extensive experience in the healthcare employee and managerial compensation field. I was able to pick up a great deal from these efforts.

Upon hiring the new compensation specialist, I took a special interest in her initial activities on the job. First, I naturally wanted to ensure that I had made a good hiring decision. Second, by keeping a close watch on her day-to-day activities, I was able to increase my knowledge of the function. While I cannot claim that I am an expert in the field, I believe I know enough about it to know what needs to be done from an organizational perspective, and how to get the most, in a general sense, from any compensation position that reports to me.

In regard to recruiting, because our organization always utilized the personnel department to do a lot of employment screening, I've interviewed literally thousands of candidates in the past eight years. Our training programs always included topics such as employee selection and interviewing techniques, and I've acquired some good practical approaches to that duty. As human resources director, I'm always involved in executive-level recruiting activities, and I believe my work record in this regard is very solid. I enjoy the interviewing process, to be honest, because I'm always interested in learning about different parts of the medical profession and different viewpoints of health-care professionals; in the case of candidates who will probably be hired, I like to determine their possible role in the organization and what their progressive development might be.

As far as basic personnel administration goes, I would not have been able to survive in my present role for any length of time if I was unable to handle that part of the job. Whether in implementing our new job grading system, or taking the lead in organizing employee-driven programs such as the United Way campaign or the medical center's annual holiday party, I believe my staff and I have been very effective.

While I've only been in my current position for two years, I think the biggest benefit for me personally is the fact that I've expanded my professional horizons across the entire human resources field, using a good base in training. From what I've learned about this position, my growth will be able to continue while my generalist expertise and specialist knowledge of the training and development functions will allow me to really provide your organization with some solid professional contributions in both the short and the long term.

Keller (after asking a few more questions): Thank you, Cecilia, for coming back to Memphis today. I've enjoyed our talk, and agree with my staff that you certainly merit strong consideration for this position. I'll discuss my thoughts with them, and we'll get back to you in less than two weeks with a decision. Are there any questions you might have for me?

Jackson: Well, perhaps you could give me some of your views about the regional director's position.
(Keller describes his quick thoughts about the responsibilities of the position. Following this, he again thanks Jackson, exchanges pleasantries, and concludes the interview.)

Jackson's answer showed a good breadth of technical expertise in the generalist role of a regional human resources director, fully addressing the topic in a manner Ray finds most credible. Her work ethic and desire to learn professionally are underscored, as is her ability to communicate directly and efficiently. Ray is duly impressed, and he, Nick Wright, and the other members of his staff who have interviewed Cecilia Jackson decide to offer her the position.

Conclusion

Because Nick Wright is the supervisor of the subject position, it is his responsibility to check the three references that

Ms. Jackson has provided. Because virtually anyone can find three people to supply good references, Nick relies more on his own interview assessment, as well as the assessments of the other members of the staff. All the interviewers feel that Cecilia is the most qualified of the candidates for the position and that she could eventually ascend into the corporate position upon Red West's retirement. Nick telephones Jackson, makes the offer orally, and immediately sends out a formal offer letter. Cecilia Jackson calls back the next day and accepts the position, giving a starting date.

By using the practical approach to healthcare recruitment and selection described in Part Two, Nick Wright has hired a regional human resources director who will grow and develop in step with the growth and development of the organization. In the process, she will exemplify the practical maximization of human resources.

Chapter 9

Requirements for Effective Performance Appraisal

In today's healthcare business environment, a great need exists for accurate performance appraisal that is both equitable and objective. The healthcare employee is challenged by an ever-changing workplace, along with the high stress and demand for consistent, top-quality performance that have always been integral parts of the healthcare work climate. Even the most highly motivated employees need regular, creditable feedback, as well as direction of their future performance. Because of the dire shortage of skilled personnel, technicians and other specialists can often find suitable employment and better wages with a competitor. An employee who does not feel that the organization values his or her services will undoubtedly feel compelled to explore outside opportunities.

The Joint Commission on Accreditation of Healthcare Organizations (JCAHO) is currently focusing a major part of its accreditation process on performance appraisal systems. In the past, many hospital administrators, as well as other healthcare executives, have failed to make their organization's performance assessment system anything more than a subjective exercise, one that does not accurately evaluate an individual employee's true performance. The current efforts of the JCAHO are intended to ensure that all member hospitals and healthcare organizations use a system that in fact is criterion-based and objective.

In the simplest terms, the performance appraisal must be constructed so that the individual employee's performance is compared objectively with the original criteria set forth in the

145

job description that is on file in the organization's personnel office. The job description should be the "guiding light" for calibration of performance and delineation of specific duties. The tenets of this approach, as well as the principles of good human resources management, dictate that the job description should be clearly constructed and define forthrightly the essential elements of the job. Furthermore, the organization should supplement the job description with case-specific examples, and the employee's adherence to the tenets of the job enumerated in the job description should be demonstrated with specific, objective evidence.

While this sounds easy and elementary, it is somewhat more complicated in the reality of the live work situation, as a glut of ineffective performance appraisal systems in the 1970s evidenced. In that decade, American managers and directors became infatuated with the Japanese style of management, and wholesale adoption of Japan's binary performance appraisal system became fashionable. In the first part of this system, the employee rates the organization and his or her supervisor; in the second part, the supervisor rates the employee's performance. While this might have proven successful in Japan, the versions of the system used in this country, where different industrial and sociological norms prevail, were little more than exercises in what we refer to as psychobabble. Many of these systems were chock-full of pseudo-psychological terms that were poorly defined and, moreover, had little practical relevance to the employee's day-to-day activities. Additionally, they lent themselves more easily to subjective and personality analysis than to true assessment of objective performance. This frequently led to crippled motivation and, in extreme cases, legal action on the part of disgruntled employees.

The need to keep employees well-motivated, as well as to withstand the increased scrutiny of governing bodies such as the JCAHO, has made it imperative for the healthcare manager to understand fully the ramifications and potential benefits of a fact-based performance appraisal system. When one considers the heavy legal attachments a poor performance appraisal system can bring, coupled with the present litigation-crazy atmosphere in all aspects of human resource management, the need for such a system becomes all the more evident. With the genesis of a new breed of lawyers who specialize in representing people who have allegedly been wronged in the workplace, a healthcare manager's responsibility to maintain an accurate assessment system is more important than ever.

In Part Three, we will discuss some common areas of difficulty in performance appraisal. We will then present a compendium of good performance appraisal principles, as well as several practical approaches that can readily be used to ensure compliance with good human resources practices as well as the unique requirements of the present-day healthcare business arena.

Common Problems in Healthcare Performance Appraisal

Several factors can creep into the performance appraisal process and discredit the accuracy and the overall quality of the assessment. Many of these problems are rooted in the expectations that an employee or reviewer has prior to the appraisal session itself. Other problems result from the organization's assessment philosophy or the practices historically used to apply it. In this section, we will review some of the common problems and discuss their effect on both the organization and the individual. Figure 24 shows the five areas—assessment, dialogue, expectations, justice, and the future—in which problems often arise from the apprehensions of both reviewer and employee.

Assessment. The true intent of the performance appraisal system is to provide assessment to the individual employee about his past job performance and to provide constructive direction that will enhance future performance and productivity. The apprehensions of both the employee and the reviewer play a big part in how the appraisal, particularly the basic assessment process, will be conducted. The reviewer often enters the performance appraisal session knowing that the employee she is about to review is a valued commodity. Obviously, if he was not at least

Figure 24. Common Expectations in the Appraisal Process.

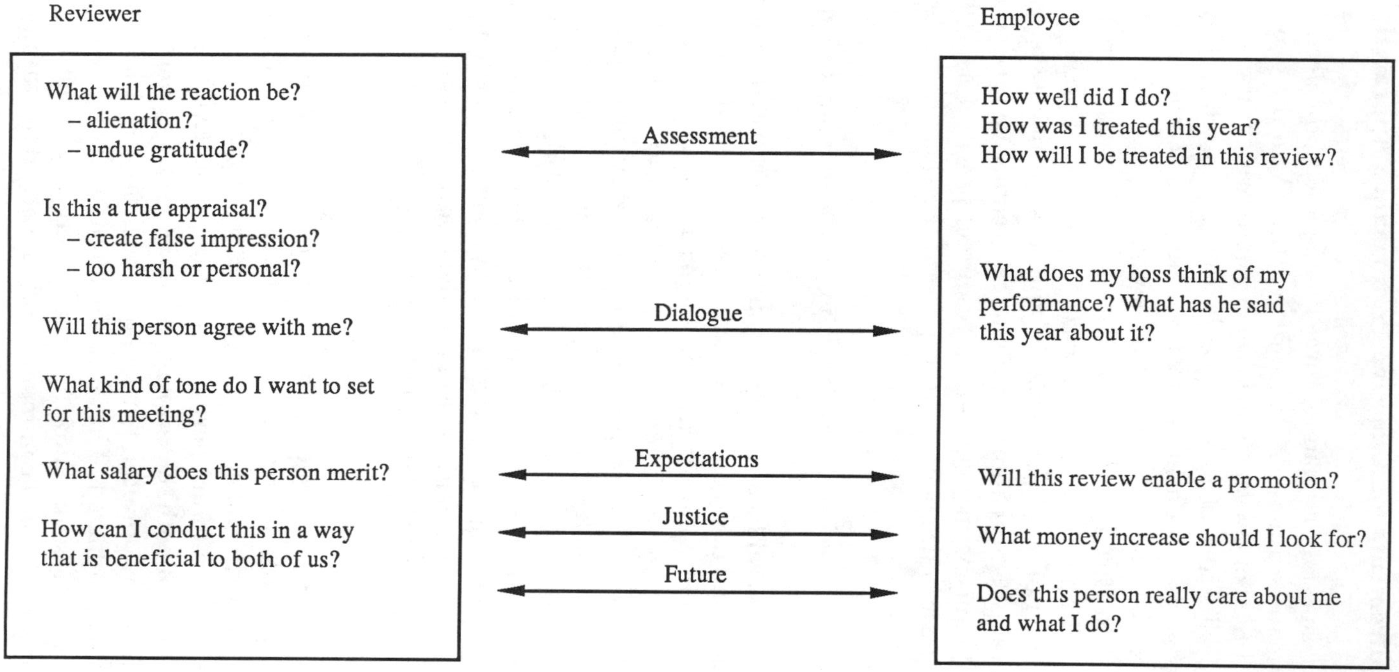

Reviewer

What will the reaction be?
 – alienation?
 – undue gratitude?

Is this a true appraisal?
 – create false impression?
 – too harsh or personal?

Will this person agree with me?

What kind of tone do I want to set
for this meeting?

What salary does this person merit?

How can I conduct this in a way
that is beneficial to both of us?

Assessment

Dialogue

Expectations

Justice

Future

Employee

How well did I do?
How was I treated this year?
How will I be treated in this review?

What does my boss think of my
performance? What has he said
this year about it?

Will this review enable a promotion?

What money increase should I look for?

Does this person really care about me
and what I do?

a satisfactory performer the session would be a probationary or even a termination discussion. Because the manager values the employee's output, she often feels that she should provide almost exclusively positive feedback and overtly "stroke" the employee so that he leaves the session with a renewed commitment to the supervisor and the organization. However, a manager can often find many opportunities for the employee to contribute even more to the organization; she must take advantage of the appraisal session to artfully present those opportunities, along with delivering positive feedback.

Despite this responsibility, the reviewing manager is usually preoccupied with the type of reaction she is going to receive from the employee in the performance appraisal session. For example, will the employee be alienated by what he perceives to be an unjustly negative appraisal? On the other hand, perhaps the employee will feel unduly appreciative because the appraisal was more favorable than he deserved. The employee might feel that the appraisal was generally off the mark and did not specifically address the key responsibilities of his work role. Coupled with this, of course, is the overall impression the appraisal leaves the employee with. If the employee feels that the assessment is too harsh or personal, or is based primarily on the subjective conclusions of the manager, he is likely to leave the session with the fixed opinion that his manager simply dislikes him. The result is the attitude that the employee might as well not apply himself fully, since he feels that no matter what he does, he is doomed to receive a negative assessment from his boss.

The employee is likely to have a similar set of apprehensions about the job assessment. If past appraisals have been nothing more than annual paper exercises, the employee may well expect another easy review. In this scenario, it is vitally important for the manager to impress upon the employee that what is past is past, and that from this point on the performance appraisal process will be important to the employee's very existence and progress in the organization.

The employee usually has a very definite opinion of how he performed in the job during the last grading period, and he will be ready to defend that opinion, complete with supporting examples. Therefore, the employee's preeminent apprehension is likely to be the question of how his perception of his performance corresponds to the manager's assessment. This is why it is important for a manager to be consistent in the manner in which she provides feedback to the employee throughout the year. She should reflect on the employee's progress and productivity throughout the entire grading period (as opposed to just the three weeks prior to the session), and consider the employee's success in accomplishing all the goals he was given at the beginning of the grading period.

Both manager and employee are likely to become defensive if the process has not been handled accurately and consistently. Both parties enter into the performance appraisal session knowing full well that what is about to occur is in reality a one-hour synopsis of an entire year of work. Accordingly, it is essential for the manager to assess the employee's efforts during the course of the year, give the employee meaningful feedback throughout the year, and give the employee ample opportunity to discuss informally any pertinent performance issues.

Dialogue. The performance appraisal process, like all human resource management functions, depends on solid communication for its success. With this in mind, it is important for the reviewing manager to remember at all times that the performance appraisal session is essentially a constructive dialogue. The manager should use approximately 75 percent of the "air time" of the performance appraisal to delineate key elements of the employee's performance; the employee should have about 25 percent in which to rejoin and express her thoughts about performance and future progress. While it is vital for the employee to have sufficient opportunity to give her input, the manager must keep in mind at all times that the performance appraisal process is intended not only to review past performance, but also to chart future performance. To accomplish this, he must take the lead in the discussion and hold it.

Many organizations utilize performance appraisal forms that do not provide the employee with any space to respond one way or another to the appraisal. This prohibits the employee from giving any useful input about her job. Not only is this impractical and inconsiderate, it is also illogical, since the person who does the job daily is the one most likely to know how its productivity might be improved. Furthermore, in not providing employees with an opportunity to participate in the dialogue, the organization is in effect telling its employees that when it matters the most, their input is not really valued. Besides hampering motivation, this suggests that the employees are there to be used and directed, that they are not intelligent, productive contributors to the organization. Failing to consider employee input, in sum, gives employees the impression that it is "us versus them" in employee relations, and it often sets the stage for third-party options such as labor unions or other so-called work coalitions for the people, the ultimate strain on productivity and human relations.

In some performance appraisal schemes, on the other hand, the individual employee is given too much opportunity for dialogue. This is true of the vast majority of binary appraisal systems, in which manager and employee complete the same form. This gives the employee a full-range opportunity to assess her boss, the organization, and her job in general. The fallacy of this approach is that the employee spends more time evaluating and critiquing her organization than she spends reflecting on her own performance, which after all is the point of the process. It also encourages the employee and the manager to play a game of "match-up," spending an inordinate amount of effort trying to make the assessments identical. If the communication between manager and employee has been stellar throughout the grading period, it is quite possible that this might occur naturally. More often, however, the attempt results in a guessing game that contributes little to a truly accurate, insightful discussion of performance.

Expectations. Both the reviewing manager and the employee enter the performance appraisal discussion with a set of expectations. These include expectations about a pay raise, the overall performance rating, and the range of goals and objectives to be set for the next year. Both will scan their memories and review their notes to try to recall any pertinent comments (by the manager) or any significant actions (by the employee) that might contribute to the overall assessment. This is easily done if the employee was given a set of objectives on the first day in the job; the manager then has merely to compare noted achievement and behavior against those objectives. If this was not the case, however, the performance appraisal session might well become a forum in which to debate what the past objectives supposedly were, and what the next year's goals should be. This can quickly become a discussion of what should have been done and what should be done, not what was actually accomplished.

The employee may also have expectations about his future development in the organization, and, of course, about any attendant compensation benefits. These expectations, whether of a pay raise, an increase in responsibility, or a promotion, may be based on the employee's evaluation of his own performance; however, they are also a reflection of how he preceives his overall worth to the organization. It is important in this regard for the manager to discuss forthrightly the types of opportunities that are available to the employee, both short- and long-term. In doing so, she not only helps to inspire the employee's motivation but also makes sure that the employee leaves the session with a clear understanding of what the future will hold for him at the organization.

The manager should in all cases consider how the employee responds to feedback and determine the best way to present her side of the appraisal. She should anticipate the employee's objectives and career aspirations on the basis of past communication and prepare herself to discuss them appropriately. She should be keenly aware of the organization's desire to determine and maximize the employee's potential for the good of both the employee and organization, and should set clear goals and objectives to enable that maximization.

Justice. The entire performance assessment scheme places a premium on justice. The manager wants to ensure that the employee is justly evaluated on past performance and is given realistic new objectives. The employee wants to be evaluated accurately and rewarded justly for her efforts. Unfortunately, because of the human element of self-perception, while both parties desire the same thing, their ways of looking at it might be radically different. For instance, what the manager thinks the employee deserves might be entirely different from what the employee feels she has coming to her.

The elements of fair play can quickly be dispelled if the appraisal is based purely on perceptions and isolated incidents. It is therefore essential for an organization to embrace a fair, objective, criterion-based performance appraisal system. Only then, when the fundamental tenets of the job are objectively scored and rated, can a realistic reward or remedial program be put into effect. The credibility of a rating system rests entirely on its ability to assess performance objectively and reward it appropriately. Many lawsuits over unjust or inaccurate performance appraisal are rooted in the inadequacies of the entire system in use by the organization.

Future. The basic question that all employees bring to the performance appraisal session is, does this person (the manager) really care about me? The answer to this question will be evidenced by the manner in which the appraisal is conducted and by the depth of thought the manager has invested in considering the employee's past performance and future opportunity. This answer also sets the tone for the manager-employee relationship from that point onward. If the employee feels that he received an unfair appraisal, he will be apt to take a malevolent attitude toward his job. He might even be impelled to seek employment at a place where he feels he can get fairer treatment.

The manager must realize that while the performance appraisal of a marginal performer will often be very harsh, it should still be anchored in objectivity. By being objective and fair, the manager will naturally weed out employees who are less than satisfactory in the accomplishment of their duties. The manager will also indicate to the above-average and exemplary performers that their efforts are indeed valued and will be rewarded in the future. Many healthcare managers and executives fail to realize that the performance appraisal is more of an opportunity to set precedents for the future than it is to provide constructive criticism of past performance. While discussion of past performance is essential and in fact helps to dictate what will happen in the future, it is not the primary part of the performance appraisal system. A solid, well-adjusted performance appraisal system will be constructed and utilized in such a way that the employee leaves the review session knowing that a course has been established for the future that will greatly benefit the employee, the manager, and the organization itself. By using creditable examples from the past and setting thoughtful objectives for the future, the healthcare manager can make this intent a reality in each performance appraisal session.

Fundamentals of a Solid
Performance Assessment System

A performance appraisal and review system must possess several characteristics in order to be as effective as possible. Many appraisal systems are criticized for being too "soft," for not being particularly job-specific, or for failing to provide direction for future performance. In our work with performance appraisal systems in hospitals and other healthcare organizations, we have identified ten traits that are essential to a fair and effective review and assessment system. The system must be:

1. Equitable
2. Individual
3. Directional
4. Motivational
5. Situational
6. Comprehensive
7. Financial
8. Continuous
9. Understandable
10. Measurable

Equitable. First and foremost, a performance appraisal system must be 100 percent equitable. All the elements considered in grading the employee must be based primarily on job performance. As in the interview, the emphasis must be strictly on that performance, not on subjective characteristics such as personality. This extends to characteristics covered by the Equal Employment Opportunity Commission (EEOC) and Title VII. An employee's ethnic or racial background, sexual orientation, age, and so on should play no part in the grading process.

In a truly equitable performance appraisal system, the employee's performance in the past grading period is objectively assessed and compared with the original set of objectives. The employee's performance is also compared fairly to that of other employees in similar positions. If the employee is part of a group of workers doing similar work, such as a housekeeping department, the manager must take into consideration both the employee's achievement of goals and how it compares to the achievement of others performing identical tasks. The primary focus, however, should be on how the employee accomplished the set objectives and goals, as evidenced by past performance.

An inequitable performance appraisal system results in misdirection, inaccurate scoring, and all too often, basic employee distrust. These maladies can quickly lead to poor motivation and ultimately to turnover, the most financially draining problem in human resources. On the other hand, an organization's performance appraisal system might be too equitable, a common phenomenon in the healthcare arena. In such a system, employees are graded strictly in respect to one another, and all have the same basic objectives, which barely stretch the employee's skills and potential. As a result, all of the employees wind up being graded at the same level and true assessment is sacrificed. It is essential to remember that equitable performance appraisal is not the same thing as giving everyone the same grade. This inhibits growth and individual employee contribution and in fact cheats the stellar employee while coddling the employee who is less productive.

Individual. Each employee's performance appraisal should be distinct from those of other employees, starting with the initial goal-establishment phase. The review, as well as the data on the form itself and the objectives established, should be tailored to the individual employee's abilities and potential. The appraisal session itself, where the manager and the employee fully discuss performance, should also be a unique, exclusive interchange between manager and employee. The employee should feel that the meeting is an exclusive discussion about his past performance, future goals, potential career steps, and any other pertinent information about his work role in the organization. The appraisal is the employee's one opportunity for the year to discuss candidly all of these important issues in an effort to set a course toward maximum performance.

In the present hectic environment, it is even more essential that each of these appraisal sessions be an individual, exclusive meeting. In such a meeting, the manager can convey to the employee a sense that his work, talents, and abilities are indeed valued by the organization. This also provides an opportunity for the manager to give the employee personal direction that will help maximize the employee's performance. If nothing else, it forces the manager to set aside at least one block of time in each grading period to sit down with the employee and chart a course for the next year, as well as review critical performance aspects of the past year. By maintaining the individuality of the performance appraisal process, the manager makes sure that the employee realizes that he is a valued organizational resource who merits individual, special attention.

Directional. The performance assessment process should provide specific guidance that will further growth and development as well as increased productivity. Many healthcare performance appraisals do not achieve this end because they are in essence little more than report cards. They merely assess the employee's past performance, usually in a very limited fashion, and cite general accomplishment of set goals. No meaningful direction is provided for the next year's performance, neither a developmental activity nor simply a well-thought-out, achievement-oriented objective. A solid performance assessment process must both review past performance and set the direction for the future. It should provide key training and development activities that are relevant to the employee's career growth and for education that will make the employee more productive. This type of education also makes the employee a greater contributing asset to the organization. Setting a direction allows both the manager and the employee to adjust future performance creatively by adding new objectives to a practical reconstruction of goals set in the preceding grading period.

The process of setting a direction should commence when the manager determines the need for the job position and sets the job description criteria. The performance appraisal process should therefore be a point on the entire continuum of management and direction. The appraisal form itself should have individual sections in which the manager can specifically delineate any developmental activities that should be accomplished in the coming grading period. It will also have a section in which old goals can be revised and new objectives added.

If the appraisal form lacks a directional aspect, the employee will feel that the appraisal process is merely a task completion game, that the manager and the organization have no real interest in the individual's development. Not only does this hamper motivation, but it also keeps the company from getting the most from its employees, or, in other words, from receiving the maximum return on its human capital investment. This neglect is definitely linked to turnover. Virtually every attrition study done in the human resources field has found that a major reason for an employee's leaving one firm for another is the well-formed impression that the former employer was uninterested in the employee's long-term development. Accordingly, it is vital for the manager to embrace equity and individual tailoring in the performance appraisal approach, and additionally to provide direction for future performance and goal achievement that will enhance the employee's professional growth and development.

Motivational. A stellar performance appraisal system is motivational in tone as well as in intent. In additional to setting an objective grade or rating for past performance, the manager expresses to the employee a level of confidence and concern for the employee's future performance. Simply stated, if the employee has done an excellent job, the organization should indicate its appreciation. In this way, the manager provides solid positive motivation and encouragement for the employee. On the other hand, if the employee's performance has been less than satisfactory, the objective performance assessment process provides a forum in which the manager can convey his displeasure to the employee in no uncertain terms and set into motion a corrective action program. In doing this, the manager can definitely apply some negative motivation to the employee, augmented appropriately with the threat of probation or termination if the employee does not turn her performance around.

The manager in either case must keep in mind that the performance appraisal session is a terrific opportunity to provide a dose of motivation that is certain to have a lasting effect. Since the employee is aware that her appraisal is linked to her compensation, there is no doubt that the manager will have the employee's complete and undivided attention. If the assessment is objectively presented and supported with tangible examples of past performance, the employee should clearly see the opportunities for improvement, as well as the importance of continuous good performance. A proviso to this approach is that all of the examples presented are objectively provable; if they are subjective or of questionable accuracy, their motivational value will be nil and, in fact, they could very well harm existing motivation. The objective nature of the appraisal will provide the manager with a presentation that the employee can easily believe and thus use to upgrade the level of her performance and productivity.

Situational. One of the most common complaints from health-care employees about every type of performance assessment system is the feeling that the appraisal is too general and does not have specific relevance to their particular jobs. This is typified by such comments in the appraisal session as "you really don't know my job," "you should give me some more specific examples," and "my work role isn't anything like you think it is." The review feels like a trial in which the employee is being tried by a prosecutor who does not have pertinent evidence. While this portrayal might appear to be overly negative, most healthcare managers who have had to work with a subjective, generic review system can attest to its validity. It therefore is essential that the review be comprehensive and use as many situational, point-specific examples as possible to ensure that the employee understands. The manager should collect as many data as possible about specific situations concerning the employee for presentation during the appraisal session. These should be presented adroitly and objectively in support of the assessment of the employee's performance.

Often, managers are able to make a quick determination on an employee's performance and do not feel an overt need to substantiate it with facts drawn from the past year's events. It is essential that the manager keep an ongoing notebook, or "leader's log," of critical incidents that have occurred in the past grading period. This concept of keeping track of significant incidents was originally developed by the Bristol-Myers Company Management Development Staff in the late 1970s. It has subsequently become a popular tool in the healthcare supply industry and has great potential for today's healthcare manager. The manager should keep a regular log of incidents that are key indicators and representations of the employee's performance. This helps prevent the situation, which exists in many organizations, in which a manager winds up evaluating only the factors that are prominent in the manager's recent memory—in essence, the last three months of the employee's performance. By maintaining a log and keeping copious notes in it about each employee's performance, the manager makes certain that each employee will receive an appraisal marked by case-specific examples of his or her individual performance. This case-specific approach gives manager and employee ample opportunity to discuss specific situations and particular approaches that will help enable increased productivity on the job.

Comprehensive. Before presenting the appraisal, the manager should sit down and ask himself, "What is the entire scope of this employee's job position?" Many times managers fail to go to the very first document they have to assist them in answering this question—the job description. In looking at the job description, the manager should then determine, first, whether the description accurately reflects what is presently needed in the position, and second, whether the particular employee is meeting all tenets of this description. The manager should subsequently review his logbook entries and all of his performance data on the employee and determine what the employee's overall performance has been.

Periodically, employees justifiably lament that managers look at only one aspect of their job and base the entire review on that. While some aspects of a work role are certainly more important than others, tunnel vision can happen either when the job description has a number of invalid aspects in it or when the manager is not seeing the total spectrum of the employee's efforts. Because some aspects of a job are more important than others, we will demonstrate later in Part Three a goal-setting scheme that encourages the placement of objectives in order of importance. The manager should still make sure that every objective cited on the appraisal form is important in some fashion; other objectives should be deleted from both the job description and the appraisal form.

In order for a healthcare organization to meet its critical need to groom employees who are versatile within their sphere of responsibility and technical competence, it must be able not only to evaluate performance completely and comprehensively but also to set broad goals and objectives. Managers must impress upon the employees the importance of attacking all of their assigned objectives diligently by giving, along with feedback, direction that is both comprehensive and all-inclusive.

Financial. Perhaps the most delicate aspect of the performance assessment process is the financial relevance of the appraisal to the employee's compensation. Like anything else, when money enters the picture areas of discussion that were previously black and white now become gray areas. Healthcare organizations tie money to the performance appraisal system in various ways. In many cases, the performance appraisal is held on the employee's anniversary date; the raises are set according to a predetermined compensation scale. In other cases, all the performance appraisals for the entire organization are held within a two-week period determined by the administration a year in advance, or in the same calendar period each year; compensation increments are addressed at the same time. No matter what system is in use, there are a few guidelines that can be applied to any scheme linking compensation and performance appraisal.

First, the manager should make certain that the financial implications of the review—whatever they might be—are kept as separate as possible from the performance review segment of the appraisal so that the conversation can remain focused on performance and future objectives. Many healthcare clients have told us that their review systems are worthless; the employee always agrees with everything so that the process can move quickly to the bottom line—the pay increment. For this reason, our staff suggests that pay raises be set for one date (such as an anniversary date) and the performance appraisal for another (such as the first week of June or January).

Second, if the performance appraisal system is integrated with the financial compensation scheme, the relationship between performance and money should be spelled out to the employee at the conclusion of the review. This allows the focus of the interview to be on performance while making clear to the employee how her compensation is affected by her performance. Furthermore, whatever the amount of the increment, the reason for the raise or lack of one (in the case of a nonperformer) should be clearly defined and tied to performance so that the employee is motivated appropriately. Many healthcare organizations are now following the example of larger industry entities and engaging the services of firms such as Hay Associates, The Hewlett Group, and the San Jose–based West Coast Industrial Relations Association (WCIRA, Inc.) to assist them in setting up performance-based compensation programs that help the healthcare organization get the most from its human resources in times of shrinking revenues.

As a starting point, we suggest a basic three-point performance appraisal scheme that rates employees as unsatisfactory, satisfactory, or outstanding in all performance categories. This scheme lends itself readily to a three-tier reward system in which the unsatisfactory employee gets no raise, the satisfactory one a medium-sized raise, and the outstanding one the maximum raise available. We will discuss this approach in more detail in later chapters.

Continuous. The performance appraisal process begins not at the end of the first grading period, but on the day the employee enters a new job, and it continues until the employee leaves the organization. At the very outset, the manager should meet with the employee and, using such tools as the job description and interview data from the employee's selection process, discuss the manager's expectations and desires on the job. Specifically, the manager should immediately give the employee five essential objectives that are to be accomplished during the first grading period. Six months after the starting date, the manager should again meet with the employee and review the progress made toward those objectives. Most important, the manager should at this time elicit from the employee five new objectives that the employee would like to incorporate into the set of goals. This engenders a feeling of job ownership on the part of the employee, and also takes advantage of the employee's knowledge and perspective on what can be accomplished in the job. Furthermore, it sets into motion a relationship between manager and employee that will foster participatory management.

Direction from the manager to the employee should be continuous; likewise, feedback from the employee to the manager should be constant. When a precedent is set from the outset, the employee will feel that his feedback is valued and that communication is a key element in accomplishing goals. The manager should provide an opportunity for constructive communication throughout the rating period in order to remain proactive in solving potential problems and to provide timely direction. If the manager communicates sporadically or inconsistently, the report-card type of performance appraisal will result. In sum, it is essential that assessment, direction, and feedback be continuous, so that the work cycle does not become a long fuse leading to a major explosion in the appraisal session.

Understandable. The need for clear communication (as shown in Resource B) in the performance appraisal system cannot be overstated. The words and concepts used in the review should be very easily understood by the employee and should have the lowest possible potential for distortion. There should be an opportunity for the employee to present his side of the story in the discussion of his performance. The appraisal form itself should be prepared by the manager well ahead of time, so that all significant data can be reviewed and incorporated into the appraisal itself.

The manager conducting the appraisal should have a clear mind-set and dedicated concentration toward conducting the appraisal. There can be no interruptions or distractions during the review, and the performance appraisal should be the only focus of the manager's attention. The reviewing manager should ensure that no ambiguous terms are used that would create any confusion in the mind of the employee. Such terms include our often-cited psychobabble language, those general, never-defined terms that are useless to the comprehension of a housekeeper or dietary worker. We suggest the reviewing manager use the sixteen Quan-Com characteristics described throughout this book, all of which are clearly defined, proven, and relevant work personality characteristics.

While the performance appraisal session is being conducted, there should be an atmosphere of absolute confidentiality and privacy that lends itself to an individual, customized appraisal. This expresses to the employee the seriousness of the review and reflects the effort that the manager is making to ensure that the session is fruitful. With this in mind, the manager should not use any room barriers, such as an inordinately big desk, or have a third party present unless the session will end with the employee being terminated or put on probation. If any area might be somewhat ambiguous and open to misinterpretation, the manager must make a special effort to ensure that the employee in fact does understand all of the information being presented. Finally, the manager should close the session with as firm a commitment as possible from the employee to meet all of the new objectives established for future performance.

Measurable. Finally, the performance appraisal should be a measurable exercise in which the employee can clearly ascertain how her performance has improved or declined in the past grading period. The performance appraisal itself should clearly reflect, in measurable terms, the level of performance the employee has provided to the organization as well as what the future "measuring stick" might be. Along with this, the manager should discuss with the employee suggested ways of improving performance and delineate specific opportunities for the employee to readily improve productivity on the job.

It is vital that any performance measurements that are provided to the employee are clearly understood and are backed up by specific examples. The more examples the manager provides, the more he helps the employee to be more productive on the job and, ultimately, to measure up more favorably in the assessment scheme.

These ten criteria are essential to the construction and implementation of a truly effective performance appraisal system. In the following chapters, we will provide specific guidance on how to apply these criteria in creating a winning, effective performance assessment scheme. The resulting benefit will be increased productivity, lower turnover, and a maximization of vital human resources talent.

Chapter 10

Setting
Performance Standards

Perhaps the most critical part of the performance appraisal process is the setting of performance standards, the initial phase of the cycle. In this phase, goals are established for achievement and standards are determined against which performance levels can be measured. Since the publication of *Managing for Results,* by Peter Drucker, in the early 1960s (Drucker, 1964), the American business community has been made acutely aware of the need to set standards and has become enamored of various schemes of setting performance goals. The most prominent of these is the "management by objective" (MBO) formula, which is probably the system most commonly employed across the entire spectrum of American industry. In this chapter, we will talk about setting performance standards and their particular application in the healthcare organization. We will also discuss ways of determining goals from organizational, departmental, and individual perspectives, as well as exploring various ways in which to maximize performance through the establishment of constructive goal setting.

Several factors in the current healthcare arena make the need for performance standards that encourage maximum performance and optimum effectiveness on the job especially urgent. First is the unique status of healthcare employees. In addition to being managers or staff members, they must also be technicians within their fields. They are responsible for maintaining a body of technical knowledge, and they must also possess a business acumen that will allow them to use that technical expertise to contribute measurably to the all-important bottom line.

165

For this reason, the successful healthcare manager will employ a goal attainment system that encourages the employee to seek out new opportunities and professional growth in both managerial and technical areas. Without growth in both of these equally important categories, the employee will soon become stale and thus less of an asset to the organization.

A second factor unique to healthcare is the high premium put on a person's ability to act independently. The healthcare worker, unlike her counterpart in other industries, is often not subjected to day-by-day, hour-by-hour direction from her manager. Whereas in other industries, manager and employee often have daily or hourly contact during a typical 9–5 shift, the healthcare worker might not even see her supervisor during a given work week—let alone have a long, detailed discussion of important objectives—because of the alternating shifts and decentralized control present in almost every healthcare organization. It becomes even more important, therefore, for the healthcare manager to ensure that his employees are given a stable, consistent set of directions and goals and the resources necessary to attain them. While manager and employee might occasionally meet to discuss work flow and objective achievement, it is vital that a general direction and a set of objectives are established from the very first day of employment. Permanently recording the goals on the performance appraisal form itself from the outset gives both the employee and the manager the same blueprint for success to work from.

A third factor, attendant on this need for independent action, is the need to delegate effectively. Because most managers, if not all, are also technical experts in their field, they rarely have the time to get involved in each and every situation that comes under their jurisdiction. With this in mind, the manager must make sure that he delegates assignments whenever possible to people who are eminently capable of completing them successfully. The combination of setting goals, selecting the best performer, and establishing performance standards is essential to successful delegation. Without this combination, the worker does not have a clue as to what the final outcome should be. The healthcare manager must be detail-oriented enough to explain to his subordinates what needs to be done, tempering this with the confidence that the subordinates will have enough independent judgment and job savvy to accomplish the task at hand. Unlike his counterparts in other industries, the healthcare executive must be especially careful in delegation, since a patient's health—and perhaps life—are riding on the results. While the healthcare arena is replete with standards for technical quality, it is up to the individual manager and the human resources staff to ensure that the same high quality is evident in the dealings with patients and their families.

A final factor in setting performance standards that is unique to healthcare is the need to develop employees as fully as possible on the job. The job itself should be the primary training and development activity, allowing the employee to grow while making the maximum contribution to the organization. Insufficiently challenging goals do not encourage growth and thus, in essence, deprive both the organization and the employee. On the other hand, unrealistic goals that are close to impossible to attain set a scenario in which the employee becomes overstressed, overworked, and ineffective. Like so many other functions of human resource management, goal setting travels on a bell curve. By setting goals that are too difficult, the manager cripples the employee's performance and receives diminishing returns on work output.

The line manager should employ the concept of Maximum Stretch Factor, or MSF, when setting work goals. Maximum Stretch Factor is a concept that we have found useful in setting goals in our work with healthcare organizations at large and in seminars for such groups as the American College of Healthcare Executives and the American Association of Homes for the Aging. MSF is simply the accurate adjustment of goals to employees' capabilities and performance expectations. Since all employees are individuals with different basic abilities in terms of work output, energy level, and technical acumen, each employee should be taken as an individual case and plotted on a bell curve continuum. The manager should consider what the employee's output was over the past grading period and ascertain whether the employee was truly utilized at 100 percent of capacity. If not, the goals set for the next grading period should be appropriately amplified. If the employee was overworked, on the other hand, the manager should strive to make the goals more realistic. Throughout this chapter we will more fully discuss MSF and how it might apply to various aspects of a goal establishment scheme.

Management Performance Planning

Performance planning does not begin on the employee's first day on the job, or six months afterward at the employee's first interim performance review. Solid performance planning begins when the reporting manager determines the need for the job. Upon reviewing the staff's capabilities and the work that the organization requires from her department, the line manager first determines the need for a particular position in her department or work group. This could be a new position or a vacancy in an existing position, perhaps as a result of turnover. Having identified an opening, the manager composes a job description and search criteria that reflect the amount of work, the standard of quality, and the type of expertise necessary in that position. In the preceding chapters on interviewing, we discussed the critical need to establish both technical qualification standards and standards for qualitative or personality traits for a given position. Likewise, it is essential for the manager to determine what hard-and-fast performance standards the position requires and how to enumerate those standards in a job description. This responsibility is essential as well to the performance appraisal form; specific job expectations and objectives should appear on the form as a directional tool, as shown in the example provided in Resource G. Good management performance planning requires the manager to analyze the specific work situation, establish objective, clearly defined goals, devise new goals at the first performance appraisal session, and continually review and revise the roster of goals.

Analyze the Work Situation. The manager should start by assessing the overall department that reports to her, its work setting and environment, and its overall intent, or mission. The manager should then look at the specific position to evaluate how it fits into the department's "big picture," review whatever organizational standards, rules, or technical regulations and requirements have been established for the specific position, and consider how the people using the services of that department or position perceive the job itself. Finally, the manager should update her present view of the job by combining this fundamental perspective with particular, current needs. Such needs depend on the people aspect of the job, the resources at hand, and the quality and quantity of output required from the position right now.

The manager must incorporate into these objective characteristics a little educated guesswork about what will be needed in the position in three time frames. First, the manager must consider what remedial action and other improvements are needed immediately. Second, the manager must try to determine what the organization's operation and the customers' needs will require in the coming year. While this can be a subjective exercise, the manager must examine critically what will be needed in the position for the next year and, as objectively as possible, construct an outline of tasks and needs that might become relevant to the particular position. In doing this, the manager is constructing a performance profile for an individual that will take into account as accurately as possible what is mandated in the position in the near future. Third, the manager should try to determine what kind of development activities will prepare the employee for the needs of the next three years. This represents an ideal merging of development on the job with basic job accomplishment; unfortunately, it may be infeasible in the present turbulent environment in healthcare.

Objective, Clearly Defined Goals. The key word here is *objective.* The goal-setting process must be as objective and pragmatic as possible so that the employee will understand fully what is expected of him in the coming year. As we mentioned, goals should be clearly stated to ensure comprehension. Additionally, it is vital for the manager to set a specific time limit for the accomplishment of each goal; in the case of a long-term goal, time parameters should be established for each stage of progress toward the goal.

Most effective healthcare managers employ a three-part process in goal setting. When an employee begins in a new position, the manager should give the employee from three to five goals, all of which are intrinsic to the job description and the original purpose of the job. Once the employee has explored the range of the new position, usually after three to six months, the manager should sit down with the employee and determine what additional goals might be added to the list of objectives. This second phase provides two tangible benefits. First, the employee becomes a part owner of the blueprint for success that the planning process should be. The employee's suggestions, as well as his knowledge of new situations and special conditions on the job, are given credibility and become as important in the achievement scheme as the goals set forth by the management. Second, the employee can grasp the relation of the Maximum Stretch Factor to his particular job. He can pragmatically understand what he can do on the job, what he would like to accomplish, and how his efforts can translate into realistic goals.

The third phase of goal setting should take place at the first formal performance appraisal session. At this time, the employee will have a set of goals that have been determined by management and another set that he himself has established. The third set of goals should therefore be developed and agreed on by both the manager and the employee. This set of goals in many cases addresses the developmental aspect that is so important to healthcare performance appraisal. By combining their knowledge and perspectives on the job, manager and employee are accurately constructing a goal roster that will expand both the parameters of the job and the amount of service provided by the employee to the organization. By encouraging the employee to take an active part in goal setting, the manager garners the additional benefits of expertise and directional control; she also provides a terrific motivation to the employee by using participatory management in its purest form.

This application can be implemented even with a housekeeper or other hourly position. While a CEO might be provided with seven to ten goals in each category, or over twenty-five altogether, the housekeeper might have three specific goals that are primary to the job responsibility. We have found that when given the opportunity to provide some input on goal attainment, housekeepers have found opportunities for cross-training, learning to use new equipment, expanding their range of effective cleaning responsibility, and a plethora of other responsibilities that are not readily apparent to the manager herself. It is especially vital at these lower tiers of the healthcare organization to provide employees with a feeling that they are in fact important members of the team, and that their input is valued and will be acted on in the same fashion as that of upper-tier employees.

Plan Strategic Action. In the third phase of good management performance planning, following the establishment of objective goals, the manager should discuss with the employee how the goals will be met in general. The manager's role should take on a couple of dimensions in this process in order to convey to the employee a sense of participation. First, the manager should suggest, not mandate, various methods that the employee might utilize in order to accomplish the goals. She should ask the employee directly about the type of approach he will employ to attack these goals.

Second, the manager should tell the employee what she expects in terms of approaches to the job and the time considerations she has in mind. As stated earlier, time parameters are eminently important in goal accomplishment, yet they are sorely lacking in many organizations. Time considerations can often be negotiated between employer and employee. For example, a manager might present an employee with a set of goals and ask the employee for an estimated time of accomplishment for each one. By not setting time parameters for each specific goal, the manager in effect relinquishes to a large extent the ultimate control and execution of the particular task. The employee must understand these time expectations and how they will affect the goal's accomplishment. Simply put, a goal that is not accomplished by a set deadline is in essence not accomplished at all; while the desired outcome might eventually be brought about, it will have lost much, if not all, of its value to the organization.

A third topic that might be discussed in planning strategic action with an employee is a list of options presented by the manager. In this case, the manager might provide the employee with some effective alternative plans. It is important to note that the manager does not change the substance of the goal or the intent of its accomplishment. Rather, she discusses with the employee various ways that the task might be accomplished and different directions the employee might take in attaining it. Again, it is essential that this discussion take the tone of a suggestion session, rather than an order-giving monologue. The employee is thus free to use his independent judgment in selecting not only the right approach but also different options to use if the first approach proves ineffective. With this in mind, it might be prudent for the manager to discuss potential pitfalls and certain obstacles that might hinder accomplishment. It is equally important that the manager and employee decide what kind of responsibilities might be delegated and what lateral resources might have to be used. For example, if the employee might have to work with another department, the manager should offer to telephone the department head (her peer) to inform him that the employee will be working with his unit on this particular project.

The entire goal-setting conversation should conclude with the manager encouraging the employee to stop by her office at any time to discuss any problems. She should also reiterate the time expectations of the specific goals to ensure that they are understood completely. Finally, but perhaps most important, the manager should express her confidence that the employee will accomplish the goals in an exemplary manner.

Measure, Review, and Revise. Generally speaking, the manager should critically monitor the employee's performance as much as possible to determine whether or not the employee is on course. This is a continuous process that begins on the first day of the employee's placement in the job. It should be augmented with occasional informal questions about the employee's progress toward goal attainment. Additionally, the manager must be flexible when unforeseen circumstances make the goal unattainable. She must apply her own adaptability as well as that of the employee to make sure that all options are being considered and that movement toward goal accomplishment is occurring despite obstacles. We will discuss monitoring and measuring performance completely in Chapter Eleven.

Performance Categories

In setting goals for subordinates, particularly if the subordinate is a supervisor, the manager must look at three categories of performance resources that he has at his disposal in the accomplishment of goals. By analyzing and exploring different ways in which to employ these performance resources, the manager can guarantee that all options for accomplishing a specific goal have been considered.

Human Resources. This category comprises the human resources that are readily available to the subject employee. The first component of this category is the line of report. The manager should examine the line of report the supervisor or employee is on, including any "dotted-line" relationships. For example, in a multihospital organization a personnel manager at a particular hospital might report not only to his boss, the hospital administrator, but also to a group personnel director at central headquarters. This double line of report provides the personnel manager with two different perspectives. The hospital administrator can provide an operational perspective on what is expected on the job, while the personnel director can express a point of view about specific technical aspects. By cooperating with the group personnel director, the hospital administrator can more accurately determine how the personnel manager's talents might best be utilized and how he can make a maximum contribution to the organization.

The concept of the line of report also applies to the subordinate himself and the number of personnel available to assist him in his everyday duties. For example, a supervisor has a number of reporting supervisors at his disposal, as well as the human resources that are within the sphere of his job responsibilities.

The essential factor the manager must consider in this regard is capability: the capability of the manager to manage, the supervisor to supervise, and the employee to perform expertly. Also applicable is the capability of a large work unit as opposed to a smaller one, a work unit with great technical expertise as opposed to a nontechnical one, and any other pertinent characteristic of a work unit. The manager must look at the entire spectrum of personnel connected to a given position when determining the employee's ability to perform successfully. For example, a personnel manager with a staff of four obviously cannot generate the output of a personnel manager with a staff of eight. Likewise, a personnel manager with a staff of four subordinates who are well-versed in human resources (one an expert in compensation, one in training and development, one in employment, and so on) will perform at a higher level than a personnel manager with four semiskilled personnel clerks.

In another sense, a personnel manager with a staff of strictly professional people and no clerical support would not be productive at all. The structure of a department is vitally important. Is the department, for instance, full of chiefs with no Indians to perform the day-to-day work? Is the department understaffed or potentially overstaffed? In planning management performance, it is imperative that the manager look at the entire spectrum of personnel available to the subject employee. The natural benefit of this is that the manager will ultimately assess the employee's performance in relation to the maximum use of the available human resources. Therefore, it is only natural that in the planning stage, optimum use of available human resources is explored fully and expertly.

Basic Logistics. This performance resource category is defined as the utilization of all of the physical resources and material systems available to the employee in the interest of goal accomplishment. The primary physical resource is the area in which the employee works. While planning performance, the manager should take into account the essential dynamics of the employee's work environment and how it might affect performance. For example, the area might be cluttered, ill-equipped, or otherwise unconducive to maximum performance. On the positive side of the coin, the area might be very well suited for maximum performance, and the employee might be failing to take advantage of it in pursuing work goals. In both cases, the manager must address in the planning cycle how the employee can best take advantage of the physical resources and logistical capabilities that are provided.

This logistical equation also extends itself to physical equipment. The manager must determine whether or not the employee has all the right tools to get the job done properly. With this comes the attendant responsibility to provide the employee with the best equipment possible, as well as the right amount of it. It is essential for the manager to look at the past year's performance and ensure that the employee is effectively using all of the available equipment as well as any new technology that comes down the pike. If new equipment or new logistical resources that the employee might use appear on the scene, the manager should encourage the employee to make their use part of the performance plan for the following year. Greater employment of such resources is part of the Maximum Stretch Factor, which demands that employees expand their work horizons in the interest of greater productivity and increased professional knowledge.

Power. This category consists of delegated responsibility within the organization. This is sometimes referred to as the "weight" a person has within an organization. Power is a terrific motivator, as well as a notable reward for the deserving employee. An employee's power is defined by the rank that the employee has within the organization and expressed by title and position. In the planning process, the manager should consider whether or not the employee is fully using her power, or perhaps abusing it in an effort to get tasks completed and objectives accomplished. The manager should set plans in the two-way fashion that we have described in order to take advantage of the employee's position within the organization. In sum, the manager must set plans that are commensurate with the employee's rank, salary grade, and tenure with the organization.

Certain assignments provide more visibility and power than other, less visible work duties in the same position. The manager should strive to give the employee opportunities that provide increased visibility within the organization as well as on-the-job growth and development. The visibility of such special assignments is also a great motivator, since it is a statement of the manager's special trust in the employee.

The special-assignment concept can be applied to health-care management and the performance planning process in several ways. For example, a nursing supervisor might become part of an operational committee that reviews plans for a new facility or perhaps an extension of a present facility. By giving the nursing supervisor this committee assignment, the manager is encouraging her to expand the scope of her job while using her special expertise in nursing to affect the design of a new facility. All of this results in professional growth (MSF!) for the nursing supervisor. In another scenario, the nursing supervisor might be progressively given more of her boss's responsibilities and power in an effort both to increase her expertise and to provide a backup for her boss's organizational slot. Both of these approaches must be accomplished without hindering the supervisor's performance of her normal duties, of course, and the new responsibilities must not be so great as to overtax her energies and thus affect her professional role. In short, the special assignment should be a solid complement to the employee's work load, not an additional burden, in order to be effective.

As we have stated, the purpose of the performance appraisal system is not only to chart progress up to this point but also to chart a course for future growth and development. With this in mind, the use of power in performance planning should incorporate whenever possible the assignment of tasks that the employee might have to handle in her next progressive position in the organization. We have found that the typical health-care manager is a terrible delegator because of his hands-on approach to management and supervision; this tendency should be strained in order to provide the subordinate employee with as much insight and experience as possible in preparation for assuming her next job. The manager should examine his own position, identify suitable tasks for delegation that will help the employee prepare for the next step, and make those assignments an integral part of the management performance plan. This practice ensures growth and development as well as providing a smooth backup or management succession plan replete with skilled replacements who can readily assume their next position within the organization.

Project Management Planning

Many supervisors and managers within the healthcare arena today utilize a project-management orientation toward task accomplishment. This involves dividing major responsibilities of the job into projects that become planned objectives. By taking major objectives one at a time in the planning phase, the manager can use the practical "I-Formula" as a guide for project management, project planning, and task accomplishment.

Inspiration. The initial phase of project planning begins with the inspiration for the project. In this phase, the manager selects a problem that can be addressed effectively by setting a plan objective. To illustrate this formula, we will use the example of a hospital credit correspondent who wants to use a new collection system for overdue hospital bills. In this case, the manager might sit down with the credit correspondent and come up with a preliminary set of task objectives.

Identification. In order to set an objective, the manager and employee must first identify a problem or an opportunity for focused attention. In essence, they must determine how and where to start on the road attacking the project. In our example, the manager and employee have identified a dire need to address an acute problem in collecting payment from past customer/patients.

Investigation. The next phase is investigation, or finding the root of the problem. This involves looking for clues that might be pertinent to the situation and indicate possible solutions. In our example, the credit correspondent has investigated the situation and has discovered that the essence of the problem is that accurate data about which payments are late is not provided on time.

Ideal. Having identified the problem and investigated its roots and potential solutions, the manager and employee must set an ideal standard for performance. This, in essence, is the goal or expected outcome of the project's efforts. In our case, the manager and the credit correspondent have identified as their ideal a system that will provide for the timely and accurate collection of key data. In setting the ideal for this project, the manager is applying the tenets of good performance planning, using the Maximum Stretch Factor and setting a goal that is within the grasp of the employee, and in whose attainment the employee will both grow and contribute significantly to the organization.

Idea. Upon identifying the ideal, the manager and employee should determine an initial solution, or basic idea. This idea will become the essence of the solution to the problem. In our example, the credit correspondent has come up with the idea that perhaps some sort of computer system with upgraded processing capabilities would provide more accurate information on the billing situation. The idea phase incorporates general, conceptual solutions to the problem that need further, more detailed development.

Innovation. The next segment of the formula is innovation, which involves taking the general idea and determining one or more potential solutions to the work problem. In our example, the credit correspondent has selected several software packages that, combined with existing hospital hardware capabilities, might enable the type of data generation desired.

Implementation. Implementation is the phase in which the idea and its innovations take a tangible form. In this phase, the employee takes a thoroughly explored concept and tests its viability in a real-life setting. In our case, the credit correspondent has researched various computer programs and will dry-run two of the most promising to see if they are the answer to the problem.

Illumination. In order to test the feasibility of a particular idea, the employee must first test its effectiveness and closely monitor the results of the experiment. This illumination will show the employee whether or not the initial idea will work and, more important, the practical reasons why. In our case, the credit correspondent has tested several software packages experimentally and two under actual work conditions. She can now decide which package is the most effective. Furthermore, she can provide illustrations to the credit manager that will give him insight into her decision, and provide the manager with an overall perspective on why the system of choice is the most effective answer to the problem at hand.

Ignition. In order for the plan to be carried out in a work situation, it must garner the interest and support of all the personnel who will be affected by it. Therefore, it is essential to ignite or spark interest in the project at hand. It is infinitely easier to install a new or different program with everyone's support than when there are many doubting Thomases ready to assault its viability. In our scenario, the credit correspondent has arranged a demonstration for key members of the hospital staff that will show how the new collection reporting software package works, replete with explanations of the benefit of its better service and reporting capability. It is critically important to remember here that any new project must be clearly shown to be a marked improvement on the status quo in order to eliminate undue negative resistance.

Introduction. With the support and interest collected in the ignition stage, the practitioner should seek to put the project into full action. This will often take the form of a pilot program, or limited but everyday use of the program to test its effectiveness completely under daily conditions. In our example, the credit correspondent has decided to utilize her new software to manage the collection activities in a certain geographical area that has been particularly troublesome in the past. She will then compare this data with the data generated in an area not using the system.

Impetus. In order for the new program or project to gain credibility and full acceptance within the organization, it must gain momentum, or impetus, as the process continues. The saying ''Nothing succeeds like success'' is a good guideline. For the more reluctant members of the staff to fully endorse a new project or program, it must have been completely proven to be beneficial and a clear improvement on the status quo. In our case, two months into the introduction stage, the credit correspondent has proven adequately that the data generated by the new system are infinitely better than those produced by the old system. Since this fact has been communicated to all pertinent people within the organization, the project has picked up the necessary support.

Importance. When a project gains the necessary momentum, it becomes more important to the organization. It must be stressed by the advocate of the new project that the initial success of the project's implementation clearly shows the need for it in the overall scheme of the organization. In our case, the system implemented by the credit correspondent has been approved for full use because it has shown itself to be an effective tool in managing the all-important bottom line.

Three subcategories help to close the project management loop of importance, namely:

1. *Intensity.* The project must provide the depth and breadth of service that are required as well as show itself to be a clear improvement on current or previous approaches.
2. *Imperative.* In order for the project to become part of the everyday routine, it must have total top-to-bottom support. In essence, it should be mandated by those in charge as a necessary, vital part of the operation.

3. *Intrigue.* Finally, the new project or program must have the capability to inspire interest continuously. Its effectiveness should help interest in it snowball from all important sectors of the organization.

A successful project will become fully installed in the organizational working scheme after meeting all of its criteria for success. With effective planning and intelligent adherence to the sequence advocated in this section, a manager and an employee can jointly establish a plan of action that will enhance their productivity, contribute to the organization, and stretch their professional growth and development.

Common Pitfalls of the Planning Process

In our healthcare consulting work, we have seen ten basic problems attendant on the planning process. These prevent the construction of accurate goals and productive planning, which can greatly damage the entire performance cycle. The ten pitfalls of the planning process are:

1. No joint, two-way participation
2. Lack of clarity and direction
3. No top-to-bottom commitment
4. No "competitude"
5. Ineffective employment of new technology
6. Insufficient contribution of employee expertise
7. Imbalance between results and development
8. No provisions for employee growth
9. Illogical plans
10. Organizational irrelevance

The healthcare line manager must always remember that without good planning, the entire range of employee performance is in jeopardy.

No Joint, Two-Way Participation. A manager can create major problems for himself in the planning process by planning an employee's goals without any participation from the employee. The problem with this is that the manager does not take into account what the employee might want to accomplish in the coming grading period. More important, the employee usually knows the job better than the manager because of her constant involvement in it.

Furthermore, the manager who is isolated from the demands and scope of a job but still "pushes down" imperative direction to the employee without the employee's input is in essence telling the employee that her input is not valued. This can cause severe morale problems, particularly if the employee's peers in other departments have the opportunity to help set their work goals. The manager thus not only hurts motivation but also loses an opportunity to get data that are vital in setting truly constructive objectives.

Lack of Clarity and Direction. Healthcare managers frequently create goals that they believe to be important but do not articulate these goals to employees in an easily comprehensible manner. The direction that the manager gives an employee must be clearly understood by the employee, and expectations of timing and outcome must be well defined.

The purpose of the planning process is to provide direction. By failing to make direction and goals understood, the manager is setting the stage for confusion and unsatisfactory performance, for which only he can be faulted. The manager should ensure that the employee understands the plans and goals fully and is not just nodding in agreement to appease the manager.

No Top-to-Bottom Commitment. If the employee does not believe that a goal is really important to a manager, then the goal will not be important to the employee. While some managers, particularly novice ones, tend to overstate the importance of a goal and perhaps to supervise its accomplishment too carefully, this approach is better than its lackadaisical opposite. If the manager underplays an objective's importance or seems to lack interest in it, the employee will always do so as well.

Most healthcare employees intrinsically understand that most of what they do in their jobs is important in some way to someone's health and well-being. This does not, however, relieve the manager of the obligation to stress the importance of each goal individually to the employee. By gaining the employee's commitment to the importance of the goal, total dedication to the task's accomplishment is achieved.

No "Competitude." Many managers feel that their charges are not as motivated as they should or could be. While most of their employees might be working at an above-average level, there seems to be a lack of desire on the part of these employees to improve to the outstanding level. *Competitude* is the term used to describe an employee's desire to perform better this year than she performed last year, rather than to perform better than others with the same job. The employee thus uses her own past performance as the benchmark for improvement, which is a constantly progressive standard for any worker, and one that truly elicits the best output.

The healthcare manager should inspire the employee to be the best she can be in comparison to her own best efforts, not those of others, who might not have the same capabilities or talents. The manager can do this simply by reviewing with the employee her own past performance and focusing the employee's attention on ways to better her performance in respect to her own abilities, not those of others.

Ineffective Employment of New Technology. The healthcare arena sees the emergence of some sort of new technology every day. The reviewing manager should examine her own work unit and incorporate any newer and better methods, machinery, or applications into the planning process. This accomplishes two goals. First, better results may be achieved at a faster rate; second, employees' interest can be generated by something new in the workplace.

If the manager ignores these new opportunities in the planning process, she will have to make special efforts to use the new technology later in the grading period. By identifying and capitalizing on such opportunities in the planning process, she ensures a more fluid and productive adoption of the new technology into the workplace.

Insufficient Contribution of Employee Expertise. Every person who works in healthcare has some range of technical expertise, be it in nursing, radiology, nutrition, or another field. Often, a line manager overlooks the opportunity to capitalize fully on the technical abilities of her assigned employees. The manager should scrutinize each employee's range of technical expertise, ask the employee for suggestions on how it might best be used, and incorporate it into her plans. By failing to do so, the manager risks hindering the employee's technical growth, as well as depriving the organization of gains that could be made if the employee's abilities were fully utilized.

Imbalance Between Results and Development. The healthcare manager should make sure that in her attempts to use new methods, no productivity is sacrificed. This simply means that the plans she constructs and the direction she gives her employees should encourage a reasonable balance between goal attainment and constructive use of new technology.

No Provisions for Employee Growth. The greatest possibility for hindering employee development exists when the manager fails to provide the employee with goals and objectives that will help the employee grow on the job. By employing the concept of Maximum Stretch Factor, in which the employee is provided with goals that encourage maximum growth on the job without harming daily performance, the manager provides the employee with goals that are motivating and interesting and whose attainment will provide both development and measurable results.

The healthcare manager must not simply tell the employee to "keep on doing a good job." She must set goals that will force the employee to make the criteria for a "good job" progressively more demanding in scope and thus more fruitful in contributive value to the organization.

Illogical Plans. In their efforts to be creative in their performance planning, managers can make the simple mistake of giving the employee illogical goals. The manager should ask himself after setting employee goals if the plans are in fact too creative, demanding, or grandiose. Again, objectivity is the key factor, as well as communication with the employee to establish goals that are both reasonable and challenging.

Organizational Irrelevance. Finally, all of the plans established by the manager should have direct relevance to the organizational mission and provide for the best contribution possible from the employee to those goals and objectives. Without this, the employee loses sight of his relevance to the "big picture" and thus loses motivation and contributes less to the organization.

Chapter 11

Monitoring and Measuring Performance

One of the major attributes of a good performance assessment system is a continuous employee performance review process. From the employee's first day on the job to the performance appraisal session itself, the manager must collect all evidence that accurately represents the level of the employee's performance and productivity. In this chapter, we will examine how to collect key performance indicators in the quantitative, qualitative, and supervisory categories, indicators that help provide the healthcare manager with all the data required to make an accurate and constructive performance appraisal.

Quantitative Performance Indicators

In the critical evaluation of ongoing performance, the manager should strive constantly to monitor all quantitative performance indicators. Quantitative performance indicators use key numbers or a significant numerical sequence to measure certain aspects of the employee's performance. There are several advantages in a performance appraisal that utilizes quantitative indicators as much as possible. Primarily owing to their numerical nature, they lend themselves to tangible analysis and provide clear-cut examples of goal achievement for use during the appraisal discussion itself. Their "scoreboard" orientation means they can be assessed throughout the grading period by manager and employee alike. Work progress can be charted visibly and can be easily and consistently referred to by both parties during the entire grading period.

Virtually all healthcare positions can be represented by some numerical scheme. A housekeeper, for example, can be charted on the number of rooms cleaned in a given period, the number of floors mopped in a given work shift, or the amount of time regularly spent cleaning a particular area of a hospital ward. A nurse recruiter can be measured effectively by the number of nurses hired in a particular time period and the length of time each nurse stayed on the job and performed well. A pharmacist can be assessed on the number of prescriptions filled during a given shift, the amount of time required to fill a typical prescription, or perhaps the number of personnel used to handle the pharmacy's daily work load. In all three cases, specific measures can be used to quantify the effectiveness of action. It is important for both manager and employee to ascertain which of these measurements most accurately reflect the quality of work output and which are irrelevant or insignificant. Manager and employee should come to an agreement in the planning process on which measurements will be considered acceptable benchmarks of quality performance standards.

In this section we will comprehensively explore a variety of quantitative performance factors that can be monitored and measured by the healthcare manager in assessing critical daily performance.

Monthly Reports. To ensure steady, constructive communication of work progress between employee and manager, many organizations use a system of employee-generated monthly reports. In this system, the individual employee is responsible for providing the manager with a regular monthly review of work performance and progress. This can take the form of a monthly meeting or a more formal written account of goal achievement and significant activity.

The first step in establishing a monthly report system is for the manager and the employee to identify which facets of the particular job position can best be portrayed by numerical measurements. With all quantitative performance indicators, it is essential to maintain quality and to avoid creating a numbers-chasing scheme. For the process to be viable, manager and employee must decide which numbers are true indicators of quality performance. For instance, if a nurse recruiter decided with her manager that a monthly reporting system would be helpful in evaluating performance, the natural inclination would be to look at the number of candidates interviewed, the number of resultant hires, and the cost-effectiveness of each placement, which could be determined by the ratio of interviews to actual hires. This does not take into consideration, however, the real quality of each hire. In any quantitative measuring system, quality can easily be lost in the race for quantity. In this case, it might be beneficial for the personnel manager and the nurse recruiter to add another quality assurance number to their scheme. This quality assurance number might be the length of time the average nurse hired actually stays on the job, the nurse's initial performance rating after the first grading period, or perhaps the turnover ratio between "good hires" (those who stay in the job and perform well) and "bad hires" (those whose poor performance shows they should not have been hired in the first place). These measurements are in fact the true quantitative indicators of high-quality output in this case.

Monthly reports can sometimes fall victim to "padding" by employees; numbers may be either deflated or inflated to present a picture that is rosier than the actual circumstances. This happens most often when the numbers do not really represent those aspects of a job that are important to the overall organization. For instance, a dietary worker might be assessed on the number of meals made during a given work shift, without any scrutiny of how many of the meals are actually needed and consumed. If the number of meals produced is high, the manager is likely to believe that the employee is productively performing a needed service, when in fact the employee may simply be wasting food, time, and energy to meet an irrelevant goal. The employee who works to produce results purely for the sake of meeting a numerical goal does a disservice to all parties involved. It is imperative for the manager to ensure that the working numbers in a monthly reporting system are true indicators of quality output and, further, that the goals established by the reporting system are of true value to both the organization and its customer/patients.

If done correctly, monthly reports prove invaluable for a couple of reasons. The first is that they provide the manager with a continuous source of information about the employee's performance. Furthermore, if the manager is astute enough to look at trends from month to month, she can find creditable indications of how the employee's performance is progressing or regressing compared to goals established at the beginning of the review period. By comparing one month to the next, or perhaps even one quarter to the next, the manager can see any significant upward or downward trends and address them quickly to ensure optimal performance. Finally, the set of monthly reports in effect provides the manager with several performance appraisals; these can be used in the review session, where it is extremely important to provide the employee with pertinent examples and illustrations of past performance. If the manager has gotten involved in the process to the point of sitting down with the employee and discussing the content of each monthly report, there will be no reason for surprise during the performance appraisal session. This will allow that session to become the constructive, developmental tool it should be, rather than a debate about evidence of work performance and indicators that define the level of performance.

Unit Performance. Another quantitative performance indicator is unit performance, which is the overall performance of the work unit of which the employee is a member. As in the case of monthly reports, a manager should regularly review the performance of his entire unit to see its overall progress and to provide feedback to his supervisor about how his reporting units are performing. For example, a housekeeping manager might look at the performance of not only his individual workers but also the entire unit so that he can inform the director of operations of his work unit's total progress. The bottom-line consideration is how well the unit is attaining its established work goals. With this in mind, it is important for the manager to evaluate each employee's contribution to the work unit.

The main indicator of unit performance as it relates to the individual is employee contribution value. Contribution value is the amount of work accomplished by an individual employee, which, when combined with the efforts of his peers, helps the unit obtain its overall goals. To illustrate this concept, let us take the example of a radiologist who has just been hired into the radiology department of a small community hospital. The department is considered to be an excellent work unit overall, with a record of consistently solid performance and low employee turnover. The work unit also enjoys cohesiveness; all team members share an esprit de corps and a sincere dedication to accomplishing all set goals.

In this instance, it would be very hard to ascertain the individual employee's contribution value. The new employee might in fact be a marginal radiologist; because the unit is such a strong one, however, it would be difficult to distinguish the marginal individual's performance from the overall unit's outstanding performance unless the new radiologist's efforts could somehow be isolated and individually examined. It would be much easier to draw conclusions if the situation were reversed. When a competent technician and productive worker joins a poor unit, the contribution value of the new employee is usually evident. It is important, therefore, for the manager to look at the quantitative measurements of each member's individual contributions—the individual's work rate, measurable output, or any other measure that can be compared to the overall performance indicators. By paying heed to the employee's individual contribution to the work unit, the manager can determine which members of the work unit are truly dedicated to accomplishing goals and which are merely along for the ride.

Goal Attainment. Perhaps the most evident of all quantitative goal indicators is goal attainment. Goal attainment or, as it is referred to in some circles, objective accomplishment is simply the practice of measuring the employee's performance against the goals that were established in the planning session at the commencement of the grading period. If the goals were set forth comprehensively, understood clearly by the employee, and measurable in accordance with the principles discussed in Chapters Nine and Ten, it is an easy task for the manager to relate performance to the established goals and objectives.

In reviewing the employee's performance on a continuous basis, it is essential for the manager to keep a copy of the originally determined goals as well as the original job description for comparison. It is equally important for the employee to have a hard copy of these goals and objectives as a guideline. As we discussed in the planning sections, it is vital that each goal that is set is also given a time frame in which to be achieved. As a checkpoint system, the manager should examine the time considerations when establishing a goal and set specific intervals at which to follow up formally to ensure that progress is being made. In our example of the nurse recruiter, it might be fruitful for the manager not only to look at the number of recruits being hired, but also to consider the time it took to hire them, the number of interviews conducted in a given time, and, perhaps, the amount of time that passes between the initial interview and the selection and placement of a successful candidate. Time considerations and goal attainment are equal factors that must be weighed together in assessing performance.

If a goal is not accomplished within the prescribed time parameters, in essence it is not accomplished at all. Often, the positive effects of a goal's accomplishment on the mission of the organization depend on its occurring by a specific date. With the rapid flow of activity in healthcare, this is particularly true; if the goal has not been accomplished in the set time, it is likely that the need for it no longer exists. Conditions change rapidly, and the employee who has not been able to reach a specific objective on time is soon overtaxed by new objectives. The resultant backlog increases employee stress and creates an unproductive work pattern.

Cost-Effectiveness. Because of heightened competition, the emergence of the multihospital chain as a powerful entity in the marketplace, malpractice and its attendant litigation, and the overall turbulence in the field, there is a premium on getting the most return from each budget dollar. With this in mind, the manager should seek as a final quantitative performance indicator the cost-effectiveness of each employee's effort. In effect, the manager is looking at the quality of the organization's

investment—in the form of compensation paid to the employee—
and determining the return on that investment as indicated by
the employee's performance.

In the case of our nurse recruiter, it is conceivable that
three quality hires could be made within one month. However,
the recruiting costs to make those three hires could have been
disproportionately high; excess travel might have been involved,
a plethora of candidates might have to have been interviewed,
or perhaps extra compensation might have been paid to attract
the three new employees. In the case of a dietary worker, it is
easy to see how much money can be wasted by making too many
meals for too few consumers. Food waste is easily translated
into lost dollars, particularly when one considers the high prices
charged by vendors like American Dietary Products and ARA
Services, Inc. To take the new radiologist as another example,
the cost of X-rays and the attendant mechanical and processing expenses are steep and thus provide opportunities for monetary waste. A radiologist who needs to take five X-rays to get
one usable one is of negligible value to the organization and
its customers.

In one form or another, every employee in a healthcare
organization has a budget of resources to use in conducting his
or her job. Abuse of resources or failure to optimize every penny's
worth of allotted money, either intentional or unintentional
because of poor self-management, will result in a shortage to
the entire organization. Each employee should be charged with
the responsibility of using the organization's capital resources
as if they were the employee's own money. An outstanding
employee will do exactly that by being fastidious in the pursuit
of goal achievement and in husbanding the money it takes to
accomplish those goals. Employees who do not grasp their role
in conserving for the good of all may simply get the job done
at any cost, perhaps merely to sate the supervisor and perhaps
to show that they have ''accomplished their set goals.'' As with
the timing considerations, employees need to understand that
if their efforts incur needless waste of monetary resources their
goal can never truly be achieved.

Qualitative Performance Indicators

Qualitative performance indicators are somewhat more subjective in nature than are quantitative ones and are assessed by the manager based on his or her experience and knowledge of what should be accomplished on the job. Qualitative performance indicators usually appear more often than quantitative ones on performance appraisal forms. If a manager uses too many qualitative indicators in the review cycle, the appraisal may be perceived as too subjective because it does not contain much objective performance evidence. However, a performance appraisal that is just quantitative will be seen to lack the scope to address developmental issues. Also, limiting appraisal to quantifiable factors can inhibit discussion of work-related personality dynamics that may need to be addressed. It is essential, then, for managers to strike a balance between quantitative and qualitative information in the conduct of performance reviews. In this section we will look at the sources of information about qualitative performance that are used by successful, effective healthcare managers.

Personal Observation. The most obvious source of qualitative performance information is personal observation. Because all managers have some form of ongoing personal contact with their employees, managers cannot help basing a large part of their evaluation on what they see and hear in the everyday work situation. In their book, *The Psychology of Visual Perception,* Ralph Haber and Maurice Hershenson of Brandeis University indicate that a human being cannot visually perceive another person without making some sort of judgment based on what they see (1973, pp. 195–220). In other words, we constantly assess what we observe. As this applies to the work situation, and in particular the healthcare setting, any committed manager will—and should—take advantage of any situation that allows a firsthand look at an employee's performance.

Firsthand observation by the manager can be one of the more valid ways of assessing performance, and managers are often tempted to rely on it exclusively. After all, the manager has typically hired the employee himself, knows the person's capabilities and limitations, and knows what goals the employee is trying to accomplish. The manager is therefore an expert in evaluating whether or not the performance standards are in fact being met. The problems are that personal observation is always in some degree subjective and that it can be difficult to substantiate. To counter these problems, our suggestion to our performance appraisal clients is that every supervisor carry a spiral notebook in which to record observations on individual employee performance. We further recommend that the manager keep a separate section in the notebook for each employee. This notebook will serve as a memory aid to the manager and provide a continuing record of performance over a given review period. Without such a tool, the manager's observations may fade or become distorted over time. With such a tool, the manager can keep at hand substantial records of all that he has seen relative to the employee's performance and can thus discuss personal observations adroitly and in depth whenever he needs to. Moreover, specific written records will support the manager's evaluation in case of legal action.

Quan-Com Traits. An essential part of ongoing critical evaluation of performance is the examination of the employee's adherence on the job to the Quan-Com characteristics, the characteristics discussed in Chapters Three, Six, and Seven and shown in Resources E and F. These sixteen characteristics should have been scrutinized when the employee was originally hired. It follows logically, then, that the manager rate the employee on how well he has embraced these characteristics and applied them to the everyday conduct of his job. The healthcare line manager should seek to employ the entire spectrum of attitude orientation, people skills, managerial aptitude (when applicable), and team orientation in assessing the employee's progress and performance on the job. If the manager, for example, sees a situation in which an employee does not show proper adaptability in dealing with a guest or patient, it should be noted accordingly in the manager's notebook and brought out in the context of the performance appraisal, if not sooner in a one-to-one discussion. Because the healthcare business is all about people relations, it is critically important for all supervisors to make sure that assessment of these characteristics is part of their everyday evaluation routine.

Many personality assessments are abused, becoming character assassinations, while others are completely ignored by managers who fear litigation or interpersonal conflict with their employees. The Quan-Com System is quantitatively based on basic communication on the job and in the workplace and ties performance to individual personality traits. The manager should feel free to utilize the entire set of factors in evaluating employee performance. For example, a dietary worker being overly aggressive with a guest in a dining facility is just as critical a mishap as an undercooked meal. A nursing recruiter who lacks perceptiveness and communication skills will soon be proven to be a totally ineffective performer, since these abilities are directly linked to her ability to recruit. An X-ray technician who lacks team orientation would obviously be unsuitable over the long term for work in a group.

In applying the Quan-Com characteristics to individual performance, the manager must be aware that she is dealing in a subjective area that can easily be interpreted by the employee as personality conflict. This underscores the need for the manager to have at her disposal objective evidence that can be matched against the standards provided in the Quan-Com System. In essence, the manager must not only tell the dietary worker that he is overly aggressive but also provide specific examples of this behavior and explain why it is detrimental to good service. This can be accomplished by describing standard behavior and showing how the employee might redirect his approach. The manager should reinforce this by telling the employee in no uncertain terms that a change must take place quickly and effectively, as this aggressiveness will not be tolerated further. By reviewing the Quan-Com characteristics continuously and mastering their application, the manager will be able to apply them naturally to the performance appraisal setting in such a manner that the review becomes not only a performance critique, but a directional tool as well.

Organizational Input. Organizational input is any information a manager receives from peers, supervisors, guests, or anyone else tied to the organization who has observed employees on the job and can provide creditable input about their performance. Several avenues of organizational input lend themselves readily to the manager's data bank on employee performance.

The first form of organizational input is internal feedback from members of the organization. For example, since most hospital workers eat in the same cafeteria as many of the guests, they can provide the dietary manager with input about food quality and the quality and promptness of service. To take another example, since all nursing managers and directors will ultimately employ the nurses procured by the nurse recruiter, they are able to assess, to a certain extent, the output the nurse recruiter is providing to the organization. By relaying their impressions to the nurse recruiter's boss, they are providing worthwhile performance feedback. In the case of the X-ray technician, it is easy to see that many people might be involved in the loop of communication between the X-ray department, the patient, and the attending physicians and nurses.

The healthcare manager should seek any type of usable evidence from any party exposed to the employee's efforts. It would probably be fruitful in many cases to ask individual managers who have contact with the employee for their considered opinions. In many instances, this information does not have to be asked for—it is often readily volunteered by people who have seen the employee perform either extremely well or extremely poorly. This type of information usually comes not only from peer group managers but also from directors and other members of the organization's hierarchy, as well as from certain first-line supervisors. A prime source might be the manager's boss, for example, who probably is reasonably familiar with both the subject employee and the job he has to perform. In all cases, obviously, the information should be taken for what it is worth, considering the source, the potential motives for providing information, and the pertinence of the input provided. Another manager who has a hidden agenda of some sort might be giving the first manager information as part of a power play. In another scenario, the information might be given strictly as part of a campaign to obtain more of the subject employee's time and efforts. By complimenting the reporting manager on her supervision of the employee and giving rave reviews of the employee's efforts, the manager's counterpart can help sway the manager into allowing the employee to work more closely and frequently with his work group.

While it is the aim of any organization to have good employees and to share information about their performance internally, the manager should realize that all input from others in the organization will tend to be somewhat subjective and perhaps tempered with personality-related perceptions. Therefore, the information should be taken as a useful contribution but not as an assessment in itself.

The second type of organizational input comes from external sources. Patients and guests are often more than willing to give feedback to individual managers about their stay in the healthcare institution, their perception of how they were treated by employees, and any other comments they feel to be appropriate. Because of the nature of a hospital stay, the healthcare customer/patient has infinitely more time and opportunity to make observations and form opinions than customers in other industries. A restaurant patron might have an hour or two in which to form an opinion; a hospital customer/patient might have a week to do so, and his opinion will be reinforced by what his visitors say. Also, the critical nature of the service being provided obviously makes the healthcare customers more alert to everything in the environment, particularly the staff members they come into contact with daily.

At New York Hospital in downtown Manhattan, all of the nursing directors and supervisors are required to check with each patient for his or her perceptions on how the attending nurses have performed. New York Hospital has one of the largest patient censuses in the United States, and its urban location and multiethnic customer community make it a truly unique facility; this attention to detail, therefore, must be considered exemplary. Interest in the customers' perceptions enhances the staff's knowledge of what the "end user" really thinks. It is little wonder, therefore, that the hospital's reputation in the local community is second to none. This is a good lesson, not only in getting feedback on employee performance, but also for the scores of hospital administrators who still are unable to understand how to obtain customers' opinions.

In this age of ultracompetitiveness, it is imperative that hospital administrators encourage their employees to find out all they can about their customers' needs, wants, and opinions of the service provided by the organization. Often, the manner in which the customer/patient is given the required treatment is more important and more easily understood by the customer/patient than the treatment itself. Managers sometimes receive letters, for instance, praising some employees or denigrating others. These are important data for the manager to consider in her performance evaluations, and by keeping these letters in her manager's notebook she can be sure of using them during the review itself. It is also important for the manager to discuss such a letter with the employee upon receiving it. This information should be given to the employee in the appropriate manner, underscored with an explanation of the weight a cusomer's opinions carry. Obviously, there are people in our world who like to complain about anything just for the sake of being heard, as well as people who are likely to be happy and complimentary in any circumstances. This should be taken into account by the manager as intelligently and practically as possible. As the saying goes, "No one likes a wise guy"; no one, likewise, should attach much importance to an overly positive "rave" that has very little substance.

When providing the employee with either external or internal organizational input, the healthcare manager should make sure that the employee clearly understands that these highly subjective opinions are not the primary sources of performance evaluation. The effects of good or poor performance are the vital factors. With this in mind, the manager should impress upon the employee that the manager is the one who is ultimately charged with the employee's performance evaluation, and that other organizational input is only a supplemental, albeit important, source of performance data. Put simply, while organizaonal input provides various pieces of evidence, the manager is the one who decides the verdict.

Significant Incidents. The final qualitative performance indicator is significant incidents, also called critical incidents. Significant incidents are occurrences that call for the employee to perform beyond the call of duty. As we all know, in the healthcare business something out of the ordinary occurs almost every day. Undoubtedly, there is no lack of opportunities for a manager to look at significant incidents in almost every job category within the healthcare organization. The level of performance that an employee exhibits during these situations truly measures that employee's effectiveness and value to the organization.

In order to illustrate significant incidents, let us take the examples of the nurse recruiter, the dietary worker, and the X-ray technician and locate them in a hospital in the Silicon Valley area of northern California. A new manufacturer in the area has designed a microcomputer that will mandate the hiring of 5,000 new workers for its production and distribution. With this influx of new people into the area, the nurse recruiter must quickly recruit more nurses to meet the forthcoming demand for medical services. The X-ray technician will have to process considerably more X-rays, and the dietary worker will be pressed by more customers needing more meals. In all three cases, the respective managers should look at both the positive and negative responses to the demanding new situation.

The employees who respond positively to significant incidents are able to utilize their adaptability and work ethic. The manager can assist the employees in meeting the new challenge with additional resources and special assistance, when possible. However, the employees should be able to motivate themselves without undue reliance on others or excessive encouragement and direction from their boss. They understand completely that the organization needs their best, unquestioning effort and put forth that effort freely. They are not overly concerned about getting extra compensation or immediate rewards for this extra effort. In his classic management book, *Managerial Psychology,* Harold Leavitt pointed to the fact that the valued employee is able to respond quickly, competently, and aggressively in work situations that are not part of the mundane, day-to-day routine (Leavitt, 1958). With this in mind, one can correctly assume that significant incidents are true indicators as to whether employees are deeply dedicated to the organization, can apply their expertise to a critical situation adeptly, and can obtain desired results despite the circumstantial obstacles.

Negative response to significant incidents is marked by an unwillingness to respond quickly and expertly to an unusual situation, constant complaining about having to make an extra effort, or an overt desire to capitalize on the situation for additional compensation or special benefit. The latter would be apparent, for example, if an employee's prime interest during this time was overtime pay, a raise, or more vacation time, rather than getting the job done. This is not to say that the employee does not deserve extra pay for extra work; the time to settle on extra compensation is after the work is completed, however, not while attacking the task at hand. Pressing for guarantees of extra compensation before or during the handling of a special situation indicates a lack of dedication and trust of the organization on the part of the employee. If an employee will summon the extra effort needed in these situations only after being promised a reward, the manager should ask himself if the employee is really needed.

In some situations, the more common malady is for the employee to "fold," or to be unable to perform at a needed level of excellence. Like a professional athlete who "chokes" under pressure, some employees cannot perform adequately when taken out of a daily, set routine. These employees are better suited for industries other than healthcare. The unique demands of the healthcare business environment place a premium on a deep commitment to people and their basic welfare, particularly in emergencies; there is no position in the healthcare firm for people who do not have the desire and fortitude to perform in dire situations.

Significant incidents, because of the demands they put on employees, are the most telling of all the qualitative performance indicators. The manager should assess all performance clues under the unusual conditions, because such performance is truly indicative not only of employees' current ability to perform but also of their growth potential in the healthcare field. The following list presents a summary of quantitative and qualitative indicators:

- Monthly reports
- Unit performance
- Goal attainment
- Cost-effectiveness
- Personal observation
- Quan-Com traits
- Organizational and peer input
- Significant incidents

Supervisory Performance Indicators

For those managers whose responsibilities include the management of other supervisors, there is a set of key supervisory performance indicators that should be assessed and addressed in the performance appraisal cycle. Because of the unique nature of management responsibility, these managers need a formula that will enhance the performance appraisal process so that their supervisors can develop in their management skills. In our consulting work with healthcare managers, we have identified four key categories of supervisory assessment.

Basic Supervisory Skills. The first and most obvious of a supervisor's duties is the basic supervision and administration of his assigned subordinates and allotted material and fiscal resources. The manager conducting the performance evaluation should look at the Quan-Com managerial aptitude factors and apply them to the supervisor's past performance. The manager should begin her assessment by evaluating the subject supervisor's ability to plan, delegate, act independently, and creatively solve work-related problems, as evidenced by his performance. Next, she should assess how well the supervisor was able to maximize his use of human resources—that is, get the most from each employee. This could be evidenced by the amount of progress each employee has made in the most recent assessment period, the unit performance and team effort of each employee group, and the supervisor's overall growth as a capable leader. While this measurement at first might appear to be highly subjective, there are several ways to quantify it.

First, the manager should examine how well the supervisor was able to plan the activities and execution of assignments performed by his subordinates. For example, the manager should look at whether the goals and timing of the plans were realistic, how well they took into account each employee's abilities, and how well the plan accomplished its goals. Next, the manager should look for good delegation skills and how they were applied to directing employee performance. The manager should evaluate how adroitly the supervisor was able to work *through* his assigned charges, rather than working *on* his employees in a negative, irritating fashion. The supervisor might have been unable to delegate much work because he felt he had to do everything himself; this indicates either a mistrust of employee performance or just an inability to assign work effectively. As we know, most first-line supervisors have a proclivity for taking ownership of all work themselves, and thus they do not give their employees enough work. Delegation is an acquired ability that, like fine wine, improves with age. Failure on the part of the manager to efficiently instill delegation into a new supervisor can inhibit that new supervisor's performance as well as professional growth.

The manager should next ascertain how creative and independent the supervisor was in running his segment of the business. There are five basic questions a manager should ask herself in this regard:

1. Did the supervisor lean on me more than he should have for support and direction?
2. Did the supervisor think well on his feet during crises (significant incidents)?
3. Did the supervisor creatively employ all of his assigned subordinates' capabilities and talents?

4. Did the supervisor make any improvements on the operational status quo that increased productivity?

5. Did the supervisor spend more time on political and "administrivia" concerns than on getting action-oriented results?

The answers to these five questions should in sum give the reviewing manager an answer about the supervisor's creativity and independent judgment. More "clues" to these areas appear in Resource F.

Another supervisory skill to be taken into account is the supervisor's ability to generate a team orientation for his assigned employees. The manager should seek to determine whether, for example, the supervisor's work unit has a few "superstars" who do the bulk of the quality work while the rest perform marginally. Another example might be a work group composed entirely of marginal performers whose mediocrity is validated by the supervisor's condoning of poor performance. The manager can encourage the supervisor to examine the group dynamics of his work unit simply by having a personnel review with the supervisor. This would simply be an informal meeting between the two in which each employee is discussed individually, with the reviewing manager making appropriate suggestions on how better to motivate each member and the work group as a whole. This should be formally supplemented with a "one-over-one" performance appraisal process. In this process all of the supervisor's performance appraisals of his subordinates are reviewed and approved by the manager. This allows the reviewing manager to monitor individual employee performance and to coach the supervisor on any dynamics that threaten work group cohesiveness. The team orientation factors of the Quan-Com formula in Resource F provide additional information on assessing team orientation.

From a developmental viewpoint, it is essential that the manager assess the supervisor's managerial skills. With attrition and unforeseen turnover reaching record levels throughout the healthcare industry, the ability to groom people within an organization and develop management candidates from within is more important than ever. Therefore, the healthcare manager must ensure that she provides adequate and accurate feedback to the supervisor about his basic supervisory skills and helps the supervisor wherever possible in honing those skills. The manager should realize that in order to move up herself, a capable backup or successor must be readily available. The manager should coach, counsel, and develop her supervisors for her own sake as well as for the entire organization's well-being and growth.

Technical Acumen. All supervisors within a healthcare organization are usually charged with certain technical responsibilities. For instance, a supervisor of a credit and collection function must know the mechanics of the collection process as well as, if not better than, the individual employees. This extends to fields such as nursing administration, in which nursing directors must be knowledgeable about procedures and practices in their discipline, and radiology, in which department chiefs must definitely know their trade. In virtually all of the healthcare operational departments, the supervisor must have a mastery of related technical applications. Unlike their counterparts in other industries, who need to be only capable managers and leaders, healthcare supervisors have the additional responsibility of being experts in their fields.

The healthcare supervisor has a primary responsibility to be a technical resource for his assigned subordinates. The quickest way for a healthcare supervisor to lose credibility with his employees is for the employee to discover the supervisor is ignorant of the technical side of his responsibilities. Furthermore, a malcontent employee could take advantage of the supervisor's ignorance quite easily. The healthcare supervisor must know his field in order to effectively direct and assess technical work efforts. With this comes the responsibility to stay current with his technical field. The reviewing manager should look at her reporting supervisor and not only assess his prior year's managerial performance, but also examine how the supervisor has increased his knowledge of his field. It is the manager's responsibility to encourage the supervisor to take advantage of any opportunities to enhance technical acumen, such as attending professional seminars or technical workshops or reading pertinent publications.

From another point of view, the supervisor is often an internal consultant to the organization in his field of expertise. For example, the accounting manager in a community hospital is also the staff consultant on accounting and financial matters. The personnel manager, to take another example, is the staff consultant on human resource issues. Likewise, the compensation supervisor is the organization's wage and salary expert, the recruiter the employee expert, and so on. The manager is at fault if one of her assigned supervisors is not well versed in his technical field. While the supervisor is responsible for staying abreast of technical developments, the reporting manager has the greater responsibility of ensuring that all of her charges are technically proficient. She must therefore make every effort to direct her supervisors to constantly upgrade their technical knowledge base by setting the example and doing so herself. During the performance evaluation process, the manager should assess the supervisor's technical progress and its application on the job. Evidence of good technical application should exist, and the supervisor should be able to readily educate and assist any employee or staff member who needs technical assistance. The reviewing manager should make note of any activities where this ability is notably present or absent and address them constructively in the performance appraisal meeting.

Organizational Responsibility. A supervisor in a healthcare organization is an organizational team member. This requires that the supervisor be able to work cohesively in a team setting with peers, managers, and subordinates. The supervisor must be receptive to all requests for information, supportive of group objectives, and unselfish in the pursuit of organizational excellence. This will head off the tendency to develop a "me-first" attitude, typified by a supervisor who is concerned only with his own performance rather than that of the organization and his overall work unit.

The individual supervisor is also a public representative of his healthcare organization. When interacting with the public, particularly in the organization's community, the supervisor represents the organization, and in the public's eye and perception he *is* the organization. Therefore, the attributes of good presence and bearing, combined with common sense and good judgment, are particularly important. The reviewing manager should take note of any exemplary or discreditable behavior in situations in which the supervisor had to conduct himself as a representative of the organization. Although this might be perceived as a subjective judgment, by utilizing the Quan-Com characteristics of presence listed in Resource F and matching objective observations and evidence to those factors, the manager can make the process more concrete. In today's age of video journalism, when media journalists seem to be making the health-care industry a prime target, it is doubly important that supervisors carry themselves professionally not only for their own well-being but also to provide a good example for their employees. If the supervisor himself does not understand the importance of doing this, it is highly unlikely that his subordinates will. If nothing else, it is good business practice for supervisors and employees to present a good image on behalf of the organization.

Fiscal Responsibilities. As we discussed above, cost-effectiveness and timeliness are essential ingredients of a successful work formula. They are essential as well to the basic fiscal responsibility with which each supervisor is charged. As we stated, every supervisor must adhere to and work with a financial bottom line in order to gain maximum productivity from themselves and their staff. By reviewing particular budgets, financial planning, and total employment of available resources, the reviewing manager should find all critical indicators of financial performance that give a picture of the supervisor's fiscal responsibility. This is particularly cited in this section because supervisors utilize individual and departmental budgets every day; as part of their development, they must grow in their ability to get the most from their allotted monies.

The manager should examine the returns each supervisor got with his budget. If the supervisor was under budget, the manager should encourage the supervisor to either plan his budget better or use his funds more fully. In the opposite case, where the supervisor overspends his money, the manager should likewise caution the supervisor. In both cases, the supervisor must be educated in the importance of using his budget dollars fully and intelligently.

In monitoring and measuring the performance of her charges, the healthcare manager should take into account all of the indicators outlined in the three categories of this chapter. In doing so, and in applying those data intelligently to the objectives and goals set in the assessment system, she ensures that the organization is developing the potential and optimizing the performance of its human resources in a sound, all-encompassing manner.

Chapter 12

Conducting the Performance Review Session

The most visible and tangible segment of the entire performance assessment process is the performance review session itself. Because of its annual nature, as well as its inevitable relationship to the employee's salary increase and promotional opportunities, the performance review session has a critical role in the ongoing relationship between manager and subordinate. As we have seen, effective healthcare managers will make performance appraisal part of their continuous managerial responsibilities. However, while this might lend clarity to the appraisal process and decrease the probability of the session becoming a debate, it does not diminish the importance employees place on the review session itself.

In this chapter, we will discuss various ways in which healthcare managers can maximize the performance review session. Figure 25 shows the essential dimensions of the review session. By examining formats for the appraisal discussion and the appraisal form, possible reactions to the review session, methods of handling such reactions, and several formulas that can be utilized in the session, we will show approaches the reader can employ to increase the probability of making the session the directional and developmental tool it should be.

Format for an Appraisal Discussion

In order to conduct the actual performance appraisal discussion expeditiously and effectively, the healthcare manager should utilize the five-step communication process delineated

Figure 25. Essential Dimensions of the Performance Appraisal Session.

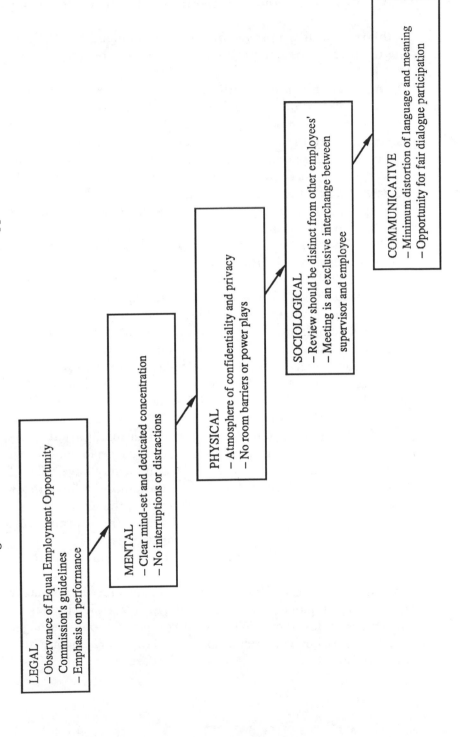

LEGAL
– Observance of Equal Employment Opportunity
  Commission's guidelines
– Emphasis on performance

MENTAL
– Clear mind-set and dedicated concentration
– No interruptions or distractions

PHYSICAL
– Atmosphere of confidentiality and privacy
– No room barriers or power plays

SOCIOLOGICAL
– Review should be distinct from other employees'
– Meeting is an exclusive interchange between
  supervisor and employee

COMMUNICATIVE
– Minimum distortion of language and meaning
– Opportunity for fair dialogue participation

in this section. It is a proven method of organizing and delivering the performance appraisal in a maximally beneficial way.

Opening and Overview. In the first phase of the performance appraisal discussion, the reviewing manager should explain to the employee in general terms what he wishes to accomplish during the meeting. In the interest of getting the employee involved in the discussion, the manager should provide the employee with a basic overview of the points to be covered in the review; if this is the employee's first exposure to the organization's performance appraisal process, he should also explain the basics of the appraisal form itself. If the employee is an hourly worker, the manager should explain that the session will take about a half hour. In the case of a supervisor, the manager should dedicate a full hour to the process and inform the employee accordingly. While reviewing the appraisal form with the employee, the manager should emphasize that the employee's active participation in the discussion is needed for both parties to get the most from the appraisal discussion, as well as for the manager to understand any views the employee has about the work situation. This will inform the employee that input is desired and valued, and will take some of the "report card" flavor out of the process.

Prior to the review itself, the manager might ask the employee to make some general notes about her performance. In a well-managed unit, the employee will naturally have a list of the objectives established for her position and will have those completely ready for the session. With this, the employee can reflect on her own performance and come to the appraisal session ready to discuss performance constructively.

Because of the legal function of the performance appraisal form as a critical source of evidence in cases of probation or termination, it becomes especially important for the manager to direct the employee to prepare for the review session by reflecting on her performance. With this accomplished, both manager and employee have in essence done their homework and are fully prepared to address the core of the appraisal.

Goal Attainment. Following the opening of the appraisal session, the manager should focus the discussion on goal attainment and performance output. This should begin with the manager and the employee jointly reviewing the job description as it appears on the appraisal. If the description is still relatively accurate and does not merit extended discussion, the manager should move on to the section describing the goals set for the prior review period. Manager and employee should review each goal as it was set, with the manager revealing his rating for each goal's accomplishment.

The manager should provide some insight into how each rating was determined by citing the objective performance evidence in each case. If good communication was evident between employee and manager throughout the year, there should be little surprise on the part of the employee concerning the ratings and the reasons behind them. The manager should get understanding—not necessarily agreement—from the employee for each rating before moving to the next one. The manager might also discuss how the importance of each goal and its relevance to the overall organization's mission were "weighed" in his estimation. This discussion of the prior period's goals should be a review in the strict sense of the word; that is, there should be no discussion at this point of new goals or amended objectives for the coming grading period. The manager and the employee are merely comparing goals with achievement in the previous grading period.

Interpersonal Assessment. The third phase of the performance appraisal discussion focuses on the characteristic or Quan-Com factor ratings as they pertain to employee performance. Simply put, in this stage the manager discusses the characteristics and how the employee's use of any particular characteristic affected performance either positively or negatively. The manager should, of course, cite as much objective evidence as possible to support his ratings.

If a characteristic was utilized by the employee in a negative fashion, it is particularly important for the manager to explain why the characteristic is important to the conduct of the job. This should be reinforced by suggestions of alternative applications of the characteristic and how it can be better used in the employee's work situation. Because interpersonal characteristics are more subjectively perceived than goal achievement, it is particularly important for the reviewing manager to use as many objective examples and illustrations of desired behavior as possible, so that the employee does not perceive this part of the discussion as a character assassination by the reviewing manager.

Developmental Direction. Developmental direction in the appraisal discussion should consist of the establishment of new or amended work goals and the planning of training and development activities for the employee for the coming grading period. It is essential for manager and employee to agree on specific goals to be established for the coming grading period, although the manager has the last word on these goals. Likewise, agreement should be reached on the plan of development activities. A good rule of thumb in this case is for the manager to designate one-third of the goals and development activities, the employee to suggest another third, and the two to arrive jointly at the final third. The manager in reality still has control of the final outcome of this process while allowing the employee ample opportunity for input that will be acted upon. In the case of an hourly employee, one developmental activity is probably sufficient; with a reporting supervisor, our consulting work in healthcare has shown, three is a good number. Three training and development activities in a yearly grading period strike a balance between a novice supervisor's daily responsibilities and the responsibility to further develop that supervisor's skills. Chapter Thirteen contains further information on this topic.

Consensus. In the final stage of a performance appraisal discussion, the manager and the employee come to some sort of consensus about the appraisal and, perhaps more important, about future work direction. Achieving such a consensus is infinitely easier when steady communication has been present. If this was not the case, the manager should use the appraisal as a new beginning and follow the appraisal session with a rededication to solid, hands-on management.

Components of an Effective
Performance Appraisal Form

Not only is it critically important for the healthcare manager to utilize an effective method of collecting performance data, setting goals, and communicating performance feedback to the employee, but it is additionally vital to have a good, workable performance appraisal form. In Resource G appears an appraisal form that has been used successfully by numerous leading healthcare organizations. It has been validated by research, quantitative measurement, and, perhaps most important, by practical use on the part of healthcare line managers. By examining this form and reviewing the components described in this section, the healthcare line manager will be able to present all critical elements of performance in a clear-cut, direct manner to the individual employee.

Administrative Data. The administrative data section of a performance appraisal form must supply several important facts. They are:

1. *Date of the appraisal*—The date on which the appraisal is actually conducted.
2. *Employee's name*—The employee's legal name as it appears on all documents in the employee file, usually accompanied by an organizational I.D. number or Social Security number.
3. *Work position*—The job title as it appears on the job description and all other significant organizational records.
4. *Department designation*—The work group to which the employee is assigned on a regular basis. If the employee is on loan to another department for a significant time, that should also be noted, particularly if his performance in that department is being assessed in this appraisal.
5. *Supervisor's name*—The reviewing manager or supervisor's name and organizational I.D. number.

6. *Start date*—The date on which the employee actually started work in the organization.
7. *Date in current position*—The date on which the employee started in the job he currently holds.
8. *Appraisal occasion*—The reason for the appraisal, usually the normal annual or semiannual review or perhaps a disciplinary or other special reason.

Job Description. The second section of a sound performance appraisal form should be the job description. This can be taken verbatim from the on-file job description, or it can be an abbreviated version of that description. The job description on the appraisal form must be criterion-based, in conformity with the guidelines of the Joint Commission on Hospital Administration as well as a plethora of federal and state employment statutes. As described in Chapter Five, the job description should include the overall scope of the current position, replete with a delineation of its major responsibilities. It should be tailored to the individual employee's actual duties as much as possible, rather than being an outdated, generic overview of the position. In all cases, the employee should be given a copy of the on-file job description on the first day on the job, and this, along with the supervisor's direction, should be the employee's guide in performing the job.

Past Year's Objectives and Expectations. The third section of a good performance appraisal form should list all of the major expectations and set objectives that the employee was to have met in the past grading period. The goals should have been set according to the precepts of Chapter Ten and understood and agreed to by the employee. In each case, the manager should rate the particular employee's accomplishment of each goal. As when rating candidates in an interview, the manager should utilize a three-tiered grading system, using one grade for poor accomplishment, a second for satisfactory performance, and a third for stellar achievement. This system discourages the manager from rating everyone in the organization as a 6 or 7 on a scale of 1 to 10, or a little higher than satisfactory. This also forces the manager to grade each goal individually and critically, rather than giving the employee one blanket rating.

By listing each objective as it appeared in the original goal-establishment format, the manager ensures continuity and consistency in the assessment and appraisal process. This also simplifies the review for the manager, since the manager then merely has to check the roster of objectives against actual performance. It further helps to show the employee clearly what is needed on the job, how it was achieved, and what should be accomplished from this point onward.

Characteristic Ratings. The next section of the performance appraisal should give some type of indication as to the employee's work-related personality attributes and how they either positively or negatively affect performance. For our clients, we have suggested the continuous use of the Quan-Com factors for this assessment requirement for all employees. In the case of a supervisor who is being reviewed by a manager, the managerial aptitude category will have particular application, while the entire range of sixteen characteristics can be relevant to any work position.

In utilizing the Quan-Com formula, the manager should review the employee's performance and decide if any of the factors was present or absent to the extent that it notably affected performance. For example, if an employee was particularly adaptable in successfully handling a unique situation, adaptability should be cited as a stellar commodity and the evidence of its positive application on the job should be supplied. On the other hand, if the employee was inflexible in that situation, the manager should grade the employee accordingly and provide insight on how to improve that rating. Average or satisfactory application of these characteristics does not need to be cited, since it is expected from the employee and does not greatly affect performance either negatively or positively.

Objective/Expectation Adjustment. Since goals change, employees come and go, and circumstances in the workplace fluctuate, a good performance appraisal form will have a section in which employee and manager can jointly construct new or amended goals for the coming grading period. The manager thus ensures that the goals are current, that they are maximally applicable to future business desires and objectives, and that the employee's interest is sparked whenever possible by new challenges. The manager should list in this section any new goals that are needed to meet emerging business demands, as well as amend any current goals according to what is needed in the future.

Development Plan. A good performance appraisal form is also a good development tool. The performance appraisal form should have a section that acts as a plan, or prescriptive prognosis, for useful developmental activities, in which opportunities for the employee's development are identified, discussed, and planned for accomplishment. By making this a required part of the appraisal form, the manager formalizes the commitment to helping the employee develop. Furthermore, the employee now has a formal plan for development that he has helped construct and that he is committed to completing for professional growth. As with the entire assessment process, the two-way planning of development activities elicits a commitment from each side as well as a true interest in employee growth. Chapter Thirteen provides an overview and compendium of development strategies the line manager can use to get the most growth from his health-care employees.

Employee Comments. On all performance appraisal forms, employees should be given the opportunity to rebut the appraisal formally and submit their impressions of their performance. Some organizations use a binary form, in which the employee reviews the supervisor on another appraisal form. Most organizations, however, simply have a section on the appraisal form in which the employee has the opportunity to give his comments. The effectiveness of each approach depends on the individual organization and its philosophy in this regard. Most state labor statutes require, however, that the appraisal form have some sort of accommodation for employee comment.

If the manager has allowed the employee ample opportunity for feedback on a daily basis, the employee comment section does not need to be very lengthy. However, there should be some sort of space on every appraisal form for employee comments, whether the employee wants to use it or not.

Overall Rating. Finally, the manager must attach an overall rating to the employee's performance. If he has in fact utilized a three-tiered system in rating each objective's accomplishment, as well as any of the characteristic ratings that might apply, the overall rating can be an easy summation process. In fact, if any numerical sequence has been used in the appraisal, it is simply a mathematical process to attach an overall rating number. The best rule of thumb in these cases is for the manager to review the entire content of the appraisal form and try to quantify the entire appraisal with an overall by-product number. Since there seem to be as many rating systems as there are appraisal forms, the reader might consult Frank J. Landy's book, *Psychology of Work Behavior* (Landy, 1985), to learn more about numerical grading systems other than the three-tiered system we advocate.

Signatures. At the conclusion of the performance appraisal form there should be space for both manager and employee to sign the form, with the date of the appraisal. This is a simple legal requirement. In some cases, usually because of a negative review, the employee will refuse to sign the appraisal form. In these cases, the manager should write in longhand on the form that the employee refused to sign, and initial and date the document. This should always be done so that an employee cannot contest the date or validity of the appraisal form in any litigation that might arise from a termination.

In all healthcare organizations, the appraisal form must be easily understood, easily read, and easily acted on in planning for future performance. Unfortunately, many existing forms are either too simplistic to be useful or too full of psychobabble and corporate jargon to be easily understood. Appraisal forms of this nature are not only a potential legal risk but also give employees no indication of their performance and invite objections from employees because of their lack of pertinent detail. By utilizing the form in Resource G, and tailoring it if necessary to an individual organization, the reader will have a legally sound, productive tool that will portray performance accurately and provide direction for development, as it has done in over fifty leading healthcare organizations.

Potential Employee Reactions in the Review Session

In our consulting work with performance assessment in the healthcare industry, we have identified ten common reactions to the performance review session, namely:

- Complete surprise
- Misunderstanding objectives
- Expecting praise
- Immediate blame
- Charging personal bias
- Strong verbal reaction
- Strong nonverbal reaction
- Complacency
- Contradiction
- Taking initiative

In this section we will identify each of these reactions, explain the root of the problem that causes it, and provide a remedy that the manager can use to get the discussion back on track.

Complete Surprise. Perhaps the most telling of all reactions to a performance appraisal is complete surprise at the content of the appraisal form and the dialogue that takes place in the review. The employee might register surprise during a particular segment of the performance discussion or from the very outset of the appraisal, and continue to show it right through to a negative conclusion. When an employee is truly surprised by the content of a performance appraisal, he usually spends the entire session dealing with his emotional reaction and thus misses much of the content of the session itself. On the other hand, an employee given an accurate negative review might feign surprise in order to communicate to the reviewing manager that he has a different opinion about his performance and past productivity.

The reason for genuine surprise is usually found in a lack of communication, typified by a dearth of feedback or direction from manager to employee. If the employee has not been told during the grading period that his performance is lacking, he will assume that his performance is satisfactory. At the appraisal itself, when the reviewing manager presents a litany of missed objectives, substandard output, and other work-related problems, the employee will be genuinely shocked. In this case, the fault lies primarily with the reviewing manager who has not utilized solid communication techniques in supervising the employee. Since the manager is at fault, the best remedy is for the manager to continue with the review, such as it is, and state a commitment to the employee to provide feedback on a more timely basis. This commitment should be supplemented by a scheduling of regular meetings between the two in the coming grading period so that communication does not again become a problem. This problem is common among newly appointed supervisors and managers, so it is important for the more senior managers in the organization to guide the novices toward making the review process a continuous one.

When surprise is feigned, the remedy is somewhat different. In this instance, the employee is using surprise as a ploy to deflect criticism or other negative feedback and to lend credibility to the employee's own view of his performance. It therefore becomes imperative for the manager to provide several pieces of concrete evidence that clearly show the employee's shortcomings on the job. These should be reinforced by references to any conversation the manager might have had with the employee in which the employee's poor performance was discussed. When faced with examples of poor performance and reminders of corrective discussions, the manipulative employee's case loses much of its veracity. The manager should seriously question such an employee's loyalty to the organization as well as his basic desire to perform well. If the employee subsequently attempts to improve his performance, the manager's actions are well rewarded. If the employee continues to perform poorly, the manager should underscore the next discussion about performance by putting the employee on probation with an eye toward termination.

Misunderstanding Objectives. Another common reaction that seems particularly to affect novice managers is simply the employee's misunderstanding what was expected on the job on a daily basis. This problem usually occurs when a manager has not set objectives from the very outset of the job. That is, no clear-cut expectations and objectives for performance are defined for the employee. This problem can also result when the employee has been provided with the objective but has not fully understood it. For example, the employee might not have been provided with the time frame for completion or might not understand the importance of a deadline. In other cases, the objective might have been fragmented and the employee therefore did not understand the scope of the assignment.

In situations such as this, the fault can lie with either the manager or the employee, or even with a misunderstanding on the part of both. The fundamental problem here is once again communication. By constructing objectives and goals in a clear-cut manner, and also by giving the employee, when feasible, a written outline of what is expected and required on the job, the healthcare manager eliminates the problem of misunderstood objectives. When the manager conducts the performance review sessions, he can ask the employee to bring his outline of objectives with him, and together they can clearly and comprehensively review goal attainment and work output.

Expecting Praise. Some managers in the healthcare industry, because of their own enthusiasm and energy on the job, have a propensity to appear overly positive about everything. They tend to praise employees throughout the year and to avoid situations in which they have to provide negative feedback. This is also true of managers who are overly concerned with being liked by their employees. A by-product of this Pollyannaish approach to management is the expectation of undue praise in the performance review session. In this situation, the employee comes into the review session expecting the proverbial pat on the back for his efforts.

In the healthcare labor market, there are more jobs for technically skilled people than there are skilled people to fill those jobs. Healthcare managers therefore take every opportunity to convey to employees a sense of appreciation for their efforts and talents. Unfortunately, for the appraisal process to be really constructive, it should not be reduced to a "stroking session" that the employee attends just to hear how terrific and valuable he is to the organization. The employee who comes into the performance appraisal session expecting the review to be 100 percent positive may be disappointed if the review is even 95 percent praise and 5 percent constructive criticism. The employee who has been spoiled by too much stroking throughout the grading period will invariably focus on the 5 percent that is constructive criticism, to the extent that the entire process appears negative. This, of course, if it is not resolved, can lead to poor performance and lack of desire on the job.

In this sensitive situation, the manager should emphasize the fact that the employee is a valued and productive organizational member. The manager should make it clear that the organization therefore has a vital interest in the employee's further development and wants the employee to become an even greater resource. Therefore, it is imperative for the manager and the employee to address aspects of the employee's overall performance that are not outstanding and discuss ways in which they might be improved. In taking this approach, the reviewing manager assuages the ego of the employee without sacrificing the critical core of the performance appraisal. This lessens the probability of damaging the employee's motivation, since the employee is still given credit for solid achievement.

In the case of employees who have performed at a substandard level in the past grading period, managers should use the review to demonstrate to the employees how incorrect their own perceptions of their performance actually are. This is evidently a clearer problem to deal with and is infinitely less delicate than the case of the good performer.

Immediate Blame. A favorite offensive tactic of employees who are aware that they have performed poorly is immediate blame. This is the practice of blaming another person, a physical resource, unusual circumstances, or anything else other than themselves as the cause of poor productivity. Peers and supervisors are prime targets for this strategy.

Employees might have several reasons for using this strategy. If the employee has received clear and timely feedback about his poor performance, he will have a feeling that a negative review is in the offing. He then prepares a suitable roster of alibis to deflect the blame to another party. Another reason might be that the employee is simply a classic "blamer" who rarely takes responsibility for his own actions and blames others out of habit. People like this have spent most of their lives blaming others, and they should have been weeded out of employment consideration in the interviewing process.

In any case, it is vital for the healthcare manager to keep the emphasis of the appraisal directly on the employee's objective work output itself. It must be stressed to the employee that he alone is responsible for his actions; if a problem exists that prevents him from performing adequately, that problem should be identified and brought to the attention of the supervisor immediately, not six months later in the review. Since many healthcare organizations are overworked and understaffed, there are an infinite number of targets for the blame of the negatively oriented, sneaky employee. For the same reason, many employees honestly believe they are indispensable. The reviewing manager must stress that no employee, in fact, is indispensable and that each employee is getting paid to produce results, not to create excuses. The reviewing manager herself should consider whether the blaming employee is really worth a paycheck. Of the ten possible reactions to a performance appraisal, this one in and of itself is an indicator of a person who would rather apply his energies toward negative ends than positive ones. A blamer in the review session will be a blamer throughout the conduct of the job. His propensity for blaming others and not being accountable for his own actions will spread to others and can cause problems throughout the work unit. If a blamer is allowed to continue this behavior, other workers will believe that it is acceptable to the manager. It is essential, therefore, for the manager to use the review session to stop the problem before it spreads. If subsequently the manager does not witness a drastic change in this behavior, termination based on poor performance and insubordination becomes a logical remedy.

Charging Personal Bias. ''You just don't like me or people like me.'' This statement is usually the answer from an employee to a manager when the employee wishes to make personal bias or prejudice an issue in the performance review discussion. Many poor performers enjoy using this cheap tactic in order to avoid discussing the essence of their bad results and lack of work output. For example, the employee can tell the reviewing manager that he feels the manager does not like him because of his clothing style or his religious, ethnic, or regional background. He might also accuse the reviewing manager of playing favorites and of persecuting him because he is not one of those favorites. Other reasons may be cited, but the common factor is that the alleged bias is subjective and difficult either to disprove or to discuss objectively.

This type of behavior is a symptom of a larger problem; the employee probably uses this type of argument whenever things get difficult on the job. While in some cases it might be true that the manager does not particularly care for the employee personally, this dislike should not affect the manager to the point of causing unfair performance evaluation. If that happens, the manager should be chastised and corrected by her own boss. However, in the more common cases, when the employee is simply using a charge of personal bias to shift blame, this must be addressed in no uncertain terms in the appraisal with the promise that it will not be tolerated as an excuse for poor performance in the future.

Strong Verbal Reaction. Another frequent response to a performance appraisal discussion is a strong verbal reaction to the information provided by the manager. The employee may raise his voice, use profanity, or otherwise verbally register disagreement with the appraisal.

The manager must first find the root of the disagreement by asking the employee why the reaction is so strong. Second, the manager should calmly explain that nothing constructive will come from shouting and hollering, and that the difference in opinion about the appraisal should be discussed in regular conversational fashion. Furthermore, the manager should emphasize that the healthcare organization is a professional setting, and the manager must insist that the employee conduct himself professionally, no matter how angry he might be. If the reaction is extremely intense, the reviewer should utilize one of the return-to-objectivity (RTO) formulas discussed in the next section of this chapter.

Strong verbal reactions can be expected from employees whose overall performance has been poor. If they have an inkling ahead of time that the review session will be somewhat negative, they will probably prepare a tirade that will both express their displeasure and shift the focus of the session from objective performance to subjective emotionalism. Whatever the case might be, it is essential for the manager to keep the performance appraisal review session on an even keel.

Strong Nonverbal Reaction. Like the strong verbal reaction, the strong nonverbal reaction conveys bitter disagreement with the performance appraisal. The employee decides to smolder, stare, or steam, in all cases intending to express displeasure to the manager rather than pay attention to the content and conduct of the review. In this case, the possibility of conducting a constructive performance appraisal is remote.

The remedy is somewhat similar to the previous one. The manager should tell the employee that she can easily see, from the employee's expressions and emotions, that he does not agree with the substance of the review. The manager should indicate, however, that while the employee obviously disagrees with the appraisal, the manager believes it is a valid assessment and will continue with it. She should then give the employee a copy of the completed review form and suggest that he review it himself for a couple of days, after which he might rebut the review in writing or at another scheduled discussion. This allows the manager to salvage an opportunity to educate the employee about his performance. It also gives the employee the chance to read the review, a permanent record of assessed performance, and come to the realization in his own way that whether he agrees or not, this is how he is being appraised, and he must improve performance quickly. The employee will also then be individually responsible to either improve performance or suffer the consequences of probation or termination.

Complacency. Many employees are naturally complacent about their jobs as well as life in general. This attitude, unfortunately, will insinuate itself into their performance and the performance appraisal session. Complacency might be expressed by a marginal employee, or perhaps by one who is a satisfactory worker and is just not interested in being a top performer. This gives the manager the very delicate task of trying to motivate an employee whose performance is acceptable to improve even further without alienating or disenchanting the employee. After all, the employee might reason, what is wrong with being graded satisfactory?

In some forms, complacency might be another hallmark of the classic poor performer. People who lack both the work ethic and loyalty characteristics we have discussed in this book will often demonstrate complacency, even in something as important as the performance appraisal session. In this case, the manager must weigh the complacency against what is desired and needed in the position and decide how much that complacency affects performance on the job. The very complacency the employee exhibits during the appraisal session becomes another piece of evidence of undesired on-the-job conduct. In citing situations in which the employee's complacency help produce negative results, the manager can add the observation that the employee seems uninterested in his own performance appraisal. With the marginal employee, the manager should seize the opportunity to take corrective action. With the average or above-average employee who just seems to have a temporary lapse of motivation, the manager should explore with the employee aspects of the job that are of greater interest to the employee and might help restore motivation. For more information on motivating the marginal employee, the reader should consult *Management and Organizational Development* by Chris Argyris (Argyris, 1971).

Contradiction. Contradiction takes place in the performance appraisal session when the employee takes exception to certain segments of the review or to the entire appraisal itself. The employee might contradict the reviewing manager when discussing what the established performance goals were, what performance was achieved as evidenced by work output, or any other aspect of the job. This obviously can cripple the validity of the performance appraisal session and greatly hinder agreement at the conclusion of the session on future goals and objectives.

The first remedy for contradiction is to prevent it by setting clear-cut goals along the parameters discussed in Chapter Ten. The second is to provide the employee with objective examples to support each negative grading. For every goal that was not satisfactorily met, the manager must have a related illustration showing why the goal was not achieved satisfactorily. The employee might try to attack the validity of the illustration itself. In this case, the manager should change the appraisal from a conversation that is becoming a conflict to a one-sided session in which the manager delivers the entire appraisal and then lets the employee respond. When compared with the overall assessment of performance and the overall dissatisfaction with the employee's output, the trivial disagreements with minor issues will pale. If the employee contradicts the overall appraisal, the manager should very simply and flatly tell the employee that his current level of performance is not acceptable, and if the employee is unable to improve that performance, for whatever reason, he would be better off seeking another employer.

It is truly amazing how many examples we have seen in our healthcare consulting work of employees who are contradictory, disloyal, and more than willing to expound their negative opinions about their boss and organization to anyone willing to listen. If this is tolerated for too long, the problem is always found in the weakness of management and an unwillingness to confront the employee. This malady is not unique to hourly employees; we have seen countless newly graduated, entry-level supervisors who were the greatest proponents of immature bad-mouthing, contradiction, and disloyalty. This undermines the authority and credibility of management, and it is very similar to union-generated ploys to gain support for organizing health-care employees. Contradiction, with its attendant game playing, is destructive and can easily become cancerous if management does not handle it forcefully and resolutely.

Taking Initiative. This is the least harmful of the ten reactions discussed in this section. Employees who take the initiative are usually highly motivated and have performed well during the grading period. They are so enthusiastic in their desire to assist the manager that they try to conduct the session for him. Additionally, they are eminently agreeable to anything the manager says.

The only problem with this is that the employees, in their enthusiasm, do not listen very well when new dimensions are introduced; they are liable to miss the point of any substantive feedback provided by the manager while trying to make the review a fluid process. The only remedy needed in this case is for the manager in essence to slow the employee up, making the employee take the time to understand the constructive information and developmental direction that the manager is trying to provide in the interest of improving performance even further. The manager must do this to make sure the good employee gets as much from the appraisal session as the marginal employee.

Using Defusers—The Return-to-Objectivity Formula

As we have discussed, there is a range of possible reactions to the performance appraisal. In some situations, the remedies covered in the previous section might be inappropriate or ineffective. With that in mind, we have designed for our performance assessment clients four basic defusing strategies, which we refer to as the return-to-objectivity or RTO formula. This formula gives the reviewing manager four practical ways to return a highly emotional performance appraisal to its objective and constructive tone.

A defuser is a communication technique that eliminates emotionalism from a work-related conversation. Defusing an emotional conversation is like defusing an explosion by either extinguishing or cutting off its fuse. The four techniques described in this section can be utilized by a healthcare manager to eliminate argument and disagreement immediately. They also allow the employee the opportunity to come to a less emotional, more objective frame of mind before continuing with the substance of the performance appraisal interview.

Pacification. Pacification is the practice of allowing the employee to ventilate her anger immediately so that the rest of the performance appraisal can continue constructively. It is the first defuser the manager might use in response to a strong verbal reaction in the initial stages of the performance appraisal. The reviewing manager might tell the employee that he understands the employee's point; after letting the employee make her point to her satisfaction, the manager redirects the conversation toward the appraisal itself. If he thinks the employee's point of contention is substantive, the manager might include a commitment to discuss that issue further in another conversation.

Pacification is a good technique if the employee has just one specific argument that she wants to make known to the manager. General or partial agreement with the employee's point satisfies the employee, who is usually responsive to the rest of the performance appraisal. This scenario might be, in fact, the only one in which pacification can be effectively employed. For instance, if an employee wishes to contest every segment of the performance appraisal, pacification will merely encourage her to turn the appraisal session into a debate. The other risk with this approach is that the employee, having gotten agreement on one argument, might get the impression that the manager will be agreeable to other issues of interest to the employee. Again, if it is a minor issue that is at stake, and the employee is sincerely interested in making her feelings known without any underlying motives, this technique is usually very effective.

Facilitation. Facilitation encourages the employee to discuss any contentions she presents in the context of the performance appraisal session. By utilizing this approach, the healthcare manager is providing the employee with a forum to discuss the full range of her disagreement. This is an extremely effective method if the employee's point of contention is related to a major issue in the performance appraisal. In fact, the intent of a performance appraisal session is to discuss critical dimensions of performance and developmental direction. Therefore, it might be entirely appropriate for the manager, using facilitation, to encourage the employee to discuss more specifically her concerns and her potential solutions to stated problems, and to come jointly to an agreement on how the problem might be better addressed in the future.

Facilitation may not accomplish this end when a malevolent employee who has major problems on the job wishes to provide a full-scale diatribe on why "things go wrong all the time." The employee is not interested in constructively discussing work solutions but probably is interested in blaming or contradicting, motives we discussed in the last section. Facilitation also may not work well with employees who are overly conversational and will seize the opportunity to present a book-length dissertation on the organization, their department, and of course, their particular jobs. Managers must call on their independent judgment in order to decide how and when to employ facilitation and to what degree to allow facilitation to become an integral part of the performance appraisal session. The manager must keep in mind that the performance appraisal is vital to individual employees and their compensation; any dialogue that takes place during this forum will be perceived as extremely serious to the employee. The manager's response to the presentation of the employee's concerns will be remembered and marked well by the employee.

When utilizing facilitation, the reviewing manager must also keep in mind the time parameters allocated to each employee's appraisal. If one employee's appraisal session is longer than average, the employee might react to the discrepancy in one of two ways. Either, in her perception, she is doing very poorly on the job and thus needs a lot of guidance, or, on the other hand, she is a favorite of the manager and thus gets extra time because she is "special." The employee who receives less time in the appraisal session than average—perhaps because there was no need for facilitation or extended discussion—might feel cheated of time spent discussing critical performance with the manager. Therefore, the manager must keep in mind that facilitation is a good practical tool but must be applied intelligently and according to the requirements of each employee's individual situation. If major issues cannot be resolved within the time allotted to the appraisal session, the manager might wish to schedule a specific time for the employee and himself to discuss the situation in detail.

Suspension. In some situations in the appraisal session, the employee becomes so highly charged emotionally that it is virtually impossible for the manager to discuss the complete review. Employees can become distraught or angry or demonstrate other emotions that prohibit sound conduct of the appraisal. In cases such as this, it is imperative that the manager employ the strategy of suspension. Suspension is the practice of putting off the remainder of a performance appraisal for a period of time, during which the employee can cool off, collect her thoughts about the appraisal, and prepare to approach the next appraisal session more objectively.

During an appraisal session on a Thursday afternoon, for example, the manager might tell an overwrought employee to forget about the appraisal until Tuesday morning at ten o'clock. In doing this, the manager gives the employee the opportunity to spend the rest of the work week and the weekend reflecting on the performance appraisal. He might, in fact, give the employee a copy of the appraisal itself so that the employee can study it and, in her own way, reconcile its contents with her perceptions of how she performed. Usually, the employee will approach the situation with a cooler head and on Tuesday morning will, ideally, have a more educated perspective on why the manager evaluated the performance as he did. An obvious proviso here is that if suspension is used, the manager must ensure that on Tuesday morning the rescheduled meeting is conducted without fail. If it is not, the employee can easily get the impression that the appraisal must not have been that important to the manager, and the manager has better things to do than to discuss the employee's performance.

An obvious pitfall of suspension is that the employee might become even angrier or more distraught between sessions. This short-term problem does, however, have the long-term benefit of showing the employee that the manager cared enough to make two efforts to discuss the employee's situation. The manager must distinguish between the employee's emotionalism and the reasons for that emotionalism, and then decide whether or not the employee's points are valid. If they are not valid, the manager should determine whether the employee's emotional outburst was part of the employee's daily work personality or was done strictly for effect. In either case, the use of suspension will probably give the manager further insight into the employee's motivation and desire to work hard for the organization.

Cancellation. The final defusing strategy, both in terms of our formula and because of its "last resort" nature, is cancellation. Cancellation is merely the abrupt halting of a performance appraisal session in which a negatively assessed employee counters the conduct of the session with negative emotionalism that is typical of her work behavior. By blowing up in the appraisal, the employee is providing the manager with a perfect example of negative, unacceptable behavior. The manager then aborts the review and uses the rest of the session to either put the employee on probation or terminate the employee.

This approach is used primarily with an employee whose continued employment is somewhat doubtful. If the employee is already on probation, any negative emotionalism, contradiction, or other detrimental ploy must be met with cancellation. This approach gives the manager the critically needed opportunity to dismiss the employee from the organization, since the employee is in essence terminating herself with her actions. The manager, if he wishes, might simply stop the appraisal and ask for a resignation; if the employee is reluctant to resign, he should just terminate the employee. While this at first might seem to be a very hard-line approach, a major problem in healthcare human resource management today is the softness of line managers toward employees who do not merit employment to begin with and who probably should have not been hired at all in a people-oriented organization. In the days of high profits and low competition, such softness did not acutely harm the bottom line, because in truth there was no bottom line. In today's environment, however, employees who are better off in other industries should not be allowed to wallow in a healthcare institution; their collective unproductiveness and subversiveness can be very costly to all concerned. The manager is doing himself, his well-motivated and productive employees, and his organization a major disservice by sheltering poor employees in the false hope that they might one day turn around. If the manager believes that an employee who has submitted poor work for two years will suddenly turn into a solid performer, he is in essence lacking independent judgment and aggressiveness and hurting his entire work unit.

While cancellation is a severe measure, being in effect a final step, it is certainly needed in these situations. Obviously, all terminations and probations must be tempered and conducted with the expertise that can be provided by a solid human resource department or legal counsel, if necessary. However, by adhering to the tenets of legal dismissal and termination, and by incorporating the cancellation method when opportune in the appraisal setting, the manager has a fortunate opening to rid the organization of human resources who are not worth their paychecks. In the words of a seasoned nursing director at a Philadelphia hospital, "Tell them our competitor has a good employment opportunity for them—that is the only way the lousy employee can help our hospital!"

Chapter 13

Providing for Staff Growth and Development

In order to maximize the performance assessment process in a healthcare organization, it is essential for the line manager to give consideration to development strategies. Development strategies are any activities that can be carried out within the normal conduct of the employee's job that will enhance the employee's growth and development as well as his or her contribution to the organization. The survey provided in Resource H can help managers determine their organization's training and development needs. In this chapter, we will discuss development strategies that can be readily implemented by the healthcare manager in order to provide optimum growth and motivation on the job.

There are several reasons that a healthcare manager should seek to provide his employees with specific development strategies at each performance review session. First, the healthcare manager can reduce turnover and help facilitate a backup system. By providing the employee with the opportunity to grow and develop on the job, the manager is preparing the employee for the next successive position in the organization as well as contributing to the employee's overall professional growth. In most cases, a developmental activity that is particularly relevant to the employee's job will give the employee knowledge that he can immediately apply to his current position, thus increasing the quality of work.

A second reason is the responsibility of each healthcare manager to ensure that all of his employees are keeping abreast of technical developments that are essential to timely progress

233

and competence in their jobs. Because of the heavily technical nature of many jobs in the healthcare sector, it is imperative that all employees have the opportunity, for their own well-being and the sake of the organization, to learn and master any techniques that will add to technical competence. Many development strategies, such as seminars and workshops, facilitate an exchange of ideas and methods related to technical approaches and applications. In this type of setting, employees have the opportunity to see state-of-the-art technology and how it might best be applied to their particular work situations.

A third reason is the motivational effects that development strategies have on employees. Development strategies are usually perceived as rewards in themselves; they indicate to employees that the organization and manager value their performance enough to make an investment in increasing their knowledge and skill. This is particularly true when an organization, for example, sends an employee to an outside seminar. In this setting, away from the confines of the organization's facilities, the employee enjoys the added importance of being, in effect, the organization's delegate at the conference or seminar. Development strategies provide other benefits, namely:

- Maximize individual growth
- Increase employee's long-term value to firm
- Enhance quality of employee contribution
- Expand managerial knowledge base
- Facilitate exchange of ideas and methods
- Ensure "state-of-the-art" progress

Areas of Development Strategies

Development strategies can be grouped into three categories. The first category comprises technical development strategies, strategies and activities that increase the employee's knowledge and expertise in their professional fields. These activities are intended to enhance knowledge about a particular aspect of a field and usually utilize much practical application and discussion of specific practices. Each technical discipline within the healthcare industry has a professional organization that conducts and sponsors seminars and other activities intended to fortify technical knowledge and ability. Most employees are members of these technically oriented organizations and thus have firsthand knowledge of seminar offerings and other opportunities for technical growth. A savvy manager in a healthcare organization will regularly ask deserving employees which activities are likely to be the most enriching, since the employees in this case are the experts on what technical knowledge is needed and how it might be best obtained. The manager will then take an active part in enrolling and otherwise encouraging the employees.

The second type of development strategy is often referred to generically as employee or managerial skills development. This category comprises nontechnical development strategies, including education about business practices or interpersonal skills development. The manager has the opportunity to provide the employee with training in such topics as supervisory skills, interpersonal communication skills, and financial training for the nonfinancial manager. This type of development is usually used to prepare the employee who has been selected to ascend to supervisory or managerial role. If a manager is truly proactive in preparing developmental activities for his assigned personnel and committed to their development, he has probably identified in advance which of these opportunities would be suitable for a particular employee. With this in mind, he can provide the employee with an incremental program of education that will progressively increase the employee's knowledge base in business and leadership practices.

For example, let us take the case of a housekeeping manager who wishes to promote a stellar employee into a supervisory, or lead person, role where she will supervise four hourly workers. The manager might utilize the performance appraisal session to tell the employee of his intent to groom her for a supervisory role. He might augment the employee's development program with three activities: a basic supervisory skills seminar, a cross-training activity with a current lead person in the department, and a locally conducted seminar about budgeting and planning. These three activities, which will be targeted for completion in the upcoming grading period, will provide the employee with a perspective on what the new position entails. They will also arm the employee with the knowledge necessary to begin in the position and fulfill its basic requirements.

The third category of development strategies is commonly referred to as organizational development. This is any type of development that increases employees' knowledge of the organization, its business practices and philosophies, and the integration with it of their positions. Organizational activities can take many different forms. The training itself may occur in an in-house educational seminar, where employees are exposed to various company policies, procedures, and practices. It can take the form of cross-training, in which employees work on an interim basis with departments or in jobs other than their own. Organizational development is usually used in large organizations, where it is more likely than in a small firm that an employee will know little about other operational areas. However, even in a small organization employees can benefit from greater knowledge of the entire organization.

Types of Development Strategies

Development strategies in each category can take several forms. Each type has its own unique benefits and applications, and obviously each is more relevant and easier to implement for some organizations and employees than for others.

Professional Seminars. The most obvious type of development strategy is the professional seminar. This is a program or workshop that is sponsored by a particular professional organization and provides new information in a specific technical field. Seminars in this grouping might include, for example, a fiscal control seminar sponsored by a state accounting association, a seminar covering a new nursing procedure conducted by a regional nursing association, or a seminar for nurse recruiters sponsored by the American Society of Personnel Administrators (ASPA). The purpose of a professional seminar is to provide specific guidance and education in a technical practice. These programs primarily cover new and improved approaches to a specific facet of technical responsibility.

Professional seminars are best utilized by people in fields in which the attainment of new technical knowledge will provide immediate short-term benefits to the organization. Many professional organizations, such as the American College of Healthcare Executives (ACHE), have accreditation powers that they employ to design curricula and study plans leading to professional certification. The healthcare manager should explore opportunities of this nature and examine with the employee which of these will best enhance the employee's development and return the most benefits for the employee in the daily conduct of the job.

Managerial Seminars. Managerial seminars are programs in which managerial and supervisory practices and approaches are discussed and explained. These include programs and workshops on interviewing skills, supervisory techniques, time management, and a plethora of other topics. Managerial seminars can be conducted either in house, by qualified members of the organization or by a contracted consultant, or at an outside setting, where employees attend sessions with their peers from other organizations.

The most telling benefit of outside seminars is the opportunity they give to get fresh information and new ideas and approaches from their peers in other organizations. The disadvantage of these seminars presents itself when an employee discovers that the other participants do not hold similar positions in their organizations or work in organizations that are not similar to the employee's place of employment. On the other hand, in-house or inside seminars can seem somewhat "stale" to employees because they are attending with people they see in the course of everyday work. Dialogue and participation may also be restricted in certain organizations because of political dynamics or nuances in individual relationships. However, employees might find the opportunity at an in-house seminar to discuss a particular work-related problem that is relevant to the program's topic; this provides an open forum for resolving the problem with organizational colleagues.

Healthcare managers must decide, first, which employees would profit most from a particular seminar, and second, whether the employees would assimilate the information best at an outside or in-house setting. While the overall cost of an outside offering is invariably higher than that of an in-house program, the benefits of the outside exposure, as well as the sense of importance an employee probably feels as the company's delegate, are good sources of motivation and rewards for the participating employee.

Continuing Education. A form of development that is often overlooked by most healthcare organizations is continuing education. Continuing education is the enrollment of employees in a traditional educational program offered by a local community college or university, usually under the egis of the adult education division. Many employees often take advantage of such offerings on an individual, informal basis for their personal benefit, and, in some cases, for work-related education. Recently, some healthcare organizations have begun to formalize their relationships with their local regional colleges in the interest of promoting employee education. Following the example set by their counterparts in other service industries, many healthcare organizations now provide remitted tuition plans and other programs to encourage their employees to enroll in pertinent continuing education programs. Since the emergence of the American community college as the leading provider of adult education, every healthcare organization now enjoys geographical proximity to some type of educational institution.

Many community colleges and universities have become aggressive in their efforts to attract students from local business organizations. For example, at Middlesex County College in New Jersey, the continuing education directors make a conscious effort to provide education to local businesses; in fact, their faculty conduct classes in the plants and facilities of their students' employers. This allows a number of employees in one organization to pursue a set curriculum together and increases group motivation and cohesiveness. It also provides the course instructor with a highly motivated, deeply committed assemblage of students. In other schemes, local colleges and universities have offered group enrollment plans to organizations in their area and have worked closely with these organizations to facilitate access and administration. The healthcare manager, with the help of the human resources staff, should investigate opportunities to give the employee the advantage of continuing a formal educational track that will increase both personal and professional growth.

Cross-Training. An individual development strategy that often pays great benefits to both the individual and the organization is cross-training. Cross-training involves the immersion of employees into another work role in order to increase their exposure to lateral positions and to enhance their knowledge of other work responsibilities. For example, employees may simply be assigned to another department or position for a period of time in which they can learn the tenets of the position itself and its application to the total organization.

Cross-training allows the healthcare manager to develop more than one backup to a position, thus providing complete coverage in case of absences or unforeseen turnover. Cross-training also helps employees on a supervisory development path to understand all of the positions that they might one day supervise. By utilizing this approach, the employee gains a perspective on how the work unit operates as an overall entity. Cross-training is a fairly simple and very cost-effective procedure. It must be reinforced by the manager's guidance and instruction on how a position must be handled, as well as by the input and knowledge of the employee who handles the position on a daily basis. Cross-training employees should be told the exact reason that they have been selected to participate in this activity and given specific guidance as to what to learn from the experience.

Individual Strategies. In many cases, it is essential for the employee to pursue a particular line of education or training in order to obtain immediate results from his or her position. In this case, an individual development strategy might be devised by both supervisor and employee to obtain the specific knowledge the employee needs to conduct the job. For example, if an employee begins a job somewhat deficient in a specific area of knowledge, a good individual development strategy might be a list of technical materials that the employee must read in a set amount of time. This reading might be augmented by regular discussions with the supervisor about the material being read and its application to the job.

Another example of an individual strategy is an approach that is often grandly referred to as "contemporary exploration." This simply involves an employee looking at the practices of a competitor or other closely related entity for new and better ideas. For example, a personnel manager and a nurse recruiter might visit a similar healthcare institution and discuss with its staff various formulas for recruitment success. This approach obviously depends on the relationship between two institutions, and often relies on the networking that has been done by the supervisor. If supervisors have maintained relatively good relations with their peers in other organizations, this approach can be utilized when lessons can be learned from a similar organization that is getting measurably better results in a specific area. The hidden benefit of this type of approach is that both supervisor and employee have the opportunity to look at a different application, discuss its potential implementation, and make a joint commitment to bringing it to their organization.

While all development strategies can be described as individual in nature, the truly individual development strategy is born from a uniquely individual need. It therefore depends on the supervisor's ability to perceive the employee's need for development, as well as the supervisor's creativity in addressing that need. Individual development strategies require the supervisor to spend an inordinate amount of time coaching the employee on specific issues and tasks. They also require more dialogue between the employee and the manager in order to ensure that new methods are being properly implemented and the desired results are being gained. For more information about coaching techniques on the job for supervisory use, the reader should explore the well-regarded manual *Coaching for Proformance in Healthcare* by J. Russell Sutton and J. V. Raines (Sutton and Raines, 1983).

Chapter 14

Rewarding Good Performance

Reward systems are approaches that a manager can employ to give the employee compensation for a job well done that does not lie in the realm of money. Many industrial psychologists maintain that while money is certainly a motivator, it is also perceived as a measurement. While most employees work primarily because they need to make a certain amount of money, money is also a measurement of their competence. For example, if the salary of a pharmacist's aide in one hospital is comparable to what other pharamacist's aides in similar institutions earn, then the salary is a fair representation of the employee's worth. On the other hand, if an employee is paid considerably less than his or her peers at other organizations, the salary is an inaccurate measurement of the employee's worth and can actually serve to discourage the employee. If employees are being paid what they are worth—and, perhaps more important, what they perceive they are worth—the healthcare manager should seek other ways to reward them for their efforts. In this chapter, we will explore several reward systems that a manager can utilize to encourage an employee's continued progress and positive results on the job.

Physical Environmental Factors

Managers can provide several environmental factors in the workplace that encourage motivation and dedication to the job. Improvements in the space in which the employee must work every day are rewards that will be most apparent to and appreciated by the employee.

Spacious Workplace. Healthcare managers must make sure that their employees have an adequate space in which to perform their work, including space to accommodate storage and any other work-related needs. Work space that is too cramped inhibits workers' ability to organize and execute their work effectively.

Healthful Workplace. Since most people who work in healthcare are very health-conscious (to say the least), it is essential that all managers in the healthcare industries strive to provide their employees with a health-promoting workplace. This includes, besides adequate space, sufficient air circulation to deal with cigarette smoke and other common pollutants one finds in any workplace. The noise level should also be controlled so that employees are not constantly hampered by loud or inappropriate noise. Another contributor to a healthful workplace is proper lighting; in today's age of computer screens and constant data analysis, lighting is even more important than in the 1940s, when the Westinghouse studies first identified inadequate lighting as a hindrance to productivity (Leavitt, 1958).

Privacy. Whenever possible, the privacy of the employee's workplace should be considered. While it is not essential for each employee to have a private office, it is a good business practice for the organization to provide the employee with an individual work space that will enhance concentration. This might be done by using partitions, or perhaps by rearranging furniture to provide the employee with a settled, private space. Such an arrangement both facilitates concentration and reduces interruptions.

Psychological Environmental Factors

There are several checkpoints that managers should examine regularly in order to provide their employees with the best possible psychological environment in which to work. Depending on specific needs and the nuances of the relationship a particular manager has with subordinates, these factors can be readily distributed in a manner that will reward employees for good performance.

High-Quality Co-Workers. As we have stated throughout this book, it is essential that a manager not only select and direct high-performance employees but also galvanize them into a cohesive team. The healthcare manager should therefore ensure that each employee hired is dedicated to the organization and will put forth maximum effort on a regular basis. By failing to do this, the manager both deters performance and sets the stage for a group loss of motivation. If employees are surrounded by co-workers who are not at least as motivated as they are, they will soon feel as though a lower level of performance is acceptable. They will also lose respect for the manager as well as for the organization. The combination of these two factors will result in slackness and, if allowed to continue, long-term unsatisfactory productivity. It is difficult for employees to feel that fair treatment is the norm if a marginal employee is given the same compensation and opportunities as an exemplary one.

By providing a solid performer with good co-workers, a healthcare line manager is giving the employee an important job benefit. As a member of a winning team, the employee has the opportunity to take pride in himself and his work unit. To take this concept one step further, it is possible to reward a stellar employee with the opportunity to select his co-workers on certain projects. This allows the employee to participate in decision making, as well as rewarding him with an opportunity to collaborate with a respected colleague who has a similar commitment to excellent work.

"The Big Picture." Each employee in a work unit should understand clearly the work unit's mission and how that mission fits into the overall organizational mission. By readily identifying with the organization's goals and objectives, and understanding precisely the relevance of their work role to the attainment of those objectives, employees feel that they are part of a successful enterprise. As Abraham Maslow (1971) determined generations ago, one of every person's critical needs is to become an integral member of a noted and respected social group. This need can be satisfied in the workplace when an employee identifies with and works toward a stated and respected organizational mission.

This feeling of belonging can be enhanced in healthcare organizations when the organization recognizes the achievements of its employees in the form of special company-related activities. Such activities might include the summer picnic, the holiday-season party, or any other activity in which the organization brings all of its members together in a somewhat informal setting and expresses its appreciation and gratitude for a collective job well done. This is not only a solid group motivator but a reinforcement of the perception that the employee is valued by the organization and has become, in essence, part of the family. As we all know, this type of activity is usually rated by employees on the amount of extravagance displayed and, in short, the amount of money spent by the organization. Furthermore, employees will often compare their company "bash" to those of their social peers at other organizations and draw a conclusion accordingly as to how much the organization really prizes its employees. In the course of our healthcare consulting activities, we have often heard that the best hospital or healthcare organization to work for is the one that knows how to "work hard and play hard," as evidenced by its performance as well as its social events for employees.

Recognition Rewards

The most readily apparent reward system, next to the omnipresent raise, is formal recognition of individual employees' performance. This system has many tangible benefits, since it demonstrates to employees that their service is valued and is recognized by management. Recognition reward systems take five basic forms.

Praise. The first form of recognition is simple praise, or positive feedback from the manager to the employee. The essential dimensions that the manager should specifically cite are the importance of the employee's doing a good job, the manager's appreciation of it, and the encouragement to continue to perform at an outstanding level. An important consideration is the timing of such praise. It should be extended immediately after the result of the effort is seen and crystallized for the employee so that the employee truly understands the appreciation being expressed.

Awards. Many organizations have a system of formal awards that are presented to deserving employees. These can take the form of an "employee of the month" designation, a citation within an individual department or work division, or perhaps a certificate of appreciation given by the administrator or other top member of the healthcare organization. These awards can be embellished by several forms of public recognition, such as a small article in a local newspaper concerning the "employee of the month," that can be conveyed to the employee's friends and neighbors.

Organizational Appreciation. Organizational appreciation can take the form of letters to the employee department heads, the administration, or any member of the organization besides the reporting supervisor that will express the value the organization places on the employee's performance. Apart from a formal award, this often takes the form of either a memo to the employee or a special meeting with a higher executive or member of the organization in which the employee is personally lauded for the contribution.

Work Unit Publicity. The employee can also be cited within the context of the work unit by the reporting supervisor. For example, in a weekly meeting the supervisor of the unit might single out a particular employee for stellar performance. By doing this in front of the employee's work unit peers, the reporting supervisor is not only rewarding the individual employee but encouraging the other employees to strive for the same high level of work. This type of informal publicity for the employee's efforts helps to encourage the employee to continue to set the example of high-quality output. It also gives the employee the additional "stroke" of being recognized by the person to whom good performance matters most—the reporting supervisor who, among other things, writes the employee's performance appraisal.

Special Activities. The final recognition reward might be a special activity in which the employee can represent the work group. This might be an organizational meeting, a professional workshop or meeting, or any other activity where the employee will function as the department's delegate. The manager in this case is indicating that good performance has merited the employee's selection as a group representative at an important meeting. This not only gives the employee another opportunity for further development but also expresses distinctly that the employee is important and considered a cut above the rest.

Job Task Rewards

The manager can employ several job task rewards that provide further positive motivation to the individual employee as well as reward the employee for solid past performance.

Assignment of New Duties. A stellar positive motivator is for a manager to relieve an employee who has performed at an outstanding level of a particular job task that she does not like and replace it with an activity that she will enjoy more and thus attack more vigorously.

Assignment of New Work Partners. The manager might on some occasions restructure the work unit so that the rewarded employee will now work with the work partners he prefers. Without disrupting the entire unit just to accommodate one employee, the manager should seek opportunities to reassign personnel so that people who truly enjoy working with each other will have that opportunity. If this opportunity is presented as a reward, the employees will be even more productive in the long run. This device must be tempered with the need to avoid showing any type of favoritism or special consideration; it must be strictly presented as a reward for solid performance.

Approval of Job-Related Requests. Another job task reward approach is for the manager to approve any pending job-related requests or changes. This might mean the utilization of a different system, use of a new work approach, or any other work-related activity that the employee has generated and considered to be an improvement on the status quo. The manager might advantageously delay approving certain job-related requests until after the performance appraisal in such a way that the employee perceives that approval as part of the reward for good performance.

Job-Responsibility Rewards. Within the context of the basic job responsibilities of a given position, the manager has several opportunities with which to reward the employee. One of these is the opportunity for more self-management. The manager, whenever possible, might reward an employee by giving her the opportunity to manage her position with less direct supervision. This can often be expressed in a statement such as ''Now that you seem to have the job down to an exact science, I'll give you a free rein in handling it.'' The manager will tell the employee that while he is always available to provide work direction, he will only do so when requested by the employee. By doing this, the manager is expressing a confidence that the employee can control her own activities and produce consistent, self-generated results. This also gives the employee the freedom to decide the best way to attack the job, as well as to try any new methods that may produce even greater results. This also makes the employee a more involved member of the decision-making process.

Management Participation. To supplement the increase of self-management on the part of a stellar employee, the manager might encourage the employee to participate more actively in the management of the department. He might, for example, make more frequent requests to the employee to provide input for decisions, and ask more frequently for suggestions and recommendations on how to attain departmental goals. He can ask an employee, for example, her opinion of different job activities, how and where priorities should be placed, and perhaps provide the employee with more information related to decision making. That is, the manager will seek to make the employee more involved not only in the decision making but in examining the data that go into making that decision.

Ancillary Financial Rewards. There are several financial rewards a manager can extend to an employee that are not part of the normal financial compensation package. These include:

- *Bonuses*—additional payments for annual goal or MBO attainment
- *Profit sharing*—stock or other ownership-type investment opportunities
- *Facility vouchers*—vouchers for such things as free lunches at the cafeteria
- *Free tickets*—such as previously donated ballgame tickets
- *Company donations*—company-paid donations in the employee's name to the employee's alma mater or favorite charity

In all of these cases, the feasibility of application depends on the various policies and regulations by which the manager and organization must abide. It is essential to remember in all of these approaches that the money is not as important to the employee as the gesture itself, which is very tangible and readily enjoyed by the employee.

Status Indicators. A manager can employ a range of status indicators within the work setting to reward a deserving employee. Among these are:

- *A larger work area,* with its connotation of increased importance
- *A promotion,* perhaps the most obvious and easily understood of rewards, and usually the most desirable from the employee's viewpoint
- *A more private work space,* which also conveys the increased importance of the employee's work contribution
- *Newer equipment,* which gives the employee the best resources possible for high-quality work output while demonstrating the organization's interest in his work and efforts
- *A marked parking space,* another facility-related reward that raises the status of the stellar employee above that of his peers
- *A new title,* which does not have to be as much of a promotion as a "position upgrade"; that is, a new title, a raise,

and some new responsibilities without a change in reporting supervisors

- *More information* about the organization's plans and "big-picture" events in the workplace
- *Longer breaks,* which for a hardworking employee are usually insurance against burnout and overwork
- *Flextime,* in which the employee can to some extent choose her own hours
- *Sick day conversion,* providing the employee with the opportunity to convert unused sick days into money or vacation days, neither of which affects compensation

In all of these cases, the manager must be sure that the reward does not generate resentment among the employee's peers, but rather that the other employees understand that stellar performance will bring special rewards. By intelligently applying these reward schemes, the manager can contribute to positive group motivation.

In the healthcare business arena, where each team member is usually integral to the success of the entire unit, it is particularly vital for the manager to make good use of reward systems in the effort to breed in employees a desire to do the best possible job every day. These rewards give the employee a number of proverbial carrots to pursue besides the paycheck and the satisfaction of being competent. Because substandard performance in healthcare can literally mean the difference between life and death, it is especially essential for the manager to utilize a creditable reward system, along with an equitable performance appraisal system, to elicit the very best efforts from the employees on each and every work shift.

Chapter 15

Comprehensive Case Study of Performance Evaluation

The following case study is provided so that the reader may further examine the practical application of the performance evaluation strategy explained in the preceding chapters. Based closely on a real situation at a client community hospital, the scenario is common in scope and solution to many situations encountered frequently by healthcare managers. By exploring the approach utilized by the manager portrayed in the case study, the reader can see the natural enhancement of productivity and management development produced by the effective employment of the performance assessment program described in this book. Managers should focus on the sequential implementation of the entire performance assessment process used by the case study's manager, and consider how best to employ the same strategy in maximizing their own assessment process.

Situation

Nancy McKay is the assistant administrator of Amboy Community Hospital, a 150-bed community hospital in rural northern New Jersey. As the assistant administrator in charge of operations and patient services, she has six managers reporting to her position. The hospital is located in an area renowned for its skiing in the winter and the output of its local tomato farms in the summer; it thus has a customer/patient base of transients during the snow season as well as a solid local populace throughout the year.

Although most of the six managerial positions subordinate to her have been filled by longtime, competent employees, Nancy has had a lot of turnover in one position, the manager of the hospital cafeteria and patient food services. This position has a total reporting staff of two supervisors and twenty-three hourly workers, and a significant operating budget; Figure 26 shows the organizational chart. As far as she can determine, the turnover results from the opportunities that exist for growth in larger institutional organizations in the area. For example, the most recent incumbent left the hospital to become director of food services for a large school district in another part of the state. After discussing the situation with Barry Micheals, the hospital administrator and her boss, she has decided to make the position eligible for bonuses, thus allowing for financial growth on the job according to merit. Furthermore, in reviewing previous food service managers, she has determined that both her predecessor and she herself hired people who had not previously been employed in the healthcare field. It is her contention that because these people did not know the hospital environment, they had inappropriate expectations for career development and future opportunities, particularly because Amboy Community is a relatively small institution that does not allow for tremendous long-term career growth. Therefore, Nancy will seek to fill the vacant position with someone who better understands the healthcare arena and will be satisfied with the bonus scheme and job enrichment possibilities.

The first thing Nancy does is to look at the internal candidates for the position, namely, Pete Fontana, the supervisor of patient food services, and Angela Morris, the cafeteria manager. After determining that the existing job description is valid, and adding to it the bonus scheme and the intention to use the performance appraisal process described in this book, Nancy considers both of these internal candidates. She begins by reviewing Pete's performance appraisal. Because he has only been in his job for one year, and the former food service manager did not critically complete his appraisal, Nancy has little to go on. She correctly feels that he should stay in his position for at least another year, after which she can consider his worth to the organization.

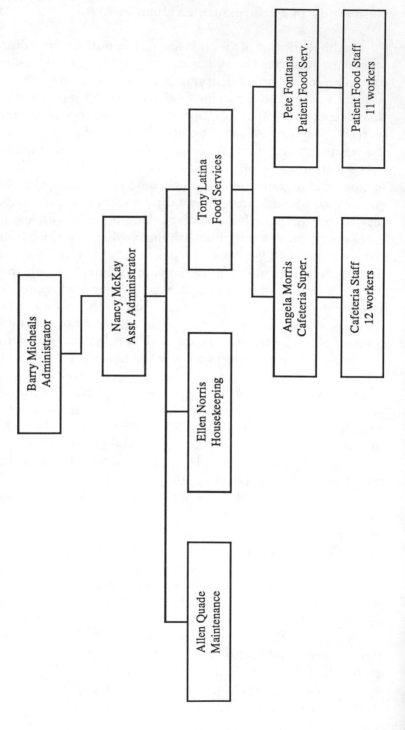

Figure 26. Amboy Community Hospital Organizational Chart.

In the case of Angela Morris, Nancy is looking at a supervisor who has performed well in her job for over eight years. She is personable but firm with her employees, demands high-quality work, and runs a cafeteria that is often complimented by staff and patients' visitors alike. She has terrific knowledge of the hospital and its specific dynamics and would be a good candidate for consideration.

A problem surfaces when Nancy meets with Angela to discuss her interest in the promotion—Angela is not interested. She prefers the nine-to-five nature of her cafeteria supervisory role; the shifting hours of the manager's position, Angela feels, might affect her home life with her three children. Furthermore, because she feels that she has her cafeteria responsibilities down to an exact science, she is not interested in taking on the demands of the managerial position. She expresses her appreciation for being considered.

Nancy realizes that it would be fruitful to include both Angela and Pete in the process of selecting a new manager from an outside source. She also believes that it would now be a good idea to utilize a goal-based performance assessment system with the two supervisors as well. In doing so, she can get true, meaningful evaluations from them as well as apply a bonus scheme that will reward long-term, well-placed employees like Angela and critically appraise relatively new employees like Pete.

Before Angela leaves the meeting, she tells Nancy of a young manager she met at a convention three months ago in Atlantic City. This manager, Tony Latina, is currently an assistant food service manager at Newark General Hospital, the largest hospital in the state. After graduating from a local high school, Tony attended Florida International University on a soccer scholarship and graduated with honors from its food services program. Since he graduated four years ago, he has worked at Newark General, receiving two promotions. Angela says he knows the hospital food business, knows the area, and is a nice guy to boot.

Nancy thanks Angela for her nomination of Mr. Latina and tells her she will consider it. She then begins a thorough selection process, using the precepts of Part Two of this book.

After determining that the job description is valid and complete, she develops a questioning strategy using her Quan-Com factors. She begins recruitment by placing an advertisement in two consecutive Sunday editions of the *New Jersey Times,* the statewide paper. This generates approximately fifty résumés, from which she selects seven for comprehensive interviews. Four candidates are interested enough to set appointments for interviews at Amboy Community, including Tony Latina, who responded to the advertisement with an impressive résumé and list of references.

Following the four interviews, Nancy has determined that Tony and one other person are the best possibilities for the position. Nancy asks Barry to interview both candidates; she also has Pete and Angela take Tony for a tour of the facility, during which they discuss their roles and staff. Nancy is inclined to hire Tony, because the other candidate, Bill Reynolds, has been in the field for eight years and might well outgrow the position quickly, which is the root of her turnover problem. This feeling is confirmed when Reynolds makes it abundantly clear that he wants several thousand dollars more per year than the advertised salary range. Therefore, with the support of her administrator and the two supervisors, Nancy extends the job offer to Tony Latina, who immediately accepts and agrees to start two weeks hence.

Setting Performance Standards

Because Nancy McKee has been in her position for over four years and during that time has had two different food service managers working for her, she has a fairly realistic idea of what is expected in the position. She also realizes that this position needs her specific attention at this time because of the turnover problem and because she also manages five other managers. Clearly it is essential to start her new food service manager off on the right track. With this in mind, she has taken the opportunity to sit down with Tony on his first day in the job and discuss a set of five objectives that he will have to achieve in his first year on the job. Nancy has constructed these objectives by applying the concept of MSF, and is presenting Tony with goals that will stretch his capabilities and talents to their productive limit while enhancing his confidence and encouraging his use of new approaches and technical applications.

Nancy has examined the work situation of the food service function in the past and determined that the first goal should be a remedial one that addresses an old problem. The problem is that the quality of the cafeteria food is consistently good, yet the quality of patient meals seems to fall on the weekend. From Monday to Friday, the food is very good; during the weekend, when visits are at a peak, patients seem to complain about the taste of the food. Knowing that Tony has special expertise in menu development and delivery, Nancy assigns as a first goal the general objective of ensuring that all meals are consistent in quality, nutritional value, and consumer appeal, and augments the presentation of this goal to Tony with an explanation of what has occurred in the past.

Nancy has assigned four more objectives based on the performance resource categories outlined in Chapter Ten of this book. In stating these objectives, she takes into account Tony's capabilities based on his experiential background as well as the potential she believes he can develop in the future. Time parameters are set for all these objectives, for the reasons described in Chapters Nine and Ten. Because Tony is new to the position, Nancy is setting a date three months hence to sit down with him and review progress, and to follow up again every three months until the yearly assessment. At that time, Nancy tells Tony, she would like him to submit five goals that he wants added to the objective scheme, and upon her approval these goals will be added to the bonus program along with the original five. She also impresses upon Tony the fact that the original five objectives will be reviewed and either kept in the program, adjusted, or discarded altogether.

While she has no specific expertise in the food service function, Nancy knows enough from her experience to give Tony some suggestions for accomplishing all of his goals. Regarding the first objective, standardizing the quality of all food service, she suggests that Tony look at the roster of people assigned to the weekend shifts as opposed to the weekday shifts in the kitchen and also check the timing of the food deliveries to see if situations in those areas might be having an effect.

Nancy's second objective is derived from both the job description and the human resources performance category for Tony's position. This objective is to determine the productivity of all the employees in his department by using the hospital's appraisal system, and to establish and maintain a high level of productivity among his staff. Although not a chronic problem, the fact that Tony's predecessor did not fill out a solid appraisal form on Pete Fontana indicates to Nancy that the entire department may not have been fully evaluated for some time. Furthermore, she realizes that the food service function is a people-intensive one, and thus wants to ensure that Tony is getting all he wants from his employees. The job market in the Amboy area is somewhat seasonal; many hourly employees work at local tomato farms in the summer and resorts in the winter for prosperous employment. Hourly workers who want a steady, non-seasonal, dependable employer that pays fair wages and offers good benefits are attracted to the hospital. Nancy explains to Tony that with this multiple job market there is no reason for him to have to accommodate marginal or unsatisfactory employees. She introduces Tony to Bernie Waters, the hospital's personnel manager, so that Tony can learn all about the employee assessment system, the hospital's recruiting process, and, if he so desires, conduct a review of existing employee files. Tony responds positively to this, and says that one of his first moves will be to learn as much as possible about the operation and staff from Pete and Angela.

The third goal Nancy establishes for Tony is to make the most of his available physical resources—for example, the full range of kitchen equipment and the delivery apparatus. Nancy encourages Tony to let her know what he thinks of the equipment and, if any changes are needed that are not covered in his budget, to inform her of that as well. She also tells Tony that the previous manager had asked for additional storage space, but did not use a storeroom with which she provided him. She specifically asks Tony to let her know at the three-month review if he really needs that space, because if not, she can assign it to housekeeping, which has a definite need for the room.

The fourth objective Nancy assigns Tony is the fundamental goal of advantageously utilizing all of his assigned financial resources. This includes the maximal use of every budget dollar and the proper planning and control of expenditures. Nancy explains to Tony that while the hospital is surviving, like many healthcare institutions in the state (and across the country, as she learned at a recent ACHE seminar) it does not have the fiscal resources of an oil sheik at its disposal. Tony says that at Newark General this was also the case. He also states that he feels that one of his strengths as a manager is to get the most from his budget dollars, and he will continue to apply frugality without compromising quality in this position. Nancy now presents Tony with a full budget sheet and explains all of its relevant points. Tony, who minored in finance and accounting at FIU, assures her he understands fully.

The fifth objective is one that Nancy has constructed with an eye to the immediate future. Because a children's hospital in the area is about to close, Amboy Community will soon be admitting more children to the facility. In fact, the hospital has recently converted an entire ward to pediatric use. Nancy charges Tony with a management project in which he should use the "I-Formula" discussed in Chapter Ten. Tony is familiar with the planning of a nutritious menu that children will especially like, since it was part of his internship project at Miami Memorial Hospital during college. In two weeks he presents Nancy with an "I-Formula" for the installation of a new children's menu, which appears below:

1. *Inspiration*—The need for a worthy children's menu that will be both nutritious and appealing to the influx of young patients.
2. *Identification*—Because of the generic nature of the current food service menu, a special effort must be made to construct a juvenile-oriented menu and food delivery system.
3. *Investigation*—Looking at the menu of the existing children's hospital is a start. I have also requested information from peers at institutions around the state that have good systems of this type.
4. *Ideal*—A good food system that the kids like and their par-

ents have confidence in and that also meets fully the directions of their attendant physicians.

5. *Idea*—The initial approach will be to create a menu of items children enjoy (such as hamburgers, spaghetti, and hot dogs) while (a) using nutritious ingredients and (b) presenting items in a festive, appealing fashion, like the fast-food joints.

6. *Innovation*—The first menu consists of three separate "WonderMeals," all of which are balanced and highly nutritious.

7. *Implementation*—Try out the "WonderMeals," with physicians' clearance, on some of the less critical juvenile patients (such as those with tonsillitis).

8. *Illumination*—Check the effect of the "WonderMeals" on (a) the children, (b) their physicians, (c) our staff (for preparation considerations), (d) the children's parents.

9. *Ignition*—Make the results of the "WonderMeals" launch known to all concerned in the hospital hierarchy, including rave reviews from the patient (the consumer), the physician (the technical reviewer), and the child's parents (the paying customers).

10. *Introduction*—Following the positive results of the test and subsequent support, seek to increase the "WonderMeals" menu to a standard seven-day, full-range menu program.

11. *Impetus*—Continue to collect positive feedback about the program and present it during the yearly managerial review to the board of directors. Also, try to present an overview of the program at the annual meeting of the New Jersey Dietary Managers Convention in Asbury Park next July.

12. *Importance*—Comprehensively demonstrate that the "WonderMeals" program is vital to the competent service provided to the child patients of Amboy Community.

    (a) *Intensity*—Show the program as a total package of significant patient nutrition specifically tailored for the child patient.

    (b) *Imperative*—Enlist the unqualified support of the physician group and the administration for its continuation.

    (c) *Intrigue*—Continue to enhance the "Star Wars" type

of packaging, the quality of the contents, and the creativity of meal construction and nutritional components.

Installation of the "WonderMeals" scheme will be reached upon successful accomplishment of all of the above steps.

After quickly summing up the five goals, Nancy presents Tony with a copy of them typed on a performance appraisal form. She stresses to Tony her confidence in him, restates the need to follow up on progress in three months, and asks him if he has any questions. Tony asks only if Nancy has any set priority for accomplishing these goals. Nancy replies that they are all equally important at this time, but that at subsequent meetings their priority might shift according to the conditions. Tony thanks her again for hiring him, and begins his first week at Amboy Community Hospital.

Monitoring and Measuring Performance

After reviewing Tony's goals and objectives with him and receiving his managerial performance plan for the children's meal program, Nancy McKay turns her attention to the monitoring and measuring of Tony's performance in the job. Using the tenets of Chapter Eleven of this book, she will assess his performance by examining quantitative and qualitative indicators, as well as his supervisory abilities as they pertain to his role as the food service department manager.

Quantitative Performance Indicators. Because the work of Tony and his department involves many situations that can be charted by numbers, Nancy has decided to use all of the critical quantitative indicators, starting with monthly reports, which she requires from all six of her managers. She requires Tony to submit the total number meals served during the month, an update of his budget expenditures, and any other significant information about the food service segment of the hospital's operations. She examines these numbers in relation to the hospital's overall census and notes that there are no major trends developing.

She notes that Tony is spending more money on equipment repair and maintenance than his predecessor, and questions Tony about this at the three-month review. Tony responds that much of the equipment is on its last legs and was not well maintained prior to his arrival. He mentions two employees, Kenny Stiles and Milton Guest, who are particularly adept at maintaining the equipment and know how to repair the refrigeration unit. If they were sent to the supplier's regular seminars on maintenance, he says, their acquired proficiency would decrease maintenance costs. Nancy encourages him to send the employees to the seminars, and tells him to let her know if he sees any more opportunities to cut operating costs.

The next category for inspection is unit performance, where Nancy must determine how Tony affects the performance of the food service department as a whole. Because he is the supervisor, his impact as a manager will be evaluated more clearly within the parameters of his supervisory performance indicators. Also, since the food service department was relatively solid in its past performance, it would be difficult to ascertain any major impact from a new employee. As a comparison, Nancy remembers that when she hired Allen Quade to be her maintenance manager, the level of performance for that previously disastrous work unit showed tremendous improvement in just two months, increasing as Quade effected necessary turnover of poor employees for skilled, motivated new hires.

The third category for quantitative consideration is goal attainment. After three months, it is apparent that Tony is well on his way to achieving all five of his initial goals. He has revamped the work schedule of his patient food services staff so that the senior members are working on the weekends more than before. While there was some initial griping, he assured the employees that once the normal weekend staff had been better trained (primarily through working with the seasoned crew), the schedule would demand less of their weekend time. Tony also found that by changing the delivery schedules of some of his suppliers, he was able to have fresher foodstuffs with which to compose his weekend meals. As a result of these two approaches, complaints about the weekend patient cuisine have already been reduced.

Tony is making definite progress toward his other goals. He has gotten Pete and Angela to use a goal system with their employees and has enrolled both in the hospital's upcoming performance appraisal seminar. As the equipment-maintenance episode shows, he is exploring cost-saving methods of using the equipment. He has not, however, decided fully about using the extra storeroom that Nancy told him about; this decision will come in the next few weeks. He is moving along rapidly on his fifth goal, the "WonderMeals" program. The initial offerings of "AstroBurgers," "Galaxy Dogs," and "Space-ghetti" are cleverly packaged, nutritionally excellent, and a big hit with the kids. Nancy compliments him on this and encourages him to take it to its "interplanetary limit."

In respect to his fourth goal, the cost-effectiveness of his operation, Nancy uses the fourth and final category of the quantitative performance indicators. Again, Tony is right on target; in fact, his cost-effectiveness to date is likely to bring him under budget for the year. Nancy tells him that while his frugality is good, he should not deprive himself or his department of anything they need. Tony states that he has not done so, but he will keep that thought in mind. In fact, he might replace some minor pieces of equipment later in the yearly cycle, which will exhaust his remaining budget dollars. Nancy has also determined that Tony has eliminated a minor problem with food waste, and expresses her approval of his efforts in this regard. As time progresses and the yearly appraisal approaches, there is little change in any of these quantitative indicators.

Qualitative Performance Indicators

Nancy McKee has decided, on the basis of the quantitative performance indicators, that hiring Tony Latina was probably a smart move. However, she also realizes that the quantitative aspects of assessment do not tell the complete story. She therefore keeps a manager's log on all of her supervisors, in which she records any important personal observations about her managers' qualitative performance. She makes observations and notations as events occur and reviews these observations on a monthly basis. After combining their content with the other two categorical indicators, she is able to complete assessment fully at each quarterly interval and in the annual assessment.

Nancy's personal observations focus on the managers' application of the Quan-Com characteristics in their jobs. Because of the nature of their positions, Nancy closely monitors her charges for behavioral clues in the categories of attitude orientation, people skills, managerial aptitude, and team orientation. She notes the incident or behavior, whether it is positive or negative in its effect on the job, and to which Quan-Com characeristic or objective it might be relevant. She also takes into account any organizational input that she receives concerning the managers' performance, as well as detailing any significant incidents and their relevance to the job. Nancy keeps this log current throughout the entire yearly grading period, monitoring the qualitative performance categories of personal observation, Quan-Com characteristics, organizational input, and significant incidents comprehensively. Nancy can thus provide her managers with a performance assessment that takes into account the "big picture" of their performance. The evidence in the notebook also provides data on the quantitative performance indicators, particularly goal attainment, as well as data on supervisory performance characteristics. Exhibit 1 shows all the notations Nancy McKee has made during the first year of Tony Latina's employment at Amboy Community.

Exhibit 1: Nancy McKee's
Managerial Logbook Notes on Tony Latina

9/1/85—T.L. starts position. Receives five goals on appraisal form.

9/17/85—T.L. submits first draft of "I-Formula" on children's meals for review. + Creativity, Aggressiveness, Energy Level, Goal 5.

9/31/85—Overhear T.L. tell Guest and Stiles that "the kitchen equipment is garbage." I counsel T.L. to bring his complaints to me for resolution, as opposed to discouraging employees, and to take positive action. – Ind. Judg., Goal 3.

10/4/85—T.L. meets with Bernie Waters (Mgr.

Per.) and begins to implement review system for employees using Angela Morris and Pete Fontana. + Emp.Rel., Goal 2.

10/9/85—Cafeteria introduces new "lite sandwich" menu, which is a big hit with employees and patient visitors. + Creativity, Aggress., Goal 1.

10/31/85—T.L. and staff decorate cafeteria for Halloween and put appropriate "special touches" on patient meals. + Employee Relations, Creativity, Supervisory Skills, Goal 1.

11/12/85—T.L. sends Guest and Stiles to equipment supplier; also purchases equipment maintenance manuals for members of staff. Has Guest and Stiles demonstrate what they learned to all members of kitchen staff, which will save maintenance dollars. + Tech. Exp., Team Orientation, Overall Supervisory Skills, Goals 2 & 4.

11/12/85—T.L. repeats success of Halloween presentation with Thanksgiving programs in both cafeteria and patient services. Other asst. administrators all compliment his efforts to date to me. + Overall Quan-Coms and Goals, Organizational Input and Supervisory Skills.

12/2/85—Conduct three-month review. All positive, but want resolution on large storeroom issue. Also encourage T.L. to temper frugality w/quality. Overall good evaluation and direction for next quarter and rest of year.

12/18/85—T.L. and staff present excellent meal at Xmas party. T.L. gets a little "tipsy" and too "friendly" with local pals attending from community. + Goal 1, – Ind. Judg., Org. Respblty.

12/29/85—T.L. puts staff on rotation for weekend patient food service, as he promised, thus relieving tenured members. + Planning and Delegation, as he now puts Fontana in complete charge of project after helping him get shifts started and resolve quality problems. Goal 1 accomplished to date.

2/6/86—Hear T.L. tell two employees that hospital's

United Way campaign is a "bunch of B.S." and he "ain't giving a dime." Counsel him on setting the right example and to keep such opinions to himself. – Loyalty, Org. Respblty.

3/1/86—T.L. take his two supervisors to Atlantic City for annual convention; conduct a positive review upon his return. He has used the storeroom for supplies needed for "WonderMeals" installation and fiscal line looks good. Encourage him to watch his comments to employees, but emphasize approval of all other job performance.

4/19/86—T.L. terminates, with proper documentation and my approval, Kate Cassell and Larry Bates, two proven "wiseguys" and marginal performers. Has both supervisors participate in the termination procedures from start to finish. + Mgr. Aptitude, Goal 2, Delegation, Aggressiveness.

4/28/86—Using T.L.'s guidance and the skills learned at the hospital's human resources management seminar, Angela Morris and Pete Fontana hire seemingly solid replacements for the departed Cassell and Bates. + Delegation, Mgr. Aptitude, Employee Relations, and Goal 2.

5/8/86—Brenda Lane, a shy but competent cafeteria worker, tells Angela Morris that T.L. told her that "you could be standing in line behind Cassell and Bates at the unemployment line if you mess up." Tell T.L. the perils of employee terrorism; he says he was having a bad day, and apologizes to A.M. for interfering with her employee, and then to Lane with A.M. present. +/– Ind. Judg., +/– Emp.Rel, +/– Delegation/Spvsy. Skills.

5/30/86—In preparation for T.L.'s third quarterly review, look specifically at quantitative indicators (goals on target, unit performance high, all monthly numbers strong, cost-effectiveness excellent, particularly considering the "WonderMeals" program, which cost little extra money), qualitative indicators (all good except occasional immature managerial and independent judgment) and supervisory skills (for the most part, again satisfactory).

6/2/86—Conduct review and present my side. Remind T.L. that at the 9/2/86 yearly review we will go into more depth and will ask for new goals and objectives from him.

6/18/86—T.L. gives full presentation to Amboy Community administration and board on "WonderMeals"; excellent job! + All people skills, Goal 5 accomplished, + Org. Respblty.

8/13/86—All of T.L.'s charges have had the opportunity to go on vacation during summer; no lapses of work quality evident. Goal 1, + all Mgr. and Supervisory qual., + Team Orientation.

8/19/86—During my yearly review, Barry cites Latina's contributions as part of my performance, particularly the good quality of patient food, apparently fresher food in the cafeteria, and the success of "WonderMeals." He reminds me that T.L.'s review should "stretch" him sufficiently for the next year, as well as reward him for this year.

8/29/86—Prepare for T.L.'s annual review; look at all numbers, monthly reports, goal attainment, fical expenditures, organizational input letters and memos, and last but not least, all of the contents of this logbook from 9/1/85 to date.

Supervisory Performance Indicators

The supervisory performance indicators, described in detail in Chapter Eleven, are particularly important in the case of Tony Latina. Because he is responsible for twenty-three workers and two supervisors, the managerial aspect of his work role is vital to his success, and, in a sense, is probably the most important. From a developmental standpoint, Nancy must keep close watch on the emergence of Tony's supervisory talents, since at his previous position at Newark General he did not have as challenging a managerial responsibility as he currently has at Amboy Community. Nancy must look closely at all four of the supervisory performance indicators.

She begins with basic supervisory skills, which describe Latina's ability to manage his fiscal, human, and physical resources effectively for the benefit of his department and, of course, the entire hospital. As a checklist, Nancy uses the five-question process outlined in the discussion of basic supervisory skills in Chapter Eleven. She then looks at Tony's technical acumen: his knowledge of food preparation, food delivery systems, equipment usage, and all other relevant technical aspects of food service. Next, Nancy explores Tony's abilities in attending to his organizational responsibilities, evidenced by the quality of his dealings with other professionals in the hospital who need his input and by his behavior as a creditable representative of the organization in public, whether at local gatherings or professional meetings. Finally, Nancy must look at the fourth supervisory performance indicator, fiscal responsibility, and consider whether Tony is taking care of all of the financial aspects of his managerial role, including budget expenditures, payroll administration, and cost containment of supply resources.

Like the first two categories of performance indicators, the supervisory indicators will provide Nancy with data essential to a performance assessment that is complete in scope and significant in detail. In the case of the managerial employee, such as Tony, it is important to pay particular attention to the supervisory category, since it deals with the potential and growth of the novice manager, an important human resource of the organization.

Conducting the Review Session

Nancy McKee now begins the final stage of Tony Latina's first-year performance assessment cycle, the actual composition and delivery of Tony's annual performance appraisal. She must first collect her thoughts and review all of her notes and supporting material in order to fill out the appraisal form. Then, having scheduled the appraisal and prepared the form, she conducts the review according to the five-part format delineated in Chapter Twelve.

Nancy opens the review by giving Tony an overview of the appraisal and telling him that this hour will be spent summarizing all of the significant performance activities of the past year as well as planning the activities of the coming year. Because this is Tony's first formal yearly review, she explains the form and its mechanics entirely, and emphasizes the need for his constructive input. Because Tony has implemented the system with his two supervisors, he has a good grasp of the form's workings. Also, since the two have met for regular quarterly reviews, he knows what to expect and has prepared his input and list of new goals ahead of time. Because Nancy has used the "Day 1" approach to the process, monitoring Tony's performance from his first day on the job, there will be no big surprises or arguments in this particular appraisal.

Next, Nancy presents Tony with a review of the past year's goal attainment, starting with a general review of the job description and focusing on the five objectives that were established for the past year. This part of the discussion includes the submission of Tony's new goals for the coming year. The next phase of the discussion assesses the interpersonal facet of Tony's job as food services manager, utilizing primarily the Quan-Com formula.

The fourth phase of the appraisal covers the developmental direction set by Nancy for Tony's completion in the next year. This includes anywhere from three to five activities that will enhance Tony's professional development from a technical or managerial perspective. Finally, the two come to a consensus on the appraisal's overall ratings as well as the future direction, represented in the next year's goals and objectives. Because Tony has proven to be a good addition to the staff and has received timely, meaningful feedback from Nancy throughout the course of the year, there are few objections on his part and an overall agreement on the content of the appraisal. However, if Nancy were faced with a marginal employee who had strong objections to the appraisal content, she could utilize the defusers described in Chapter Twelve to handle negative reactions.

Exhibit 2 shows the complete evaluation given to Tony Latina by Nancy McKee, using the form described in Chapter Twelve and completely illustrated in Resource G. Nancy uses the three-level (1, 2, and 3 or −, ✔, and +) system to indicate marginal, satisfactory, or outstanding performance in each aspect, as well as in the overall rating of Tony's performance.

Exhibit 2: Tony Latina's
Performance Appraisal from Nancy McKee

Part 1—Administrative Data

a. Date of Appraisal—9/2/86, first anniversary of hiring date
b. Name of Employee and I.D. number—Anthony R. Latina, Empl. I.D.# 324-50-4718
c. Work Position—Manager, Hospital Food Services Department
d. Department Designation—Food Services Department
e. Supervisor's Name—Nancy D. McKee, Empl. I.D.# 254-89-7650
f. Start Date—9/1/85
g. Date in Current Position—9/1/85
h. Appraisal Occasion—Annual Review Date

Part 2—Job Description

The manager of the food services department is comprehensively responsible for all of the food services provided by the hospital cafeteria and the patient food services function. The manager shall be responsible for all personnel management, equipment usage, and fiscal responsibility in this regard. The manager shall ensure that the food provided is of the highest nutritional and esthetic quality possible, and fully supports the medical and humanistic mission of Amboy Community Hospital. The manager shall expand and augment services as needed, and effect any programs necessary to comprehensively support the patient and visitor services accorded by the hospital, as well as providing the nutritional support of its employees.

[*Both Nancy and Tony have decided at the yearly appraisal that the job description is relatively current and accurately reflects the overall mission and purpose of Tony's work position, as well as the general intent of his department.*]

Part 3—Goals and Objectives

1. Maintain consistency of meal quality, nutritional value, and consumer appeal, with a special emphasis on correcting the problem of inconsistent patient meals. [*Nancy has decided, based on her monitoring of this problem, that Tony has adequately resolved this inconsistency. His restructuring of the shifts and rescheduling of food deliveries was the key to the solution. However, this solution was suggested by Nancy herself, so she scores this goal attainment as a satisfactory or* ✔.]

2. Determine the quality of existing human resources and maintain a managerial program to get the maximum organizational benefit from their employment. [*This was also accomplished fairly well in Nancy's estimation. She cites as support for this opinion Tony's use of technical training for his people, the Bates and Cassell terminations and replacements, and the development of Morris and Fontana, which Tony initiated at her suggestion. In the overall scheme, the situation with Brenda Lane is not all that significant, since it was corrected quickly by Tony. Again, Tony rates a satisfactory or* ✔ *rating. He will be provided with more human resource goals for the next year-long grading period, as we will see.*]

3. Make optimum use of physical resources, with a specific proviso to check all existing equipment and to employ the large storeroom or relinquish it to another department. [*Because Tony used the storeroom for longer than was expected for the "WonderMeals" program, this objective was not met in time. Overall, however, this was balanced by Tony's solid use of the equipment*

and by the equipment training and preventive maintenance program he has installed. Again, he receives a satisfactory or ✓ rating.]

4. Advantageously utilize all assigned financial resources. [*Tony met this goal by using the initial excess in his budget toward the development of the "WonderMeals" program. Tony's statement at their initial meeting about possessing financial savvy was further validated by his ability to use his available monies to install the new "lite sandwich" menu at the cafeteria, for which he also used the experience of Angela Morris. Although tempted to give Tony an outstanding rating, Nancy correctly realizes that while he met her expectations, he did not particularly exceed them. Hence, another satisfactory or ✓ rating is given.*]

5. Execute a management project for a children's menu, an objective that all the evidence indicates has been met outstandingly. [*By following the "I-Formula" and aggressively pursuing a solid plan of action, Tony indeed exceeded Nancy's expectations regarding this goal. He has established a program that not only meets the need but actually serves as a model for creative excellence in children's food service, as supported by the opinion of everyone from the administration on down. Nancy rightly gives Tony an outstanding or + rating.*]

[*After reviewing these five general goals and agreeing that they should remain objectives for next year after some modification, Nancy asks Tony if he has goals he wants to add. The two review seven suggestions from Tony and agree to add five of the suggestions as objectives for the next year. A total of ten goals for the next year are thus established and placed in the goals section of a new appraisal form for the next grading period. This also takes care of the fifth requirement of a good appraisal form, the adjustment of objectives and goals in accord with business changes. Tony Latina's goals and objectives for the next grading period (9/86–9/87) are determined and agreed on by Nancy and himself.*]

1. Maintain consistency of all food services.
2. Maintain a maximally effective human resources program.
3. Make optimum use of available physical resources.
4. Advantageously budget and utilize all fiscal resources.
5. Maintain the high quality of the "Wonder-Meals" program.
6. Create and implement a technical cross-training program, which will allow for the exchange of knowledge between hourly employees of both work sectins. This will help in shift assignment and "cross-fertilization" of job knowledge and technical acumen.
7. Implement a stellar vending machine service in the cafeteria, so night-shift employees and emergency room personnel and visitors can obtain nutritional essentials when the hospital cafeteria is closed.
8. Install a supervisory development system by making training available to Angela Morris and Pete Fontana, as well as by designating Kenny Stiles and Milton Guest as team leaders on their respective shifts, thus grooming them for promotion to supervisory roles.
9. Replace the antiquated refrigeration system, which is beyond reasonable repair. This will involve an "I-Formula" approach and more technical training for the workers upon installation. Tony will budget for this accordingly and have the new system in place by 6/87.
10. Designate a quality control team in both work sections, with a rotating membership of four workers. Each group of four will be on the quality control team for three months, during which time it will make monthly suggestions to Tony and his two supervisors about improving quality and any other pertinent suggestions.

Because all of these goals have direct relevance to Tony's job and will give him the MSF (Maximum Stretch Factor) Nancy feels he needs, they are approved and put into motion for the following year's accomplishment.

Part 4—Characteristic Ratings

Using the Quan-Com formula and evidence from the past year, Nancy follows the instructions of the performance appraisal form and selects only the characteristics that have critical negative or positive applications to Tony's performance. She has selected the following three:

(a) Creativity. Tony's approach to all assignments, notably "WonderMeals" and the technical training programs on kitchen equipment, support a rating of outstanding or + in this characteristic.

(b) Employee Relations. The heightened effectiveness of existing employees, the positive development of the two supervisors and Stiles and Guest, and the replacement of two negative people had the overall effect of maximizing motivation and human resources productivity, meriting an outstanding or + rating.

(c) Independent Judgment. The Lane incident, the Xmas party joviality, the United Way comments, and the equipment criticisms all indicate that Tony's employee relations program sometimes is harmed by lapses in good independent judgment. Although they are primarily a result of inexperience, managerial immaturity, and being a little too far to the + side of his employee relations bell curve (see Chapter Three), the problem must be cited for correction with a negative or − rating.

Part 5—Objective and Goal Adjustment

This was adequately addressed with the establishment of Tony's ten new goals.

By following the guidelines described in Chapter Thirteen, Nancy is able to complete the rest of the performance appraisal form and provide Tony with the developmental direction he needs to make the next grading period a fruitful one.

Part 6—Development Plan

Nancy has identified four activities for Tony to undertake in the next year's grading period to maximize his development:

1. Attend a professional seminar, in this case one that Nancy will allow Tony to choose. Since he is the technical expert, and also because he merits a reward for his solid first year's performance, she is allowing him to select a program that will help enhance his technical competence. Tony expresses his appreciation for this, and has in mind a course at New York's renowned School of Culinary Arts, which will provide him with some fresh perspectives on original menu items.

2. Attend a managerial seminar, which in this case is one that Nancy has selected. The program is called "Maximizing Managerial Performance" and is sponsored by the American College of Healthcare Executives. This program will help Tony better understand how to maximize his staff's productivity and give him some insight into his managerial style and approach.

3. Pursue a continuing education course, in this case one that Nancy has selected. She has determined that the local four-year college, Centenary College of New Jersey, has an excellent management development course. Tony will be able to get new ideas on managerial processes and time management skills both from the course material and from his fellow students, who are managers and supervisors in other industries.

4. Assume the duties of the assistant administrator

of operations for two weeks, namely, the two weeks in November when Nancy and her husband, Frank, take their annual vacation to San Francisco. This will give Tony an idea of what his next promotional position might be and help him decide if he is interested or if Nancy should continue a course of adding job enrichment and expansion to his current work role. Of course, during that two weeks he will not have to make any decisions that are outside his understanding of the position, and he will have been well briefed ahead of time by Nancy.

Part 7—Employee Comments
    Tony's only comments on the appraisal form are "fair and complete review; I understand my future goals."

Part 8—Overall Rating
    Because Amboy Community utilizes a bonus scheme, Tony receives a 5 percent bonus, the maximum amount for which he was eligible. He is given a rating on the overall line slightly to the positive side of satisfactory.

Part 9—Signatures
    Both Tony and Nancy sign the appraisal form, as does Barry Micheals, since the hospital uses a "one-over-one" approval system (discussed in Chapter Twelve).

Both Nancy and Tony leave the session pleased with the appraisal; thanks to Nancy's competent use of the comprehensive performance assessment process, past performance has been accurately assessed and future direction is effectively charted. By using the approach advocated and described in detail throughout Part Three of this book, readers can enjoy similar success in their performance appraisal process.

Results of a
National Survey of
Patient Needs and Desires

CHR/InterVista conducted an environmental survey of five regions of the United States in order to determine common customer/patient needs and desires in healthcare. The following data are a recapitulation of the results of that survey.

The reader can see readily from the survey results the high premium that the average customer/patient places on the interpersonal dynamics attached to the delivery of healthcare. Also apparent is the correlation between the perception of excellence in healthcare service and the presence of these interpersonal dynamics.

Study Objectives

Hospital bed occupants and those of us who visit a friend or family member are no longer "just patients" or strangers in healthcare institutions. We are all consumers of hospital services and, with today's high cost of medical care, should be treated properly. This statement reflects the reason and purpose behind the O'Connor Hospital Survey Project. The principle objective of this survey is to determine what people's expectations may be in respect to hospital service and personnel in today's healthcare institutions.

The survey is an important part in the assembly of the CHR/InterVista Market Survey Profile System. Each company and industry has its own hiring criteria based on industry characteristics, performance standards, established job criteria, and other pertinent factors. All of these characteristics constitute the data base for formulating the Quan-Com System. The survey provides the consumer expectation information used in the total data base.

Methodology

The surveys were distributed to a random sample of 500 adults ranging in age from eighteen to well over sixty-five in five geographical regions across the United States. The precise geographical breakdown is as follows:

Region	Number of surveys distributed	Number of surveys collected	Response rate
New England	100	100	100%
Southern Calif.	100	97	97%
New York State	100	76	76%
Midwest	100	99	99%
Central U.S.	100	98	98%
Total	500	470	94%

Although a small percentage of the surveys were distributed by mail, the majority of the surveys were directly handed to the respondents and personally collected by a member of the survey team at a later date. This is the main contributing factor to the high (94 percent) response rate.

All surveys were completed and returned between March 2 and April 30, 1984.

The sampling error for the total sample size is estimated at less than 5.0 percent.

Table 1 shows the frame of reference the national customer/patient utilizes when considering healthcare services. The table illustrates the experiences the respondents have had in acquiring healthcare services, the factors they consider in making a decision, and their basic perceptions of healthcare services.

Table 1. Experience and Perceptions
of Healthcare Services, by Region.

Survey Question	Total	New England	Southern Calif.	New York	Midwest	Central U.S.
1. What was your most recent experience in a hospital?						
Short-term patient	22.3%	18.0%	23.2%	28.9%	26.5%	13.1%
Long-term patient	11.8	4.0	6.1	12.4	22.4	14.5
Emergency/Minor care	21.0	22.0	18.2	20.6	15.3	30.3
Visiting friend/family	38.2	42.0	47.5	30.9	34.7	35.5
Other	6.7	14.0	5.0	7.2	1.1	6.6
2. Which of the following factors is most important in selecting a hospital?						
Close to home/ Convenient	23.8	30.0	24.2	19.8	25.0	17.3
Been there before	4.3	4.0	5.0	5.2	4.2	2.7
Doctor affiliation	43.5	36.0	37.4	46.9	50.0	49.3
Religious affiliation	1.1	—	4.0	—	1.0	—
Hospital reputation	24.2	28.0	22.2	24.0	19.8	28.0
Other	3.1	2.0	7.2	4.1	—	2.7
3. During the past few years, do you think personal healthcare and service have increased, stayed the same, or decreased?						
Increased	20.7	26.0	16.2	16.7	24.0	21.0
Stayed the same	34.6	42.0	29.3	35.4	35.4	30.3
Decreased	22.4	14.0	20.2	30.2	28.1	19.7
Don't know	22.3	18.0	34.3	17.7	12.5	29.0
4. Do you agree or disagree that personal attention provided to patients is an important part of medical treatment?						
Agree	97.6	96.0	98.0	99.0	99.0	96.0
Disagree	1.7	4.0	1.0	1.0	1.0	3.0
Don't know	0.7	—	1.0	—	—	1.0

Table 1. Experience and Perceptions
of Healthcare Services, by Region, Cont'd.

Survey Question	Total	New England	Southern Calif.	New York	Midwest	Central U.S.
5. Do you agree or disagree with the idea that "Today's hospital personnel are unable to adjust to unique patient situations. They treat each patient in the same manner and sometimes fail to understand that we are all different"?						
Agree	41.2%	42.0%	37.4%	57.3%	33.0%	35.5%
Disagree	33.7	34.0	37.4	16.7	40.0	42.1
Don't know	25.1	24.0	25.2	26.0	27.0	22.4

Table 2 shows the importance survey participants attach to each of eleven common healthcare organizational traits, rated on a scale from 1 (lowest) to 5 (highest).

Table 2. Importance of Eleven Common Healthcare
Employee and Organizational Traits, by Region.

Trait	Scale	Total	New England	Southern Calif.	New York	Midwest	Central U.S.
1. Friendly	1	0.4%	—	—	1.0%	—	1.3%
	2	8.3	10.2%	7.1%	12.4	4.1%	8.0
	3	47.2	47.0	43.4	60.0	48.0	34.7
	4	34.4	32.6	37.4	23.6	31.6	50.7
	5	9.7	10.2	12.1	3.0	16.3	5.3
2. Shows concerns	1	1.1	—	2.0	1.0	1.0	1.3
for patients	2	10.9	10.2	10.1	21.6	6.2	5.3
	3	44.4	40.8	44.4	48.4	45.4	42.1
	4	34.1	40.8	34.3	22.7	34.0	40.8
	5	9.5	8.2	9.2	6.3	13.4	10.5
3. Provides	1	10.0	10.2	5.0	10.3	12.4	13.1
prompt service	2	29.7	22.4	29.3	37.1	31.9	27.7
	3	37.6	42.9	38.3	36.1	35.0	34.2
	4	17.9	24.5	23.2	10.3	13.4	18.4
	5	4.8	—	4.2	6.2	7.3	6.6

Table 2. Importance of Eleven Common Healthcare Employee and Organizational Traits, by Region, Cont'd.

Trait	Scale	Total	New England	Southern Calif.	New York	Midwest	Central U.S.
4. Listens to	1	5.2%	9.2%	6.2%	6.2%	4.2%	5.3%
patients	2	19.3	20.8	21.6	19.6	15.8	18.4
	3	50.6	52.1	51.5	52.6	48.4	47.4
	4	19.2	22.9	10.3	17.5	23.2	23.7
	5	5.7	—	10.4	4.1	8.4	5.2
5. Hardworking	1	1.9	2.0	—	3.1	4.1	—
employees	2	8.3	12.2	6.1	10.3	6.2	6.6
	3	37.8	28.6	40.4	46.4	27.8	6.7
	4	40.5	47.0	38.4	33.0	42.3	42.7
	5	13.5	10.2	15.1	7.2	19.6	16.0
6. Honest	1	1.9	2.1	3.1	3.1	—	1.3
	2	6.9	8.3	11.2	8.3	2.1	4.0
	3	34.6	31.2	35.7	51.0	24.7	28.4
	4	42.2	48.0	37.7	30.2	49.5	47.3
	5	14.4	10.4	12.3	7.4	23.7	19.0
7. Cost-conscious	1	15.7	18.7	23.7	18.9	3.1	12.0
	2	35.1	25.0	37.1	47.4	35.8	29.3
	3	34.4	37.5	25.8	25.3	43.1	42.7
	4	9.1	12.5	9.3	5.3	11.6	6.7
	5	5.7	6.3	4.1	3.1	6.4	9.3
8. Good job	1	3.2	4.1	3.0	1.0	3.1	5.3
communicating	2	20.8	20.4	22.2	28.1	19.6	11.8
with patients	3	49.2	53.1	46.5	59.4	44.3	40.8
	4	21.4	20.4	19.2	10.4	26.8	32.9
	5	5.4	2.0	9.1	1.1	6.2	9.2
9. Helpful	1	0.6	—	1.0	1.0	1.0	—
	2	10.3	8.2	12.1	13.5	5.1	13.3
	3	43.8	42.9	38.4	55.2	47.4	32.0
	4	34.8	42.9	35.3	27.1	30.9	38.7
	5	10.5	6.0	13.2	3.2	15.6	16.0
10. Courteous	1	1.9	2.0	3.0	2.1	1.0	1.2
	2	11.5	12.2	11.1	18.5	6.2	9.2
	3	37.4	34.7	36.4	46.4	36.1	31.6
	4	39.1	44.9	38.4	27.8	40.2	46.0
	5	10.0	6.2	11.1	5.2	16.5	12.0

Table 2. Importance of Eleven Common Healthcare
Employee and Organizational Traits, by Region, Cont'd.

Trait	Scale	Total	New England	Southern Calif.	New York	Midwest	Central U.S.
11. Appearance	1	1.1%	2.0%	2.0%	1.0%	—	—
	2	4.3	6.1	3.0	5.1	1.0%	6.7%
	3	28.5	24.5	31.3	43.3	10.4	33.3
	4	47.6	53.0	46.4	42.3	51.0	45.3
	5	18.5	14.4	17.3	8.3	37.6	14.7

Tables 3, 4, and 5 indicate which three of the eleven common organizational traits the respondents felt were the most important.

Table 3. Most Important Organizational Trait, by Region.

	Total	New England	Southern Calif.	New York	Midwest	Central U.S.
Friendly	2.6%	4.1%	3.1%	3.1%	—	2.7%
Shows concern for patients	37.0	32.6	27.8	39.6	43.1%	44.6
Provides prompt service	32.3	28.6	29.9	30.2	43.1	29.7
Listens to patients	5.6	10.2	6.2	4.2	4.2	2.7
Hardworking employees	3.2	4.0	4.1	5.2	—	2.7
Honest	3.2	4.0	7.2	2.1	—	2.7
Cost-conscious	3.7	4.0	7.2	6.2	—	—
Good job communicating with patients	10.0	12.5	9.3	7.3	7.4	13.5
Helpful	2.4	—	5.2	2.1	2.2	1.4
Courteous	—	—	—	—	—	—
Appearance	—	—	—	—	—	—

Table 4. Second Most Important Organizational Trait, by Region.

	Total	New England	Southern Calif.	New York	Midwest	Central U.S.
Friendly	3.0%	2.1%	7.4%	1.0%	3.1%	1.3%
Shows concern for patients	25.9	33.3	16.8	26.8	24.2	28.0
Provides prompt service	23.7	25.0	20.0	22.7	30.5	20.0

Table 4. Second Most Important Organizational Trait, by Region, Cont'd.

	Total	New England	Southern Calif.	New York	Midwest	Central U.S.
Listens to patients	11.8%	12.5%	7.4%	12.4%	13.7%	13.3%
Hardworking employees	3.5	2.1	6.3	3.1	1.0	5.3
Honest	3.9	2.1	5.3	6.2	3.1	2.7
Cost-conscious	4.1	2.1	6.3	6.2	—	6.7
Good job communi-cating with patients	20.3	18.7	25.3	18.5	21.0	17.3
Helpful	3.8	2.1	5.2	3.9	3.4	5.4
Courteous	—	—	—	—	—	—
Appearance	—	—	—	—	—	—

Table 5. Third Most Important Organizational Trait, by Region.

	Total	New England	Southern Calif.	New York	Midwest	Central U.S.
Friendly	6.3%	4.5%	11.2%	5.5%	4.4%	5.5%
Shows concern for patient	12.2	13.6	21.3	12.2	4.4	9.7
Provides prompt service	12.5	13.6	12.4	11.1	12.2	13.9
Listens to patients	16.3	27.2	10.1	16.7	17.8	8.3
Hardworking employees	7.0	6.8	7.9	8.9	4.4	7.0
Honest	6.0	9.1	6.7	7.8	—	7.0
Cost-conscious	5.3	2.3	9.0	5.5	4.4	4.2
Good job communi-cating with patients	22.5	18.2	12.4	21.1	33.3	29.2
Helpful	11.9	4.7	9.0	11.4	19.1	15.2
Courteous	—	—	—	—	—	—
Appearance	—	—	—	—	—	—

Table 6 reflects respondents' ratings of the adequacy of specific visitor and guest services at the hospitals they visit, on a scale from 1 (most adequate) to 4 (least adequate).

Table 6. Adequacy of Hospitals' Visitor and Guest Services, by Region.

Service	Scale	Total	New England	Southern Calif.	New York	Midwest	Central U.S.
Personal attention	1	12.4%	14.3%	9.1%	9.3%	14.3%	16.2%
to patients	2	72.0	71.4	75.7	71.1	70.4	70.3
	3	14.3	12.2	14.1	18.5	14.2	10.8
	4	1.3	2.1	1.1	1.1	1.1	2.7
Personal attention	1	7.7	8.2	6.1	6.2	6.2	13.5
to family/friends	2	56.0	55.1	48.5	55.7	58.8	63.5
	3	30.7	30.6	38.3	34.0	30.9	16.2
	4	5.6	6.1	7.1	4.1	4.1	6.8
Enough chairs and	1	7.3	6.1	12.1	7.2	4.2	6.7
spaces for the	2	35.9	40.8	29.3	40.2	40.6	27.0
number of people	3	53.8	51.0	57.6	49.5	48.0	64.9
in the room	4	3.0	2.1	1.0	3.1	7.2	1.4
Service at the	1	11.4	14.3	12.1	7.2	11.4	12.2
information desk	2	61.7	71.4	61.6	77.3	40.6	56.8
	3	16.3	12.2	23.2	12.4	14.5	20.3
	4	10.6	2.1	3.1	3.1	33.5	10.7
Keeping visitors	1	10.7	8.2	14.1	10.3	8.3	13.5
informed of prog-	2	50.0	44.9	52.5	59.8	41.2	51.3
ress of patient	3	32.8	40.8	29.3	25.8	41.2	25.7
	4	6.5	6.1	4.1	4.1	9.3	9.5

Table 7 reflects some more perceptual judgments as well as the objective data supplied by the participants.

Table 7. Perception of Healthcare and Respondents' Demographic Data, by Region.

	Total	New England	Southern Calif.	New York	Midwest	Central U.S.
When I check into a hospital, the staff usually makes me feel:						
Very comfortable	7.1%	2.0%	9.3%	7.4%	8.3%	9.4%
Comfortable	55.1	54.0	47.4	58.9	66.7	42.3
Somewhat uncomfortable	17.7	16.0	18.5	17.9	15.7	21.7
Very uncomfortable	2.0	2.0	5.1	—	9.3	2.6
I have never checked into a hospital	18.1	26.0	19.7	15.8	—	19.0

Table 7. Perception of Healthcare and Respondents' Demographic Data, by Region, Cont'd.

	Total	New England	Southern Calif.	New York	Midwest	Central U.S.
Would you be willing to pay more for healthcare institutions to hire people who are better skilled in dealing with people?						
Yes	41.5%	32.6%	30.3%	43.7%	60.4%	41.3%
No	42.3	55.1	46.5	39.6	28.1	42.7
Don't know	16.2	12.3	23.2	16.7	11.5	16.0
(If yes) Would you be willing to pay more in direct taxes or direct costs to the patient?						
Taxes	35.2	6.2	31.0	46.7	50.0	26.0
Direct costs	50.7	81.3	55.2	46.7	30.0	60.0
Other	13.1	12.5	12.8	6.6	20.0	14.0
What is your sex?						
Male	46.3	60.0	40.0	49.0	36.0	45.0
Female	53.7	40.0	60.0	51.0	64.0	55.0
What is your age?						
Under 25	22.1	4.0	36.4	29.2	18.3	22.4
25–34	39.1	62.0	21.2	43.7	26.5	43.4
35–44	19.8	22.0	16.2	12.5	26.5	22.4
45–54	9.4	6.0	16.2	8.3	7.2	9.2
55–64	7.0	6.0	6.0	6.3	13.3	2.6
65 or over	2.6	—	4.0	—	8.2	—
Which of the following best describes your total family income?						
Less than $5,000	5.8	2.0	8.2	7.3	7.3	4.0
$5,000–$9,999	6.5	—	8.2	5.2	12.5	6.7
$10,000–$14,999	10.4	—	12.2	8.3	28.1	1.3
$15,000–$24,999	20.8	23.0	15.3	19.8	33.3	12.0
$25,000 or more	56.5	75.0	57.1	59.4	18.8	76.0
Do you or any member of your family work in a hospital or healthcare institution?						
Yes	27.0	49.0	22.0	20.0	19.0	25.0
No	73.0	51.0	78.0	80.0	81.0	75.0

Glossary of Communication Factors in the Selection and Evaluation Process

In our extensive work in healthcare consulting, we have compiled a practical glossary of factors of communicology, or the practical psychology of communication, as it manifests itself in the healthcare work environment. The following is a complete presentation of the "C-Formula." Healthcare managers have found the formula useful as a guide to communication dynamics that might affect work progress. They have also found it to be a stellar checklist of communication factors that make themselves present, either positively or negatively, during the selection or performance evaluation process. To use this checklist effectively, the reader should look at each of its elements and determine: (1) How does each factor weigh in my management style? (2) How does each factor commonly present itself in my interviewing style? (3) How does each factor present itself in the typical job candidate I interview? (4) How does each factor affect the performance assessment process?

The Practical "C's" of Communicology

CALIBRATION: How effectively measured is the message?

CLARITY: How clear is the message?

COMPASSION: What amount or kind of emotion is involved?

COMPLETENESS: Is the message totally comprehensive?

CONFIDENTIALITY: What amount is necessary for maximum effect?

COMMONALITY: What similarities are involved?

COMEDY: Is humor used and for what purpose?

CONJECTURE: What are facts and what are arbitrary or subjective conclusions?

CONCLUSION: Does the message have a fruitful and natural ending?

CONVICTION: How much force and confidence are displayed by the sender?

CONFUSION: Is the message in any way muted or distorted?

CONSTRUCTION: How well is the message presented?

CAUTION: Is there any hesitancy (and why) in the delivery?

COUNSEL: Is the message sent to accommodate or to provide worthwhile advice?

CIRCUMSTANCE: What business or environmental issues are in action?

CONSISTENCY: How does this communication fall "in sync" with everything else?

CONCISENESS: Is the message effectively edited?

CLEVERNESS: Has style taken precedence over action?

CONTENT: What is the core message?

CHANGE: How does this business dimension relate to the message?

CONNOTATION: What secondary or hidden agendas are being assisted?

COMPLEXITY: Are technical or other issues clouding the primary message?

CHALLENGE: Is the message involved in the discussed situation?

CULTURE: What ethnic, nationalistic, or regional considerations are required?

CYNICISM: Is sarcasm or negativity a paramount factor in the delivery of the message?

CHARADE: Are you, the receiver, in some way being set up?

CREATIVITY: What level of ingenuity is applied to the message and its scope?

CONFORMITY: Is the message structured to comply with something or someone?

COMMITMENT: How dedicated is the sender to the message?

COMFORT: How comfortable is the sender in the message forum?

CONFIDENCE: What level of true confidence does the sender exhibit?

CHARITY: Is the sender saying this "just to be nice"?

CREDIBILITY: How much credibility do the sender and the message have relative to the business?

CONDUCIVE: How does the message fit with current business practice, policy, and plans?

CONTINUITY: Does the message fall in sync with all other considered factors?

CRAZINESS: Is the message, the sender, or the consequences "too far out"?

CONNIVANCE: Is the message meant to manipulate?

CUSTOMIZATION: Has the message been tailored or altered to fit the current situation?

COURAGE: Is the sender forthright and truthful in his or her delivery?

CLASS: Is the delivery professional and noninflammatory?

CLOSURE: Does the message lend itself to a business or commercial conclusion?

CONTRADICTION: Does the message oppose current fact or previously collected data?

COMPREHENSIVE: Is the message understandable, well organized, and complete?

CONFRONTATION: Is the message an invitation or introduction to battle?

CONFLICT/COMBAT: Is the message part of an ongoing battle?

CONTRAST: Hoes does the message match up to similar data?

COMPARISON: What other information is similar to this message?

COLLABORATION: Is the message intended to be part of a persuasive package?

CLIMATE: Are all relevant environmental factors being considered?

CRITICISM: Does the communication become a harangue?

CLUB: Is the message motivated by friendship with an individual or group?

CHUMS: Is the message structured with regard to friendship between sender and receiver?

COMBINATION: Does the message act in concert with another one to cause action?

COMPROMISE: Does the message suggest a meeting at a median position?

CEREMONY: Is more consideration given to relative position rather than message power?

CRITERIA: What significant factual data is the message based on?

CHUMP: Is the sender playing the receiver for a sap?

CONTRACT: Does the message set up a mutually beneficial action and set of results?

CHARTER: How does the message fit into the organization's overall mission?

CERTAINTY: How valid are the message and its circumstances?

CLOCK: How are timeliness, timing, and time parameters involved?

CHARISMA: How much is personal charm part of the message and its effectiveness?

CHEER: How much enthusiasm does the sender have for the message?

COUNTER: Is the message a direct response to a challenging statement?

CASH: What are the financial implications and circumstances of the message?

CONTEMPLATION: How much thought went into the message?

CANNED: Is the message too well rehearsed? Are there reasons for excessive prep time?

CHOICE: Does the message ask for a selective decision?

CHECK: Is the message a verification of something?

CURE: Does the message help solve a problem?

CONSTERNATION: Does the sender seem too worried given the situation?

CONSERVATIVE: Does the message signal a reluctance to take a calculated risk?

CONDEMNATION: Does the message chastise or denigrate?

CONDONEMENT: Is the message an endorsement of something or someone?

COMPLEMENTARY: Is the communication a supplement to some other message?

COMPLIMENTARY: Is the message an overt appeal to ego?

CORE: Does the message get to the heart of the matter?

COMMAND: Does the sender have control of the message and its attendant circumstances?

CROCK: Is the message 100 percent baloney?

CLOUT: Does the sender have the power to make the message happen?

COMPETITION: Is the message providing worthwhile info or is it meant to compete?

CHARACTER: Does the message reflect the integrity of the sender?

COLOR: What are the "fiber"/"qualitative"/"music" implications?

COHESION: How tightly does this information fit with other information and data?

COORDINATION: Does the message help the execution of a business event?

COLLUSION: Is the message forcefully allied with other provided information?

COMMAND: Is the message an imperative direction?

CONTROL: Does the message provide direction?

CHAOS: Does the message represent potential cause for organizational upheaval?

CONCEALMENT: Is any potentially damaging information being harbored?

CODE: How is the information communicated with regard to organizational parlance?

CONTORT: Is the message reshaped to strike a particular chord?

CONTEMPT: Is the message flavored with malice?

COMPILATION: Does the message represent a collection of ideas or input?

CONDENSE: Has the message been abbreviated for any reason?

COMPLY: Is the message stated in order to appease a particular business facet?

Sample Survey Instrument for Measuring Organizational Standards

Healthcare managers must analyze their environment and their organizations in order to establish well-calibrated factors for selection and performance evaluation. Many of the client organizations of CHR/InterVista have utilized our survey group to help determine organizational norms for the Quan-Com Formula discussed throughout the book. One such organization is the Rorer Group, the pharmaceutical giant with which every reader of this book is probably familiar. By examining the following survey instrument and adapting it appropriately to their organizations, readers can accurately assess the sixteenth Quan-Com factors in their own organizations and personnel selection and evaluation schemes.

The Rorer Group Survey
for Employee Attitude Measurement

In the interest of planning support for your managerial efforts, the Rorer Group personnel department has retained our services to help measure your perceptions and opinions regarding your organization, job, and work environment. Please take about fifteen minutes to complete the enclosed survey and return it to our attention by February 15 utilizing the stamped envelope provided. In addition to the objective statements, we would appreciate your providing any and all ancillary information you feel appropriate in the blank space provided. No identification is required, although space is provided if you wish to identify yourself; the survey forms are color-coded by organizational divison only for our numerical purposes.

Thank you for your cooperation in this effort.

I. The Organization

Please indicate your level of agreement with the following statements using this rating scale:

Strongly Agree — A +   Neutral — N   Strongly Disagree — D +
Moderate Agreement — A   Moderate Disagreement — D

1. In general, our organization has proven to be readily able to react advantageously to change in our business arena. _____
2. The work ethic in general in our organization is high and reflects dedication to success at all job levels. _____
3. Our firm has been appropriately aggressive, as reflected by all levels of management, in pursuing business goals and suitable opportunities. _____
4. Communication is an effective tool in our organization, and most communication channels are open and readily usable. _____
5. I have a clear idea of the goals and mission objectives of the Rorer Group and understand the company's future direction. _____
6. To work here and be successful, one must have a high degree of energy and self-motivation. _____
7. Our organization is "people-oriented" and genuinely concerned about the development and welfare of management and the rank-and-file. _____
8. Most people who work here are team-oriented, cooperative in dealing with others in the organization, and loyal to the company and their fellow managers and employees. _____
9. Most people here have an exemplary degree of knowledge in their particular field of expertise. _____
10. I feel that most people who work for Rorer are proud of the firm and believe strongly in its goals and objectives. _____
11. I feel that most Rorer managers and employees are fairly satisfied with the company and their job. _____
12. Despite a lot of recent organizational change, most managers and employees are relatively satisfied here. _____

I. The Organization

Please use the following space to comment on any other facet of the organization aspects of the Rorer Group you feel appropriate to our study.

_____

_____

_____

_____

_____

_____

_____

II. The Job

Using the agreement scale, rate the following statements relative to your specific position at Rorer.

Strongly Agree — A +   Neutral — N   Strongly Disagree — D +
Moderate Agreement — A   Moderate Disagreement — D

1. I feel that I am given clear objectives and performance goals. _____
2. If I need additional human resources for my staff, I can obtain them readily if I can justify the reason(s). _____
3. I feel my compensation is fair, given my expertise in my field, my level of responsibility, and what peers in similar positions earn at their firms. _____
4. I believe I get the training both my staff and myself need for our professional and managerial development. _____
5. I get the support I need from my management to achieve my goals and objectives. _____
6. Rorer management is truly interested in what my staff and I do and believe it to be essential to the company. _____
7. I can give appropriate feedback to management when necessary. _____
8. When I give management feedback I consider necessary, I am listened to and not just "heard" or politely accommodated. _____
9. I currently have most of the resources (financial, personnel, and operational) I need to accomplish my 1987 objectives. _____
10. I feel confident that I will have all the resources I need to "get the job done" by early 1987. _____
11. My job allows me to work on things I really enjoy at least 60 percent of the time. _____
12. I believe there is ample opportunity for me in my job to grow and learn. _____
13. Likewise, I believe there are positions here I can aspire for which will provide me with future professional growth. _____
14. Simply put, I enjoy my current job here at Rorer. _____

II. The Job

Please use the following space to comment on any other facet of your job that you feel appropriate to our study.

_____

_____

_____

_____

_____

_____

_____

III. The Environment

Using the agreement scale, rate the following statements relative to the work environment at Rorer.

Strongly Agree — A +   Neutral — N   Strongly Disagree — D +
Moderate Agreement — A   Moderate Disagreement — D

1. Considering all the recent change, the company has still operated well and progressed successfully.   _____

2. The Rorer-Revlon situation was more of a takeover than a merger.   _____

3. The Rorer-Revlon situation was more of a merger than an acquisition.   _____

4. The Rorer-Revlon situation caused some turbulence, but in the long run will be mutually beneficial for everyone.   _____

5. There is typically a lot of change here anyway, and most people adjust well and work in spite of it.   _____

6. The business year 1987 will be a very good one for most of the Rorer organization.   _____

7. I have a good idea of what type of place this will be to work at in the next couple of years.   _____

8. All things considered, the firm will make money and most of us will benefit.   _____

9. Compared to other places I've worked, the Rorer environment is a pretty good one in which to work.   _____

10. As I reflect on it, when I discuss Rorer with people I feel relatively good about working here and the opportunities the future holds for both the organization and myself.   _____

III. The Environment

Please use the following space to comment on any other facet of the Rorer environment you feel appropriate to our study.

_____

_____

_____

_____

_____

_____

_____

_____

Sample Forms for Administering the Personnel Selection Process

The execution of a good bidding system, an internal search system, and external recruitment strategies requires the use of solid administrative forms. This resource contains several administrative forms that can be used readily by the reader in completing job descriptions and conducting effective job searches.

Personnel Selection Administration Forms

1. Job Position Analysis Form
2. Job Description Form
3. Internal Bid System Posting Form
4. Internal Candidate Application Form
4a. Employee File Review Checklist
5. External Candidate Application Form
5a. Résumé/External Application Review Checklist
6. Interview Cuesheet, Hourly Employee Candidate
7. Interview Cuesheet, Managerial/Professional Candidate
8. Interview Scoresheet, Hourly Employee Candidate
9. Interview Scoresheet, Managerial/Professional Candidate
10. Goals and Objectives "Day 1" Worksheet

1. Job Position Analysis Form

In order effectively to begin the progression toward hiring a successful employee, the manager must first comprehensively analyze all of the important components of the job position he or she is seeking to fill. By utilizing the form shown here, the healthcare manager can conduct a methodical and encompassing review of the critical dimensions of the subject job position.

Job Position Analysis Form

Department: _____

Title of position: _____

Salary grade or range: _____

Primary supervisor: _____

(name and title)

Main objective of position: _____

_____

Three major goals or performance objectives of the job position:

1. _____

_____

2. _____

_____

3. _____

_____

Requisite education: _____

Required experience level: _____

Existing position replacement? _____   New position? _____

Potential promotional opportunities: _____

Number of employees in department: _____

If supervisory position, briefly describe number and technical classification of reporting subordinates: _____

_____

_____

Desired start date for position: _____

2. Job Description Form

A job description form is an active reference for anyone who might have an interest in the position or a working role in filling the position successfully. This would include other department heads, who might have candidates for the position, and the human resources department, which uses the job description in advertising and other recruiting approaches. By using a form similar to the one presented here, the healthcare manager can provide necessary information to both potential candidates and organizational allies in the recruitment process.

Job Description Form

Title of position: _____

Department: _____

Salary grade or range: _____

Date of this update: _____   Previous update: _____
(user must indicate the date of this description and the last update of this particular job description, to ensure content is still valid)

Reason for opening: New position: _____   Promotion: _____

                             Termination: _____   Resignation: _____

Title of primary supervisor: _____

Name of current primary supervisor: _____

Job description: _____

(construct a narrative description using the main objective and three goals listed

on the job analysis form, as well as any special requirements for the position,

supervisory responsibilities, and any other information that will help in the cali-

bration of recruitment efforts) _____

_____

Required education level and background: _____
(degrees, diploma, and/or certifications needed) _____

Required experience level and special technical expertise needed: _____
(experience level in years and types of work activity) _____

Potential promotional opportunities: _____

_____

Special circumstances of job position: (any unique aspect of the job

position that needs to be addressed in the selection and evaluation

process) _____

Point of contact: _____ (individual with the selection decision) _____

3. *Internal Bid System Posting Form*

To maximize the recruitment process, the healthcare manager must look first at the possibilities within the organization. The organization should use a bidding system similar to the one described in Part Two. Here the reader is provided with a posting form that will inform interested employees adequately of an open job position and state the essential elements of the job position in a manner that will encourage only qualified internal candidates.

Internal Bid System Posting Form

Title of position: _____

Department: _____

Salary grade or range: _____

Title of primary supervisor: _____

Job description: _____

_____

(construct a narrative description of the job, using the main objective and three

goals listed on the job analysis form) _____

_____

Required education and experience level: (represent by educational level and

years required of job-specific experience) _____

Point of contact: _____ (individual to contact to apply for position) _____

Application deadline: _____

4. Internal Candidate Application Form

This form is designed to facilitate the application of internal candidates for open positions that have been posted in the organization's facility. The top half of the form should be completed by the applicant and the bottom half by the personnel department. The healthcare manager is thus provided with a control sheet on each internal candidate's application. By using this form in tandem with the candidate's personnel file, the manager can quickly and effectively evaluate each internal candidacy.

Internal Candidate Application Form

Name:_____

Current position:_____

Current work group or department:_____

Organization anniversary date:_____   First day in current job:_____

Position desired:_____

Department of open position:_____

Special qualifications for open position:_____

_____

I request that the personnel department of __(organization's name)__ forward

my personnel file to the appropriate manager for consideration for the above-

named open position.

_____   _____
   Date   Employee's Signature

_____

For Personnel Dept. Action:

1. Personnel file sent on __(date)__ to __(manager with selection decision)__ .

2. Employee's current salary range/grade is _____ .

3. Current supervisor is _____ . Has been notified of

    employee's interest in open position on __(date)__ .

4. Screening interview by personnel conducted on __(date)__ .

5. First interview with reviewing manager scheduled for __(date)__ .

6. Ultimate decision (complete at appropriate time):

Interviewed:__(date)__   Hired:__(date)__   Rejected:__(date)__

4a. Employee File Review Checklist

In order to ensure that the line manager fully evaluates the internal applicants for a job position, he or she should follow the review process shown in this checklist. By doing so, the manager can methodically assess all of the essential attributes in determining candidate qualification.

Employee File Review Checklist

1. Years employed in organization:_____

2. Years in current position:_____

3. Most recent job position title:_____

4. Most recent performance appraisal rating:_____

5. Current supervisor's comments:_____

_____

(any pertinent comments from current supervisor)

_____

6. Meets educational requirements?_____

7. Meets experiential requirements?_____

8. Apparent qualifications for the job:_____

_____

_____

9. Potential shortcomings or disqualifiers:_____

_____

10. Level of interest by candidate: High_____ Moderate_____

                                            Uncertain_____ Marginal _____

_____

11. Will interview on_____

12. Essential Quan-Com characteristics: 1._____   2._____

                                  3._____   4._____   5._____

13. Ancillary interviewers: 1._____   2._____

(other staff members who will interview candidate)

14. Special areas of focus for technical expertise:_____

_____

15. Other areas of special attention:_____

_____

5. External Candidate Application Form

Virtually every business organization uses some sort of application form, even in the selection process of professional personnel and management candidates, who usually submit a résumé with the application form. A generic job application form containing all of the essentials of an application is illustrated. By adapting it to a particular organization's selection process, the manager can meet all the important legal and administrative requirements of this step.

External Candidate Application Form

1. Administrative Data

Name: _____

Address: _____

_____

Phone number: (____) ____ - ____

Position applied for: _____   Department: _____

Salary desired: _____   Availability to start: _____

2. Educational Background: List all educational institutions attended and degrees, diplomas, or certificates awarded, beginning with the most recently attended.

a. *Name and address of institution*   b. *Types of studies*   c. *Diplomas & dates att'd*

1. _____

_____

2. _____

_____

3. _____

_____

List all technical, professional, or educational honors, certifications, or affiliations not listed above: _____

3. Experience: List the last three professional positions you have held, starting with the most recent. Submit a résumé with this application if it contains important additional information.

a. *Job title*   b. *Description of duties*   c. *Dates of employment*
& organization

a. _____

_____

b. _____

_____

c. _____

_____

3a. Outside Activities: List any community-oriented, recreational, or social activities you participate in during your spare time away from work.

_____

_____

4. References: List three references who will provide information about your ability to perform well in the position for which you are applying in our organization.

1._____   2._____   3._____
(name and title)

_____   _____   _____
(organization)

_____   _____   _____
(phone number)

Please enclose any prepared written references with this application.

I hereby attest that all information given in this application is true to the best of my knowledge, and understand that the knowing submittal of false information will result in my later dismissal from __(your organization)__ . I also consent to waive any privacy rights and allow __(your organization)__ to confer directly with any submitted references.

_____   _____
Applicant's Signature   Date

5a. *Résumé/External Application Review Checklist*

In order to ensure that the line manager is carefully evaluating the résumés and applications submitted for an open position, the guideline on the next page is provided. By using it, the manager can systematically evaluate candidates' qualifications and set initial standards for the selection process.

Résumé/External Application Review Checklist

1. Clear and complete résumé/application?_____

2. Logical progression of career movement?_____

3. Years in current position and brief description of job:_____

_____

4. Level of education:_____

5. Level of experience:_____

_____

6. Overqualified?_____   Underqualified?_____

   Comments:_____

7. Apparent qualifications for job:_____

_____

_____

8. Apparent long-term potential and possibilities:_____

_____

9. Potential shortcomings or disqualifiers:_____

_____

10. Candidate availability:_____

   (potential start date and accessibility of candidate for interviews)

11. Will interview on_____

12. Essential Quan-Com characteristics: 1._____   2._____

        3._____4._____   5._____

13. Ancillary interviewers: 1._____   2._____

14. Special areas for questioning:_____

_____

6. Interview Cuesheet, Hourly Employee Candidate

In order to conduct an expedient screening interview of an hourly candidate utilizing the questioning strategies described in this book, the cuesheet on the next page is provided for the reader's use. By utilizing the cues provided along with specific cues from the formula appearing in Resource E, the healthcare manager can make an accurate, logical assessment, questioning the candidate systematically and evaluating the responses according to the assessment principles and interpretive clues of the Quan-Com System.

Interview Cuesheet, Hourly Employee Candidate

1. *Attitude Orientation*

   a. Tell me about job tasks or assignments you had to handle at your last job that were not part of the original job description.

   b. Tell me what you think makes a good worker.

   c. _____ (cue selected by manager) _____ .

2. *People Skills*

   a. Tell me about your co-workers at __(current or previous job)__ .

   b. Who was the most important person at your last/current job? Why?

   c. _____ (cue selected by manager) _____ .

3. *Team Orientation*

   a. What is your opinion of your current/past work organization?

   b. If you were a manager and had to hire people to work for you, what would you look for?

   c. _____ (cue selected by manager) _____ .

General Directions:

1. Conduct screening interviews for hourly candidates in 10–15 minutes.

2. Augment with technical expertise cues/clues from Resources E and F and ask specific questions about specific technical acumen if necessary.

3. Send copy of cuesheet and scoresheet to any ancillary interviewers and keep copy in job position file.

7. Interview Cuesheet, Managerial/Professional Candidate

The cuesheet depicted here is a practical tool for the reader to use in the managerial and professional interviewing process. By coupling the questions on the cuesheet with additional cues from Resource F, the manager can make a thorough assessment of a candidate. Like the other forms in this section, this form should remain in a file specifically dedicated to this job position. By maintaining such a file, the manager can handily evaluate job performance needs and conduct an effective, systematic selection process whenever necessary.

Interview Cuesheet, Managerial/Professional Candidate

1. *Attitude Orientation*

a. Tell me about a unique managerial problem you had to solve at your last/current position.

b. What are the things you look for in prospective employees?

c. _____ (cue selected by manager) _____ .

2. *People Skills*

a. Who was the most important person at your last/current job? Why?

b. Tell me about your last/current organization's "people philosophy."

c. _____ (cue selected by manager) _____ .

3. *Managerial Aptitude*

a. Tell me about your managerial philosophy, and give me some examples of how it has worked for you.

b. Who was the best manager you ever worked for? What made him or her so good?

c. _____ (cue selected by manager) _____ .

4. *Team Orientation*

a. What is your opinion of your past/current organization?

b. Tell me about some great teams, work-related or otherwise, that you've been associated with.

c. _____ (cue selected by manager) _____ .

General Directions:

1. Conduct interview in 30–40 minutes.

2. Augment with any special technical expertise cues or any point-specific factors from Resource F.

3. Send copies to ancillary interviewers and keep one copy in file.

8. Interview Scoresheet, Hourly Employee Candidate

The purpose of this form is to assist the healthcare manager in the assessment and scoring of hourly job applicants. Used by numerous healthcare and service organizations in several countries, this scoresheet will be a solid practical tool in assessing hourly talent.

THE SELECTION PROFORMANCE:™ QUAN-COM™ SCORESHEET

CANDIDATE_____ PHONE_____

ADDRESS_____

COMPANY_____ INTERVIEWER_____

POSITION_____ INTERVIEW DATE_____

ORIG. COPY   —
CANARY COPY —
0 – Marginal • 1 – Satisfactory • 2 – Strong Evidence   PINK COPY   — CHR.

1. Performs well under changing circumstances, high stress, or adverse physical conditions; can absorb different processes and new methods with practicality.	**INTERVIEWER NOTES:**	Adaptability	
2. Commits to hard work for the organization, consistently representing its best interest by giving its needs top priority; intrinsic dedication to cause and duty.		Loyalty	
3. Pursues work tirelessly to a successful completion despite obstacles; willing to go the distance consistently.		Perseverance	
4. Displays a sound, positive attitude and a "can do" approach; capable and ready to perform for the good of the organization.		Work Ethic	
	ATTITUDE ORIENTATION	Subtotal	
1. Can express needs and desires to co-workers and superiors appropriately; deals courteously and tactfully with external parties.	**INTERVIEWER NOTES:**	Communication	
2. Displays a steady, fast pace consistently, and an ability to increase activity effectively as necessary. Suitable vitality and endurance.		Energy Level	
3. Willing to discuss situations and circumstances, consistently honest, candid, and direct. Does not harbor needed information.		Openness	
	INTERPERSONAL TRAITS	Subtotal	
1. Ability to analyze quantitative and qualitative data and make logical determinations and educated perceptions; pragmatically applies intellect to the work situation.	**INTERVIEWER NOTES:**	Raw Intelligence	
2. Possesses an adequate range of appropriate experience with similar responsibilities thereby providing a realistic frame of reference.		Work Experience	
	PROFORMANCE QUALIFICATIONS	Subtotal	
1. Highly motivated toward selfless service toward co-workers, customers, and organizational goals; looks at tasks as a commitment to others and organizational excellence.	**INTERVIEWER NOTES:**	Cooperation	
2. Capable of ascertaining direction and goals, self-starting; can make judgments, decisions, and executions without much reliance on others.		Indep. Motivation	
3. Demonstrates poise and self-confidence to assume tasks and responsibilities appropriately; accepts responsibility and produces on a timely basis.		Responsiveness	
	TEAM ORIENTATION	**Team Orientation**	
	© 1984	**TOTAL SCORE**	

Optional Additional Demographic Data to be completed after decision based on employee records and applicant flow data for validation purposes only.

(1)_____ (4)_____   REJECTED ☐
(2)_____ (5)_____   ACCEPTED ☐
(3)_____ Position_____   HIRED   ☐

9. Interview Scoresheet,
Managerial/Professional Candidate

This form is a generic version of a scoresheet used by over fifty leading healthcare organizations. Its simple purpose is to assist the manager in assessing and scoring each candidate for a subject position. By using the scoresheet in conjunction with the cue and clue system displayed in Resource F, the healthcare line manager can efficiently score job candidates.

Quan-Com Interviewing Scoresheet

Candidate Name _____   Date _____

Position Applied for/Department _____

TOTAL SCORE _____

---

1. *Attitude Orientation*

   a) Adaptability   Ad: _____
   b) Aggressiveness   Ag: _____
   c) Perseverance   Per: _____
   d) Work Ethic   W/E: _____
                                                   Category Score _____

---

2. *People Skills*

   a) Communication   Com: _____
   b) Energy Level   E/L: _____
   c) Perceptiveness   Per: _____
   d) Presence/Bearing   P/B: _____
                                                   Category Score _____

---

3. *Managerial Aptitude*

   a) Creativity   Cr: _____
   b) Delegation   Dl: _____
   c) Independent Judgment   IJ: _____
   d) Planning   Pl: _____
                                                   Category Score _____

---

4. *Team Orientation*

   a) Cooperation   Cp: _____
   b) Employee Relations   ER: _____
   c) Loyalty   Ly: _____
   d) Technical Expertise   T/E: _____
                                                   Category Score _____

General Instructions

1. Score all Quan-Coms separately, then add up for category score.
2. Tally all categories for total score.
3. Comment appropriately in each section and/or set standard cues in each section.
4. Return copy of scoresheet to applicant file.

10. Goals and Objectives ''Day 1'' Worksheet

It is imperative for the healthcare manager to convey immediately to the newly hired employee the objectives for initial attainment in the subject position. To do this, the manager might use the form on the next page, which sets a comprehensive timetable for goal achievement, including a description of the goals and objectives as well as an introduction to the important aspects of the position that will be measured in the performance appraisal. In using this systematic approach, the manager makes certain that the new employee is given thoughtful direction at the outset of the job and understands what is expected in terms of initial job performance.

Goals and Objectives "Day 1" Worksheet

Job title:_____

Department:_____

Start date/day "1":_____

Initial Goals and Objectives

1._____

_____ Due date:_____

2._____

_____ Due date:_____

3._____

_____ Due date:_____

(first three objectives should be taken from job analysis form)

4._____

_____ Due date:_____

5._____

_____ Due date:_____

(second two objectives should be based on candidate's particular abilities)

Critical Performance Dimensions

1._____ (manager should list three essential

2._____ Quan-Com characteristics for subject

3._____ position and explain to new employee)

Development Activities

1._____ (manager should list two initial development

2._____ activities for employee, if necessary)

Date for first follow-up session:_____

Date for regular performance appraisal:_____

Quan-Com
Selection System
for Hourly Employees

The following guide is provided to assist the reader in the interviewing and selection of nonexempt or hourly employees. The reader should first assess the open position to determine which of the characteristics are most needed, and then select questions from the following sheets that will help form a determination on the candidates for the position.

Attitude Orientation

Quan-Com Factor 1—Adaptability

Adaptability—Proven ability to perform well under changing circumstances, high stress, or adverse physical conditions; ability to relate to different processes and absorb new methods with excellent practical results.

Cues:

1. What duties did you handle on your last job that were not part of the original job description?
2. What processes were used at your last job that were unique to the industry?
3. What radical changes took place at your last job that affected you directly?
4. Have you ever worked in a foreign place or different city?

323

Clues:

1. Previous adaptations to significant change, such as a new boss, processes, or facility.
2. Geographical change tempered with stability.
3. Response to change in the interview.
4. Demonstrated ability to work with different types of people.
5. Consistent past performance under adverse conditions and circumstances.

Attitude Orientation

Quan-Com Factor 2—Work Ethic

Work Ethic—Displays a consistently sound attitude and a positive "can-do" approach to all situations; manifests an aura of being capable and ready to perform any tasks that will contribute to the good of the organization.

Cues:

1. How do you feel toward your current employer?
2. How do you feel about your current work situation?
3. How do you feel about the way your career has gone up to the present?

Clues:

1. Perceived image stays the same throughout the interview.
2. Words chosen to describe sensitive situations.
3. Realizes customer/client is number 1, organization is number 2, and individual is number 3.
4. Always willing to give something extra when mandated by work situation.
5. Prides self on professionalism and values it in others; almost intolerant of those who do not put in an equal effort.
6. Strives for quality, not just for quantity, in all endeavors.
7. Takes genuine pride in work and company.

Attitude Orientation

Quan-Com Factor 3—Perseverance

Perseverance—Pursues established work schedule and goals tirelessly and to a successful end despite any minor obstacles; willing to go the distance every time.

Cue: When confronted with an immediate problem on the job, what course of action do you take?

Clues:

1. Persistent in answering questions, even if thrown a curve.
2. Willing to work through problems and stress rather than avoiding them.
3. Believes in treating all goals and objectives as if they were the most important.
4. Flexible but persistent in achieving results.
5. Does not bend to surrounding negativity or ill feeling.
6. Can bounce back readily from adversity.

Interpersonal Traits

Quan-Com Factor 1—Communication

Communication—Can express needs and desires effectively to co-workers and superiors in a professional manner; deals courteously and tactfully with external parties.

Cues:

1. What avenues of communications were available for your use at your last job?
2. Detail an aspect of a particular procedure.

Clues:

1. Syntax, grammar, and tones utilized effectively.
2. Style of nonverbal communication.
3. Overt listening abilities.
4. Questioning process used by candidate when given the opportunity in the interview.
5. Brevity, conciseness, organization, and verbal style.
6. Succinct and adroit with sensitive information.
7. Does not embellish, alter, or slant objective information.
8. Appears capable of preparing and developing required oral reports.

Interpersonal Traits

Quan-Com Factor 2—Energy Level

Energy Level—Displays a steady, fast pace in executing assignments, a notable positive approach to work, and an innate ability to increase activity effectively when necessary; possesses suitable vitality and endurance for job assigned.

Cues:

1. What kind of activities do you participate in away from your job?
2. How many hours a day do you usually spend working?

Clues:

1. Animated in conversation, responds quickly in verbal interaction.
2. Discusses situations and experiences positively and looks at future optimistically.
3. Expresses reasonable degree of emotion in discussions.
4. Appears more than willing to expand parameters of job scope and amount of activity.
5. Maintains a zealous, earnest manner in answering interviewing probes and explaining information.

Interpersonal Traits

Quan-Com Factor 3—Openness

Openness—Willing to discuss situations and circumstances in a manner that is consistently honest, candid, and direct. Does not deliberately harbor information relative to poor decision making.

Cues:

1. Do you find it difficult to convey your opinions to peers or supervisors?
2. Tell me about a specific situation where you made a wrong decision. How did you remedy the problem?

Clues:

1. Free flow of communication between interviewer and interviewee.
2. Honest, candid portrayal of past performance.
3. Not hesitant in responding to point-blank questions.
4. Appears genuinely at ease in interview.
5. Willing to discuss past mistakes and what was learned as a result.
6. Capable of directly approaching supervisors with pertinent information.

Performance Qualifications

Quan-Com Factor 1—Raw Intelligence

Raw Intelligence—Demonstrates ability to analyze both quantitative and qualitative data, make logical determinations, and develop educated perceptions of relevant situations; able to pragmatically apply intellectual strengths to the work situation.

Cue: Explain fully a process you were involved with from design through reality.

Clues:

1. Verbal skills: vocabulary, syntax.
2. Academic record: types of coursework pursued.
3. Displays analytical thinking in explaining processes and procedures.
4. Displays conceptual thinking when presenting ideas, opinions, and perceptions.
5. Exhibits depth of knowledge as well as breadth.
6. Capable of utilizing creative thinking when solving a unique problem.

Performance Qualifications

Quan-Com Factor 2—Work Experience

Work Experience—Brings an adequate range of past experience to the position, notably in positions that are similar in scope and responsibility to the subject job; has practical experience and appropriate frame of reference.

Cue: Explain your range of experience in our industry.

Clues:

1. Prior healthcare experience.
2. Broad-based exposure to healthcare industry.
3. Worked in high-stress environments.
4. Worked in physically demanding circumstances.
5. Has worked in positions that require high physical endurance.
6. Appears physically fit, as evidenced by past job requirements.

Team Orientation

Quan-Com Factor 1—Cooperation

Cooperation—Highly motivated toward selfless service to coworkers, customers, and the goals of the organization; handles assigned role not as a job, but as a commitment to others and to excellence.

Cues:

1. In your last (or any previous) position, did you work as an integral member of a team?
2. What do you foresee as your goals and objectives if you get this job?

Clues:

1. Total commitment to the goals and objectives of the work group and organization.
2. Able to act as a resource to others needing technical or peer assistance.
3. Willing to help others who are making a solid effort but need assistance.
4. Consistently puts group priorities ahead of personal ones.
5. Does not blame others for mistakes; takes appropriate responsibility for actions.
6. Does not perceive self as individual star or as an autonomous performer.
7. Stresses "we," not "I."
8. Direct and free in sharing essential information with peers and others.

Team Orientation

Quan-Com Factor 2—Responsiveness

Responsiveness—Demonstrates the poise, demeanor, and self-confidence necessary to assume responsibility of assigned role; willingly accepts responsibility and produces results on a timely basis.

Cues:

1. Have you ever felt that you have been given more responsibility than you can handle?
2. How do you follow up to make sure you are getting the results you want?

3. Tell me of an operational problem you resolved.
4. Tell me of a personnel problem you resolved.

Clues:

1. Has achieved past goals on time or ahead of time.
2. How quickly and honestly does candidate respond to probes?
3. Turnaround time on projects cited as part of accomplishment.
4. Displays a willingness to get involved with tough situations.
5. Can reflect on past experiences and objectively discuss what was learned or achieved.
6. Has proven record of working well with peers on critical projects.

Quan-Com Selection System for Managerial and Professional Personnel

In order to accurately interview and select professional and managerial candidates, the reader should use the guide provided in this section in conjunction with the approaches explained in the selection chapters of this book.

Attitude Orientation

Quan-Com Factor 1

Adaptability—Proven ability to perform well under changing conditions, high stress, and adverse physical conditions; ability to relate to varied personalities and absorb new methods with excellent practical results.

Cues:

1. Have you ever lived or worked in a place different from your hometown?
2. In your last (current) position, give me some examples of jobs you were asked to do that were not part of the original job description.
3. Detail a unique product (or aspect of a product) as if I were a potential customer.

331

4. Tell me about an unusual situation you had to handle at your last/current position.
5. What radical changes took place at your last job that affected your role in the organization or your daily activities?
6. Tell me about a job situation where you had to handle several things at one time.

Clues:

1. Willing to expand on original duties, wants to contribute and learn as much as possible to enhance performance.
2. Previous successful adaptations to significant change, such as new boss, new product, or new approaches.
3. Consistent past performance under adversity or major negative change.
4. Demonstrated ability to work with a wide spectrum of people.
5. High level of achievement under high stress and pressure.
6. No apprehension about a multidimensional or wide-range work role.
7. Effective response to change in the interview flow.
8. Demonstrated ability to read, react, and readjust effectively.
9. Geographical change tempered with success and stability.

Attitude Orientation

Quan-Com Factor 2

Aggressiveness—Takes command appropriately in all situations; enterprising, direct, and effectively persuasive in all business dealings.

Cues:

1. What leadership roles have you held in school, job, or community? How did you get them?
2. What tactics do you employ to sell a point or product in a business situation or "hard sell" circumstance?
3. How do you open up dialogue when you first meet a new prospective customer or client?

4. Give me an example of a selling situation where your customer initially wanted nothing to do with your product or services.

Clues:

1. Held leadership roles that demonstrate ability to inspire and manage people, was picked by competitive selection.
2. Utilizes a good balance of tact, aggressiveness, and persuasiveness in dealings with others.
3. Establishes initial rapport with others (and the interviewer) appropriately, professionally, and with ultimate impact.
4. Creditable assertiveness in the interview forum.
5. Stays with point when challenged.
6. States case forcefully but tactfully.
7. Does not hesitate to challenge the norm when necessary.
8. Prohibits aggressiveness from becoming obnoxious, offensive, or pretentious.
9. Does not wait to be led or fed; "gets off first" and makes point.

Attitude Orientation

Quan-Com Factor 3

Perseverance—Pursues established work schedule and goals tirelessly and to a successful end despite any situational obstacles; willing to go the distance every time.

Cues:

1. When confronted with a major obstacle in a business situation, what course of action do you take?
2. Many times, the circumstances under which a goal is established change. In this case, would you change your approach or change the goal itself?
3. Give me an example of a situation at your last/current job that required a lot of persistence or perseverance.

4. Tell me about someone you have worked with who really impressed you with their attitude about their job.

Clues:

1. Defines problem, analyzes possible solutions, selects a plan of attack, and resolves dilemma.
2. Provides a credible example of working through a tough problem by fully utilizing all of the resources at hand.
3. Persistent in answering all cues, even if thrown a curve.
4. Willingness to positively attack problems directly, rather than working around them or avoiding them completely.
5. Proven ability to function well in a stressful situation or environment.
6. Believes in treating all goals and objectives as if they were the most important.
7. Appropriately flexible but persistent in obtaining desired results.
8. Does not bend to surrounding negativity or ill feeling.
9. Can bounce back readily from adversity.
10. Does not tend to become tunnel visioned or overly hard-headed.

Attitude Orientation

Quan-Com Factor 4

Work Ethic—Displays a consistently sound attitude and a positive "can-do" approach to all situations; manifests a realistic aura of being capable and ready to perform any tasks that will contribute to the good of the organization.

Cues:

1. How do you feel about your current employer?
2. How do you feel about your current work situation?
3. Besides yourself, who is the hardest worker at your current workplace?

4. How do you feel about the way your career has gone up to the present?
5. In your mind, what constitutes a good work ethic?

Clues:

1. Relatively satisfied with accomplishments at present job, but looking for a more substantial challenge or career opportunity.
2. Feels this position will be a logical next step, but takes reasonable pride in accomplishments to date.
3. Perceived image stays the same throughout the interview.
4. Words chosen to describe sensitive situations are appropriate.
5. Realizes customer/client is number 1, organization is number 2, and the individual is number 3.
6. Always willing to give something extra when mandated by the work situation and maintain utmost quality.
7. Prides self on professionalism and values it in others; almost intolerant of those who do not put in an equal effort.
8. Strives for quality, not quantity, in all endeavors.
9. Takes genuine pride in work, company, and self.
10. Provides realistic, practical definition of constructive work ethic.

People Skills

Quan-Com Factor 1

Communication—Can express needs and desires effectively to co-workers and superiors in a professional manner; deals tactfully but advantageously with external parties.

Cues:

1. What avenues of communication were available for your use in your last/current job?
2. Detail a procedure or product, starting with a general overview and then going into specifics.

Clues:

1. Good style of nonverbal communication.
2. Nonverbal style is natural supplement to verbal style.
3. Utilizes syntax, grammar, and tones effectively.
4. Seems appropriately natural and comfortable in interview forum.
5. Possesses superior listening skills; listens in "technicolor."
6. Solid questioning procedure when given opportunity in interview.
7. Uses brevity, conciseness, and organization in verbal style.
8. Succinct and adroit with sensitive information.
9. Does not embellish, alter, or slant objective information.
10. Appears capable of preparing and developing required written and oral reports, as evidenced by past job requirements.

People Skills

Quan-Com Factor 2

Energy Level—Displays a steady, fast pace in executing assignments, and an innate ability to increase activity to the maximum when necessary; possesses suitable vitality and endurance for present and future assignments.

Cues:

1. What kind of activities do you participate in away from the job?
2. How many hours, on the average, do you spend on the job?
3. How would you rate your endurance and stamina in your work?

Clues:

1. Animated in conversation, responds quickly in verbal interaction.

2. Discusses situations and experiences positively and looks at future optimistically.
3. Expresses reasonable degree of emotion in interview.
4. Appears more than willing to expand parameters of job scope and amount of work-related activity.
5. Maintains a zealous, earnest manner in addressing cues and explaining information; maintains consistent enthusiasm.
6. Appearance of active, balanced life-style away from work-place.
7. Always works the required amount of hours as a minimum, often works additional hours to ensure excellence.
8. Applies energy intelligently; works smart, not just hard.

People Skills

Quan-Com Factor 3

Perceptiveness—Has a comprehensive understanding of the human quotient as it relates to the workplace; good dexterity in both internal and external interpersonal dealings.

Cues:

1. Give an example of a tough people problem you had to handle.
2. What do you believe is your self-image?
3. How would your current/past manager characterize your business style?
4. Where do people fit into your equation for success?

Clues:

1. Provides solid examples of dealing with a tough problem successfully while maintaining the best possible interpersonal relations.
2. Is eminently aware of self-image and how it affects others.
3. Stresses people and their intangible qualities as important, in a sincere, nonplastic manner.

4. Appears to be considerate of others and their needs and open-minded to their opinions.
5. Can relate to other viewpoints; adjusts self accordingly without vacating personal ideals.
6. Stresses other people in conversation.
7. Has a feel for varied personalities and good dexterity for people.
8. Enthusiastic when discussing people from past work experience.
9. Has a good sense of humor and appropriately warm style in interview.
10. Never allows perception to cloud objective facts.

People Skills

Quan-Com Factor 4

Presence/Bearing—Creates a positive impression and makes presence felt in any given situation with favorable results.

Cues:

1. Do you make a conscious effort to convey a certain image?
2. What kind of feedback have you received about your image?
3. Tell me about a customer or organization that has a business image you can or cannot relate to.

Clues:

1. Tempers being his or her self with a solid business style.
2. Not overtly concerned with presenting a certain act.
3. Not a devout advocate of a portrayed organizational style or rigid manner of external presentation.
4. First impression: what would I think of this person if they were dealing with me in a business relation?
5. Communicological style is in sync with personality.
6. Does not project an elitist or aloof presence but more of a down-home, natural style.

7. Conveys a winning combination of appropriate warmth with dependable professionalism.

Managerial Aptitude

Quan-Com Factor 1

Creativity—Can innovatively employ both qualitative and quantitative strengths to set policy, construct plans, and provide results-oriented direction; unafraid to take risks on new programs that can provide improved benefits, more expedient service, or a better product.

Cues:

1. What new approaches have you used in selling your products or services in the past six months?
2. Explain fully a process you were involved with from design through reality.
3. What factors did you consider when you made the decision to _____?
4. Tell me about a project you worked on where you really had to utilize your imagination.

Clues:

1. Routinely looks for and utilizes new approaches which are both effective and produce better or more results.
2. Can expediently but efficiently detail a working process in a step-by-step progression to a productive end.
3. Academic background—types of courses, net yield of education, intensity of study, ability to apply knowledge base to job needs.
4. Heavy reliance on input from others in decision making and plan implementation; constant reliance on mentor figure in thought process.
5. Looks for creative openings and resultant opportunity; does not have to be pushed into "thinking."

6. Willingly takes risks, even if decision to do so is unpopular or considered unorthodox.
7. Does not appear to need a lot of guidance or positive reinforcement.
8. Takes control of interview in terms of thought range and idea presentation.
9. Displays analytical thinking in explaining processes and procedures.
10. Displays conceptual thinking when presenting ideas, opinions, and perceptions.
11. Exhibits breadth of knowledge as well as depth.

Managerial Aptitude

Quan-Com Factor 2

Delegation—Can assign responsibility and authority in the interest of improving expedience of action; can effectively work through people to accomplish desired ends.

Cues:

1. What methods do you use to measure and assign work for others?
2. How do you follow up on work you have assigned others?
3. Do you think you are a good delegator?
4. When assigning work, what criteria do you consider?

Clues:

1. Stresses the achievement of others in unit task achievement.
2. Maintains a set procedure for work measurement, task assignment, and timely completion; stays cognizant of all phases of operation.
3. Considers self to be a good delegator, but can explain reasons, methods, and examples to support that opinion.
4. Clearly is capable of assembling and managing team as evidenced by past performance.

5. Appears to be able to give work out rather than maintain a high level of ownership.
6. Demonstrates perceptiveness of subordinates' capabilities and limitations.
7. Has been able in past roles to obtain maximum project performance from assigned subordinates.
8. Maintains responsibility for work given out; not a shuffler.

Managerial Aptitude

Quan-Com Factor 3

Independent Judgment—Capable of ascertaining direction and goals utilizing individual talent and ability; basically self-starting, makes judgments and decisions and executes without undue reliance on other parties.

Cues:

1. Tell me about an operational or personnel problem you resolved.
2. What programs have you conceived and implemented in your career?
3. Have you ever felt as though you have been given more responsibility than you can handle?
4. Tell me about some gambles you have taken in the past that paid off for you. Why did you take the chance?
5. What do you analyze when pressed for a decision? How do you get your data or the facts?
6. Would you say you rely more on facts or gut vibes? (Have candidate defend choice.)

Clues:

1. Utilizes an effective mechanism to ensure results are being generated.
2. Details a resolution of a problem that required quick and accurate response.

3. Has achieved set goals ahead of time or on time consistently.
4. Responds to probes without undue hesitation and with apparent honesty.
5. Turnaround time is cited as part of project accomplishment.
6. Displays a willingness to get involved with tough situations.
7. Can reflect on past experiences and objectively discuss what was achieved and learned.
8. Has a proven record of working well independently without alienating co-workers, subordinates, or superiors.
9. Virtually unafraid to take risks if overall result will be favorable to all concerned, notably the organization.
10. Has logical backup reasoning for actions taken; delineates data analysis and decision rationale without hesitancy, ambivalence, or retraction.

Managerial Aptitude

Quan-Com Factor 4

Planning—Establishes short- and long-range objectives, course of action for achievement, and syllabus of specific tasks; proactive in setting targets and task accomplishment.

Cues:

1. What are your career objectives, both short- and long-range?
2. When you assign a job for your employees to work on, do you let them know exactly what actions they should take?
3. How do you plan a (sales call, unit meeting, interview)?
4. Who was the best planner you ever worked with?
5. This year's "hot topic" for business professionals seems to be strategic planning. What does that mean to you and how has (or how will) that fit into your daily activities?

Clues:

1. Has established a reasonable but challenging plan for career.
2. Calibrates work direction and related planning efficiently.
3. Routinely analyzes situations and formulates a plan accordingly.
4. Conveys the future goals he or she has set in a clear-cut manner, and can detail steps that will lead to those goals.
5. Comes well prepared to interview; knows what he or she wants to present and how it relates to the subject position.
6. Seems to have charted logical course of action in attaining goals.
7. Capable of explaining plans and the benefit of their implementation.
8. Has had to plan daily activities for self (and work units) in past roles.
9. Not overly tied to a plan to the point where changing factors are ignored or optimum performance is sacrificed.

Team Orientation

Quan-Com Factor 1

Cooperation—Highly motivated toward selfless service to co-workers, customers, and organizational goals; looks at tasks as a commitment to others and organizational excellence.

Cues:

1. In your last (or any previous) position, did you work as an integral member of a team?
2. What do you foresee as your goals and objectives if you get this job?
3. What do you like about working with people?
4. What activities or jobs have you been in that required a lot of people contact?

5. Tell me about a specific situation where you made a wrong decision. How did you remedy the problem?

Clues:

1. Total commitment to the goals and objectives of the work group and organization.
2. Able to act as a resource to others needing technical or peer assistance.
3. Willing to help others who are making a solid effort but need assistance.
4. Consistently puts group priorities ahead of personal ones.
5. Does not blame others for mistakes; takes the bad with the good.
6. Does not perceive self as an individual star or as an autonomous performer; stresses the "we" more than the "I."
7. Direct and free in sharing essential information with peers and others; does not harbor potentially critical information.
8. Not hesitant in responding to point-blank questions; honest, candid portrayal of past performance.
9. Appears genuinely at ease in interview; maintains a free flow of communication.

Team Orientation

Quan-Com Factor 2

Employee Relations—Creates and maintains a workplace relationship with assigned subordinates that generates maximum effectiveness and productivity while enhancing motivation and growth; uses human resources as an integral factor in accomplishing goals.

Cues:

1. What types of motivation do you use to help encourage your employees to do their best at their jobs?

2. What kind of relationship do you feel a manager should have with subordinates?
3. Give me an example in your past work experiences where success was predicated on your effectively training your employees.
4. Tell me about your managerial philosophy and where people fit into the equation.
5. Who was the best employee that ever worked for you and what made them so good?

Clues:

1. Values same tenets in employees that the company does; acutely aware of need for superior human resources.
2. Possesses sound principles of management that would have practical use in new position.
3. Employee(s) cited as exemplary in past jobs have valued traits of our organization.
4. Fosters relative system of participatory management when advantageous.
5. Can present change openly to employees to a positive end.
6. Enthusiastic when discussing personnel from past roles.
7. Past roles have produced high productivity, tangible goal results, and low turnover from employees.
8. Clearly and concisely delivers work direction to subordinates.
9. Conveys a sense of comfort and confidence in establishing a fair but firm relationship with subordinates.

Team Orientation

Quan-Com Factor 3

Loyalty—Commits to a firm contract to work hard for the organization, represent its best interests at all times, and give its needs and overall performance top priority; has an intrinsic dedication to cause, organization, and mission.

Cues:

1. Why do you work? What are your basic motives in pursuing your career objectives?
2. What were your reasons for leaving (or wanting to leave) your position at (last or current employer)?
3. What do you think of the people you work with at present?
4. What is your opinion of your current firm or past employer?
5. What kind of commitment do you look for from a firm or customer?

Clues:

1. Length of time spent in each career progression.
2. Unwilling to speak negatively about other people; no bad-mouthing.
3. Does not go overboard in criticizing current/former employer.
4. No disproportionate desire to gain money, achieve social status/personal recognition, with corresponding uninterest in group effort and reward.
5. Ego does not take precedence over all.
6. Always seeks to give organization maximum return on salary.
7. Primary loyalty lies with family and work rather than softball career, bowling team, political causes, and so on.
8. Seems honest in interview.
9. Not a "guppy"; loyalty is true fidelity to maximum performance.

Team Orientation

Quan-Com Factor 4

Technical Expertise—Possesses a superlative degree of accrued and formal knowledge of the assigned facet(s) of the business; able to draw from and succinctly apply that knowledge in a proficient manner.

Cues:

1. Explain your range of work experience in (specialty).
2. What do you know about our firm and our business?
3. How do you keep up with all of the new innovations in our/your field?
4. Give me an example of a business situation where your technical knowledge enabled success.

Clues:

1. Prior experience in high-stress situations where customer/ patient service is of paramount concern.
2. Substantial range of practical knowledge in the subject field, as evidenced by all indicators.
3. Proficiency at technical terms.
4. Good technical questions asked when given opportunity in interview forum.
5. Expressed interest in learning more about specific area of business.
6. Strives to keep abreast of newest trends in field through course work, reading, professional seminars, and so on.
7. Active affiliation and participation in recognized professional organizations.
8. Attainment of certain specific certifications, degrees, credentials, or related technical or professional recognition.
9. Can explain technical concepts and processes so nonrelated personnel can understand and utilize them.

Resource G

Model
Performance Appraisal
Form

This resource contains a performance appraisal form designed by CHR/InterVista for the world-renowned Estelle Doheny Eye Hospital. It is totally comprehensive in scope, meets all legal and professional requirements, and can be used immediately by the reader according to the direction provided in the last five chapters of this book.

Estelle Doheny
Eye Hospital
1537 Norfolk Street
Los Angeles, California 90033
(213) 224-5000

Performance Appraisal Form

Date of Appraisal:_____

I. Administrative Data

Name:_____

Position:_____

Department:_____

Supervisor:_____

Start Date:_____

Date in Current Position: _____

Appraisal Occasion:_____

II. Job Description

Detail major responsibilities and general scope of current position.

_____

_____

_____

_____

_____

_____

_____

_____

_____

_____

III. Past Year's Objectives/Expectations

List all major expectations and set objectives, rating the degree of accomplishment in each case. Utilize additional sheets as required, and narratively comment on any facets.

Rating Key: - Below Expectations
√ Meets Expectations
+ Exceeds Expectations

1. Objective/Expectation: _____

   Accomplishment Rating: _____
   Comments: _____

2. Objective/Expectation: _____

   Accomplishment Rating: _____
   Comments: _____

3. Objective/Expectation: _____

   Accomplishment Rating: _____
   Comments: _____

4. Objective/Expectation: _____

   Accomplishment Rating: _____
   Comments: _____

5. Objective/Expectation: _____

   Accomplishment Rating: _____
   Comments: _____

6. Objective/Expectation: _____

   Accomplishment Rating: _____
   Comments: _____

7. Objective/Expectation: _____

   Accomplishment Rating: _____
   Comments: _____

8. Objective/Expectation: _____

   Accomplishment Rating: _____
   Comments: _____

9. Objective/Expectation: _____

   Accomplishment Rating: _____
   Comments: _____

10. Objective/Expectation: _____

    Accomplishment Rating: _____
    Comments: _____

IV. Quan-Com Ratings

Using the Doheny Quan-Com Factors, list all factors in which the reviewed employee is either particularly deficient or noteworthy. In the accompanying narration, stress the reasons why this factor became an integral part of the performance of the employee.

Factor:_____   Rating:_____
Performance Narrative:_____
_____
_____

Factor:_____   Rating:_____
Performance Narrative:_____
_____
_____

Factor:_____   Rating:_____
Performance Narrative:_____
_____
_____

IV. a) Leadership Quotient

If the reviewed employee is a supervisor of others, attach an additional rating sheet and narrative on the management skill of the employee and its effect on departmental performance and progress.

V. Objective/Expectation Adjustment

List below all additional objectives/expectations for the coming year, and/or any amended objectives/expectations based on this year's performance and strategic goals.

Objective/Expectation:_____
_____

Objective/Expectation:_____
_____

Objective/Expectation:_____
_____

VI. **Prescriptive Prognosis**

List activities the employee will undertake in the coming year that will
enhance knowledge and professional development, thus increasing
the employee's total value.

I) Activity:_____
Development Value:_____

II) Activity:_____
Development Value:_____

III) Activity:_____
Development Value:_____

VII. **Employee Comments:**

The space below is provided for any appropriate comments from
the employee. Attach any additionally needed pages.

_____
_____
_____
_____
_____

_____
Employee's Signature

VIII. **Overall Rating**

Considering the above ratings, subjectively plot the employee's overall
rating on the lineal scale below.

-	✓	+
Below	Meets	Exceeds
Expectations	Expectations	Expectations

_____
Manager's Signature

Survey Instrument for Determining Training and Development Needs

In order to determine training and development needs, the reader can use the following survey instrument, designed by the CHR/InterVista staff in conjunction with Syracuse University for the Bristol-Myers Company. The instrument will assist the reader in ascertaining the training and development needs of an entire work group organization of any size.

A. *Communication Skills*

This kind of training could include writing skills/strategies, interpersonal dialogue, self-expression, clarity, and communicating to different audiences.

1. Please list information about any communication skills training you have ever attended. Include as much information as possible. Place a * next to the best one.

   a. Seminar name _____
      Place/date held _____
      Group presenting seminar _____
      Topics _____

   b. Seminar name _____
      Place/date held _____
      Group presenting seminar _____
      Topics _____

   c. Seminar name _____
      Place/date held _____
      Group presenting seminar _____
      Topics _____

d.   Any others? _____
_____

2.   Please number from 1–5 the communication skills which you feel are most needed.

☐ Self-expression   ☐ Written communication
☐ Communicating with staff   (clarity, brevity)
☐ Communicating with supervisors ☐ Technical writing

3.   Describe your own biggest problem with communication.

_____
_____
_____
_____

4.   The best seminar on communication skills you've attended has content that is: (Check the response that is closest to your feeling.)

Pure theory (psychology)	Mostly theory (some skills)	Half theory half skill	Mostly skills	Pure hands-on skills
1	2	3	4	5
☐	☐	☐	☐	☐

5.   Ideally, what type of theory (psychology)/practical skills combination would help most with day-to-day management (and make life easier at work)?

Pure theory	Mostly theory	Half theory half skills	Mostly skills	Pure skills
1	2	3	4	5
☐	☐	☐	☐	☐

B.   *Motivation Skills*

These skills include such topics as: leadership, personality types, rewards, group interaction, direction, and theories ''X'' and ''Y.''

1.   List any motivation skills seminars you have ever attended. Include as much information as possible. Place a * next to the best seminar.

a.   Seminar name   _____
Place/date held   _____
Group presenting seminar   _____
Topics   _____

    b.   Seminar name   _____
         Place/date held   _____
         Group presenting seminar   _____
         Topics   _____

    c.   Seminar name   _____
         Place/date held   _____
         Group presenting seminar   _____
         Topics   _____

    d.   Seminar name   _____
         Place/date held   _____
         Group presenting seminar   _____
         Topics   _____

    e.   Others _____   _____

                               _____

                               _____

2.   The best motivation seminar has content that is:

Only psychology of motivation	Mostly psychology/a few skills	Mostly skills, examples of techniques	Only skills
☐	☐	☐	☐

3.   What type of emphasis would you prefer in a motivational management seminar?

All psychology/principles	Mostly psychology/a few skills	Mostly skills	All skills
☐	☐	☐	☐

4.   Motivation skills which would be most useful to me would be:

☐ *Self* motivation   ☐ "Problem" employee
☐ *Group* motivation   motivation
☐ Morale building   ☐ Motivation isn't
                               a major need for me

☐ Others (describe): _____

_____

_____

5.   What three things would you like to change in the operation of your department, to make life a little easier, and better run?

_____

_____

C.   *Technical Skills Training*

The purpose of this training is to maintain a high level of subject matter expertise in managers, as well as in staff members. The topics of technical skills training seminars are many and varied. Your answers to this section will help provide skills training in key areas for *your* department.

1.   What department do you manage? _____
     _____

2.   How many people work for you? _____

3.   About how many training seminars/sessions has your department attended in the last year?

     0–1 _____   2–4 _____   3–7 _____

4.   Are any of these seminars worth repeating to your department on a regular basis? If so, please list those you would like repeated.

     Yes _____   No _____
     Seminar name(s): _____
     _____
     _____

5.   Please list the most *important areas* for technical skill development in your department. (In descending priority.)

     a. _____
     b. _____
     c. _____
     d. _____
     e. _____

D.   *Time Management Skills/Planning*

These skills will help a manager prioritize activities, allocate time and other resources for activities, and develop schedules for achieving goals. They will also provide strategies for implementing plans.

1.   In general, time management skill development would:

     Solve most of my
     management problems   Help somewhat   Probably not help
              ☐   ☐   ☐

2.   Please check the importance of time management skills to you in the areas of work specified.

Time management skill development would be:

Work area	Extremely useful	Helpful	Not really necessary for me
Coordinating work for my staff	☐	☐	☐
Coordinating my *own* duties	☐	☐	☐
Predicting/ meeting time deadlines	☐	☐	☐

3. List any management seminars you've been to that dealt with planning and time management. Include as much information as possible. Place a * next to the *best one.*

   a. Seminar name   _____
      Place/date held   _____
      Group presenting seminar _____
      Topics   _____

   b. Seminar name   _____
      Place/date held   _____
      Group presenting seminar _____
      Topics   _____

   c. Seminar name   _____
      Place/date held   _____
      Group presenting seminar _____
      Topics   _____

E.   *Attitude Formation*

Attitude formation skills and seminars training deal with identification of "peer attitudes," diagnosis of their causes, and specific counseling techniques for fostering "healthy" work attitudes in subordinates.

1. Please list management seminars you've attended that dealt with attitude formation or similar topics. Place a * next to the best one.

   a. Seminar name   _____
      Place/date held   _____
      Group presenting seminar _____
      Topics   _____

   b. Seminar name   _____
      Place/date held   _____
      Group presenting seminar _____
      Topics   _____

   c. Seminar name   _____
      Place/date held   _____
      Group presenting seminar _____
      Topics   _____

2. Please check all statements that describe the work attitude of your subordinate group most of the time. (Remember, everyone has lousy days!)

   a. ☐ All personnel have a "healthy" attitude. Morale is excellent.
   b. ☐ There are a few (less than 20%) morale problems in my group.
   c. ☐ The only times I can detect poor morale is during times of *stress* (impending deadlines, personal problems, overwork).
   d. ☐ Morale is a challenge for our department. In fact, it's a problem: I could do with some advice.

3. I would like/attend courses that explain: [Check as many as you wish, or better yet, write your own suggestions.]

   —How attitude problems develop   ☐
   —How a manager can identify potential   ☐
     attitude problems
   —How to develop an ongoing "attitude   ☐
     development" plan to use with my staff
   —How to identify an attitude problem   ☐
     in myself
   —None, I have no problems with staff   ☐
     attitude
   —Others (please specify) _____
                         _____
                         _____
                         _____

4. The most *persistent* type of attitude problem among people here at Bristol is (please describe) _____
_____
_____
_____

5. What factors cause this problem? (If you have any immediate ideas.)
_____
_____
_____

F. *The Ideal Seminar*

The following questions pertain to the *single best* seminar you've ever attended, in *any* topic. The answers you provide will help us design/select seminars that will be of most benefit to you.

1.   What was the name of the *best* seminar you ever attended?

   _____

2.   What were the topics of the *best* seminar? _____

   _____

3.   The topic(s) of the *best* seminar were: (check one in each category)

   a.   Fascinating   Okay   Somewhat dry

           ☐   ☐   ☐

   b.   Vital to my work   Sometimes   Primarily

           immediately   applicable   conceptual

           ☐   ☐   ☐

4.   Please rank the following areas of the best seminars (1–5 from good to bad).

	1	2	3	4	5
	Outstanding		Average		Poor
Speaker's ability to hold interest	☐	☐	☐	☐	☐
Effectiveness of audiovisual displays	☐	☐	☐	☐	☐
Consistency of topics to your expectations	☐	☐	☐	☐	☐

5.   The things the speakers did that most impressed me were:

   _____
   _____
   _____
   _____

6.   What audiovisual aids do you remember being used?

   Movies _____   Slide tapes _____

   Audiocassette _____   Models _____

   Hand-out references _____   None _____

   Others _____

   _____

7.   During the seminar the "practice time" provided for new skills/strategies was:

   More than sufficient   Average   Not enough   Not provided

         ☐   ☐   ☐   ☐

8.   Are you comfortable with the use of the following techniques in training seminars?

	Yes	No
Group practice sessions	___	___
Roleplaying	___	___
Lectures	___	___
"Charismatic" presentations	___	___
Presentations attended alone (no other company people)	___	___
Presentations attended with other Bristol employees	___	___

9.   *SUBJECT*—Using the following scale, please rate the following topics of interest.

4—Very pertinent, absolutely needed/high interest
3—Pertinent, needed/definite interest
2—Somewhat useful/marginal interest
1—Not needed/little interest

Managerial

_____ Absenteeism
_____ Budget/financial training
_____ Decision evaluation
_____ Employee discipline
_____ Employee selection
_____ Executive effectiveness
_____ Interviewing skills
_____ Job assignment/enrichment
_____ Negotiation skills
_____ Performance appraisal
_____ Productivity
_____ Supervisory psychology
_____ Technical writing
_____ Time management
_____ Work measurement

Interpersonal

_____ Affirmative action
_____ Attitude formation
_____ Behavior modification
_____ Climate setting
_____ Counseling techniques
_____ Delegation skills
_____ Executive communication
_____ Language training
_____ MBO formation
_____ Morale measurement
_____ O.D./team building
_____ Presentation skills
_____ Psycho-emotive motivation
_____ Stress management
_____ Writing skills

10.   What are your suggestions for descriptions of the *ideal* training seminar?

_____
_____
_____
_____
_____

11.   Other general comments: _____

_____
_____
_____
_____

Selected References

The following compendium includes books I have referred to in this text and used as theoretical bases in constructing the systems described and demonstrated in this volume. It is provided for readers who wish to learn more about the integrated process of industrial psychology and human resources management as it relates to selection and performance appraisal. All of the texts cited in this section have also been chosen for the practical nature of their content and the large amount of ready-to-use information that they provide.

Albanese, R. *Management*. Cincinnati, Ohio: Southwestern, 1987.

Albano, C. *Transactional Analysis on the Job and Communicating with Subordinates*. New York: AMACOM, 1974.

Argyris, C. *Management and Organizational Development*. New York: McGraw-Hill, 1971.

Baird, J. E. *The Dynamics of Organizational Communication*. New York: Harper & Row, 1977.

Berne, E. *Transactional Analysis in Psychotherapy*. New York: Grove Press, 1968.

Bormann, E. G., and Bormann, N. C. *Speech Communication: An Interpersonal Approach*. New York: Harper & Row, 1972.

Brooks, W. D., and Emment, P. *Interpersonal Communication*. Dubuque, Iowa: Brown, 1976.

Brown, J. D. *The Human Nature of Communication*. New York: AMACOM, 1973.

Bursten, B. *The Manipulator: A Psychoanalytical View*. New Haven, Conn.: Yale University Press, 1973

Caplan, G., and Cibovici, S. *Adolescence: Psycho-Social Perspectives*. New York: Basic Books, 1969.

Carlson, R. O. (ed.). *Communication and Public Opinion*. New York: Praeger, 1975.

Cassata, M. B., and Asante, M. K. *Mass Communication: Principles and Practices*. New York: Macmillan, 1979.

Champion, D. J. *The Sociology of Organizations*. New York: McGraw-Hill, 1975.

Combs, A. W. *Helping Relationships*. Newton, Mass.: Allyn & Bacon, 1978.

Condon, J. C. *Semantics and Communication*. New York: Macmillan, 1975.

Condon, J. C. *Interpersonal Communication*. New York: Macmillan, 1977.

Conference Board. *Behavioral Science: Concepts and Management Application*. New York: The Conference Board, 1969.

DeFleur, M. L. *Theories of Mass Communication*. New York: Longman, 1975.

Desatrick, R. L. *Innovative Human Resource Management*. New York: AMACOM, 1972.

DeVito, J. A. *Interpersonal Communication*. New York: Harper & Row, 1976.

Dinsmore, F. W. *Developing Tomorrow's Managers Today*. New York: AMACOM, 1975.

Drucker, P. F. *Managing for Results*. New York: Harper & Row, 1964.

Drucker, P. F. *Management*. New York: Harper & Row, 1973.

Eisenberg, A. M. *Understanding Communication in Business and the Professions*. New York: Macmillan, 1978.

Flamholtz, E. G. *Human Resource Accounting: Advances in Concepts, Methods, and Applications*. (2nd ed.) San Francisco: Jossey-Bass, 1985.

Giffin, K., and Patton, B. R. *Fundamentals of Interpersonal Communication*. New York: Harper & Row, 1971.

Gumpert, G., and Cathcart, R. *Intermedia: Interpersonal Communication in a Media World*. New York: Oxford University Press, 1971.

Haber, R. N., and Hershenson, M. *The Psychology of Visual Perception*. New York: Holt, Rinehart & Winston, 1973.

Hampden-Turner, C. K. *Radical Man: The Process of Psycho-Social Development*. Garden City, N.Y.: Doubleday, 1971.

Hampton, D. R. *Organizational Behavior and the Practice of Management*. Glenview, Ill.: Scott, Foresman, 1978.

Hellriegel, D., and Slocum, J. W. *Organizational Behavior—Contingency Views*. St. Paul, Minn.: West, 1976.

Huber, G. P., and Williams, J. C. *Human Behavior in Organizations*. Cincinnati, Ohio: Southwestern, 1986.

Landy, F. J. *Psychology of Work Behavior*. Homewood, Ill.: Dorsey Press, 1985.

Leavitt, H. J. *Managerial Psychology*. Chicago: University of Chicago Press, 1958.

Litwin, G. H., and Stringer, R. A. *Motivation and the Organizational Climate*. Boston: Boston University Press, 1968.

Lombardi, D. N. *Social Dynamics of Communicative Psychology*. St. Louis, Mo.: University Publications, 1978.

Lombardi, D. N. *Selection for Proformance*. Costa Mesa, Calif.: Center for Human Resources Press, 1984.

Lombardi, D. N. *InterVista Performance Appraisal Series*. Costa Mesa, Calif.: Center for Human Resources Press, 1985a.

Lombardi, D. N. *Leadership Qualities: Quantification of Crucial Characteristics*. Chicago: American College of Healthcare Executives Publications and Audio-Tapes, 1985b.

Lombardi, D. N. *The Quan-Com Selection Series*. Costa Mesa, Calif.: Center for Human Resources Press, 1985c.

Lombardi, D. N. "Intrapreneurs: Finding Diamonds in the Rough." *Healthcare Executive*, 1986a, *5*, 43–48.

Lombardi, D. N. *Managing Intrapreneurs: The Challenge and the Rewards*. Chicago: American College of Healthcare Executives Publications and Audio-Tapes, 1986b.

Lombardi, D. N. *Maximizing Managerial Performance*. Chicago: American College of Healthcare Executives, 1986c.

Lombardi, D. N. *Selection and Performance Appraisal Systems: Practical Applications for Maximum Performance*. Chicago: American College of Healthcare Executives, 1986d.

Lombardi, D. N. "Maximizing Human Resources." *Administrative Radiology*, 1987, *6*, 45–48.

Maslow, A. H. *The Farther Reaches of Human Nature*. New York: Viking Press, 1971.

Mead, M. *Culture and Commitment*. Garden City, N.Y.: Doubleday, 1970.

Melio, N. "Healthcare Organizations and Innovation." *Health and Social Behavior,* 1971, *11,* 163–174.

Miller, G. A. *Communication, Language and Meaning.* New York: Basic Books, 1973.

Morgan, T. *F.D.R.—A Biography.* New York: Simon & Schuster, 1985.

Musgrave, P. W. *The School as an Organization.* London: Macmillan, 1968.

Nash, M. *Managing Organizational Performance.* San Francisco: Jossey-Bass, 1983.

Newman, W. H., and Logan, J. P. *Strategy, Policy and Central Management.* Cincinnati, Ohio: Southwestern, 1975.

Odiorne, G. S. *Strategic Management of Human Resources: A Portfolio Approach.* San Francisco: Jossey-Bass, 1984.

Palmer, F. R. *Semantics—A New Outline.* London: Cambridge University Press, 1976.

Pember, D. R. *Mass Media in America.* Chicago: Science Research Associates, 1977.

Perlman, R., and Gurin, A. *Community Organization and Social Planning.* New York: Wiley, 1972.

Perrow, C. *Organizational Analysis: A Sociological View.* Monterey, Calif.: Brooks/Cole, 1970.

Phillips, J. D. *For Those Who Must Lead.* Chicago: Dartnell Press, 1966.

Raths, L. E. *Values and Teaching: Working with Values in the Classroom.* Westerville, Ohio: Merrill, 1967.

Schantz, W. T. *The American Legal Environment.* St. Paul, Minn.: West, 1976.

Schein, E. H. *Organizational Psychology.* Englewood Cliffs, N.J.: Prentice-Hall, 1972.

Schein, E. H. *Organizational Culture and Leadership: A Dynamic View.* San Francisco: Jossey-Bass, 1985.

Schiller, H. I. *Communication and Cultural Domination.* New York: International Arts and Sciences Press, 1976.

Scott, W. G., and Mitchell, T. R. *Organizational Theory: A Structural and Behavioral Analysis.* Homewood, Ill.: Irwin, 1976.

Sullivan, H. S. *Clinical Studies in Psychiatry*. New York: Norton, 1973.

Sutton, J. R., and Raines, J. V. *Coaching for Proformance in Healthcare*. Costa Mesa, Calif.: Center for Human Resources Press, 1983.

Tart, C. T. *Altered States of Consciousness*. Garden City, N.Y.: Doubleday, 1972.

Toffler, A. *Future Shock*. New York: Random House, 1970.

Tubbs, S. L., and Moss, S. *Interpersonal Communication*. New York: Random House, 1978.

Twomey, D. P. *A Concise Guide to Employment Law*. Cincinnati, Ohio: Southwestern, 1986.

Van Doren, C. *Benjamin Franklin—A Biography*. New York: Bramhall House, 1938.

Waelder, R. P. *Basic Theory of Psychoanalysis*. New York: Schocken Books, 1964.

Whetmore, E. J. *MediaAmerica*. Belmont, Calif.: Wadsworth, 1979.

Yablonsky, L. *Synanon: Tunnel Back*. New York: Penguin Books, 1965.

Index